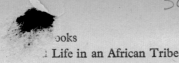

ooks

Life in an African Tribe

WITHDRAWN

Isaac Schapera, F.B.A., was born in 1905 in South
Africa and educated at South African College School in
Cape Town and at the Universities of Cape Town and
London. Since 1969 he has been Emeritus Professor of
Anthropology at the London School of Economics.
Between the years 1929 and 1950 he participated in
many anthropological field expeditions to Bechuanaland
Protectorate. He was Chairman of the Association of
Social Anthropologists of the British Commonwealth
from 1954 to 1958 and President of the Royal
Anthropological Institute from 1961 to 1963. He has
published many books about African tribal societies and
has edited the journals and letters of David Livingstone
in six volumes.

Isaac Schapera

Married Life in an
African Tribe

Penguin Books

Penguin Books Ltd, Harmondsworth,
Middlesex, England
Penguin Books Australia Ltd, Ringwood,
Victoria, Australia

First published by Faber & Faber 1940
Published in Pelican Books 1971

Copyright © Isaac Schapera, 1940

Made and printed in Great Britain by
Cox & Wyman Ltd,
London, Reading and Fakenham
Set in Intertype Plantin

Contents

Preface

This book describes marriage and family life in a South African tribe: the Kgatla of the Bechuanaland Protectorate. The Kgatla have been exposed for just over a century to the influences of contact with Western European civilization, locally represented by the White inhabitants of South Africa. The old tribal culture has in consequence become greatly modified, and in the process of transformation the traditional domestic institutions were also affected. In working up my material, I decided to make this phenomenon of change the main theme of the book. Accordingly, while describing in considerable detail the life of the modern Kgatla family, I have tried wherever possible to record the ancient usages also, to indicate how far they survive or have been displaced, and to ascertain the reasons for the changes that have taken place.

It seemed to me that a social history of this kind would be more generally acceptable than any attempt to add to the many theoretical discussions of either 'primitive' family and kinship problems, or the psychological problems of married life. I hope that my description will be found to contain material serviceable to students of these problems, but I have not tried to do more than set down the facts they may want. My object has been rather to describe in a straightforward manner how the Kgatla family has changed and what sort of life it leads today. I have felt that I could thus provide comparative data of some interest to sociologists dealing with the transformations of family life in contemporary Western society. I have felt also that an analysis of the effects produced upon the Kgatla family by contact with Western civilization may be found useful and suggestive by Administrations, Christian Missions, humanitarians, and others, to whom the future of indigenous African society is a matter of grave concern.

The material presented in this book was collected in the course of a general ethnographical study of the Kgatla. I visited the people on several occasions during the years 1929–34, spending in all just over fourteen months among them. Since then I have studied in the field other tribes of the same cultural group; but, except for one week's visit in 1939, I have done no further work among the Kgatla, although I have remained in touch with some of my friends there. I have described, in two earlier publications,* the methods I used in making my inquiries, so that there is no need for me to do so here again. I wish only to say that at the time I was interested in the tribal culture generally, and not in the family alone or even specially. The result, as I now realize, is that I failed to get all the information I should, and could, have got on various aspects of sexual life and other domestic relations. I am painfully aware of the defects in my description, and can only hope that some other worker will follow me into the same field to check and supplement what I have here written.

Since the book is designed more for the general reader than for the professional anthropologist, I have tried to avoid as far as possible the use of Native terms, preferring instead the nearest English equivalent. The only one I have consistently employed is *bogadi* (the giving of cattle at marriage by the bridegroom's family to the bride's father), which itself is now almost a technical term in the literature on South African ethnography. I have also not followed the practice, now so commonly adopted by anthropologists, of quoting statements in the original text as well as in translation. There may be some justification for this practice where the language of the people has not yet been studied, or where the writer wishes to direct special attention to some linguistic usage; but in my reading I have generally found it more annoying than helpful, especially where it serves no

* 'The BaKxatla baxaKxafêla: Preliminary Report of Field Investigations', *Africa*, vol. vi, 1933, pp. 402–14; 'Field Methods in the Study of Modern Culture Contacts', *Africa*, vol. viii, 1935, pp. 315–28.

obvious purpose other than to lend an air of greater authority to what is said. The few readers of this book likely to be familiar enough with Tswana dialects to check my translations will find the Native terms for such phrases as 'council-place', 'substitute wife', 'entering the hut', 'mourning sickness' etc., in my *Handbook of Tswana Law and Custom* (Oxford, 1938), where I have also given the original texts of many of the proverbs quoted. I may refer them also to the collection of longer Kgatla and other Tswana texts on ethnography separately published by me in my book *Mekgwa le Melaô ya BaTswana* (Lovedale Press, 1938).

Here and there I have deliberately altered or omitted the names of informants or of people referred to in case-histories, who might have been embarrassed by actual identification. Education has progressed far enough among the Kgatla to enable some of them to read my writings about their people; and while it does not much matter to the outsider whether Modise, Rathipa, or Makgantane was the name of the man who said or did this or that, it may make some difference to the latter himself, if it becomes generally known in the tribe. Past experience has shown me that this precaution is not an unnecessary affectation. Unfortunately, however, it means that the writers and recipients of the letters quoted in the book must also remain anonymous. I regret this. They gave me what I consider among the most valuable evidence of what the people feel and say to one another in private, and I would have liked to indicate my sources more precisely.

Married Life in an African Tribe was written in 1939, when what is now the Republic of Botswana was still the British dependency of Bechuanaland. Consequently all references to administration, the political situation in other countries etc., apply to the period of my fieldwork (1929–35) and not to the current situation. Almost all the persons named in the book (including Chiefs Isang and Molefi) are now dead.

Cape Town   I.S.
November 1939

1. The People and their Culture

While working on this book, I received from two of my Kgatla friends communications that provide as good an indication as could be desired of some modern trends in the marriage customs of their people. Sedimo Phaphane wrote to me (in English) from Johannesburg, where he was working as a messenger in a big newspaper office:

I wish to tell you I have dropped my love with Miss Romela Kgosina of Mafeking. I did so because I discovered she was too considered [sic]. She thought too much of herself, and she was very expensive to marry, hark, where ever we went we should buy sweets or chocolates at 4s. 6d. lb. What do you think of that? And we should always travel by taxi instead of by tram or bus at 5d. or 3d., but taxi at 2s., oh, no, I had to cut it off.

He had met this girl in Johannesburg and courted her there. They belong to different tribes, and both had left home in order to earn money by working for Europeans.* Had they been with their own people, their marriages would by traditional usage have been arranged by their parents, and not by themselves; nor, considering that Mafeking is 120 miles from the Kgatla Reserve, is it likely that they would ever have met in the normal course of events. The use of writing, and in English at that, indicates the presence of other new factors in Kgatla life, while the extravagant tastes of the girl friend are of a kind that could as easily dismay a young European citizen of Johannesburg as the Bantu tribesman who is here so distressed.

The other communication came from Mochudi, the tribal

*In South Africa the term 'European' is commonly used for a white person, and 'Native' for any one belonging to a Bantu or other African tribe. For convenience I shall follow the same usage.

capital of the Kgatla. It was a gilt-edged invitation card reading as follows:

The Marriage of
MAGANELO D. PILANE
Treasurer, Bakgatla Native Administration, to
MAMOREMA,
daughter of ex-Rent Chief and Mrs Isang Pilane,
will take place either at
Dutch Reformed Church or District Commissioner's Office,
Mochudi,
on the 21st day of Sept., 1939, at 11 a.m.

All Friends, both European and African, are cordially invited to attend.

A reception will be held after the ceremony at the residence of ex-Rent Chief Isang Pilane.

P.O. Mochudi Village, via Pilane Station, Bech. Protectorate

Such a printed formal invitation is itself a complete novelty. Other instances of change are the official position of the bridegroom, the expectation that European guests will be present, the use of the word 'African' instead of 'Kgatla' or 'Native', and the existence of a post office at Mochudi and of a railway station at Pilane, fairly close by. Then, also, the ceremony is to be performed either by the missionary or by the District Commissioner, who are both marriage officers of the Bechuanaland Protectorate Administration. The marriage will therefore be in accordance with the European civil law of the Territory, imposing upon the couple a series of obligations that do not prevail in tribal law. If the wedding takes place in church, it will also involve religious rites not known to the Kgatla of old, but introduced as part of Christianity. The missionary is a new element in tribal life, and so are the District Commissioner and the Administration that he represents. In fact, the only item corresponding at all to traditional practice is the feast given by the bride's parents. The words 'ex-Rent Chief', incidentally, are an unfortunate misprint for 'ex-Regent Chief'.

These two illustrations show rather strikingly the way in

which Kgatla culture has been influenced by Western civilization. Even the most casual visitor to the tribe cannot but notice the many features of European origin now forming part of its life and environment. The railway line from the Union of South Africa to Southern Rhodesia passes through the heart of the Kgatla Reserve. Pilane Station is only five miles from Mochudi, with which it is connected by a passable motor road. Apart from the railway buildings, it contains a post and telegraph office maintaining communication with the outer world, a trading store, and dwellings for the several Europeans employed by the railway administration or making a living by selling goods to the Kgatla. On the slopes of Phaphane Hill, midway between Pilane and Mochudi, there has been recently built a Government 'camp' containing the offices and homes of the local District Commissioner and his staff. In Mochudi itself are a church, two schools, two trading stores, a small hospital, a post-office, a smithy and the dwellings of the Europeans serving the tribe as missionaries, medical practitioners, veterinary officers, traders, and blacksmiths.

Such obvious manifestations of cultural change are reinforced by what one observes among the Kgatla themselves. Practically all adult members of the tribe, and many children, wear clothing of European pattern and material. Their dwellings are often built rectangular in shape, after the European fashion, and such European articles as ploughs, buckets, axes and other hardware utensils, lanterns, candles, and matches are commonly used. Ox-drawn wagons and sledges have become the chief means of transport. The water supply of Mochudi during the dry season comes mainly from bore-holes, through which underground water is pumped into cement reservoirs. English and Afrikaans, the two dominant European languages of South Africa, are spoken fairly widely, and the European visitor ignorant of the local vernacular need not search far or long for people to understand him.

More intimate acquaintance with the Kgatla brings to light many other indications of white influence. The tribe is no longer politically independent. Its territory forms part of the Bechuanaland Protectorate, a possession of Great Britain, and it is subject in all its external relations to the authority of the Protectorate Administration, to which it must also pay taxes. The traditional powers of the chief and his subordinate headmen have been considerably curtailed by the Administration, which exercises the ultimate control over tribal government and jurisdiction. Christianity, in the form professed by the Dutch Reformed Church, is the official religion of the people. Many children attend the schools controlled by the Administration, where they receive an education modelled on the European pattern. White traders have become part of local economic life, providing the Kgatla with the manufactured goods of the Western world, and buying from them their cattle and other produce. Money is now the principal medium of exchange. Large numbers of men, and some women also, go periodically to work for Europeans in the Transvaal and other white areas, supplementing in this way their income from produce.

Marriage and the family have shared in this transformation, with the result that the traditional structure of domestic life has been altered. Polygamy has become so exceptional that perhaps only one married man in thirty has two wives or more. But an important consequence has been the spread of concubinage. Many men now have mistresses whom formerly they might have married. This means that the children of these unions are illegitimate. It means also that wives have greater cause for jealousy, so that quarrels due to sexual infidelity have become a fairly common feature of married life. The relations between parents and children have also changed. Formerly children were wholly subject to their parents, whom they had to obey without hesitation or question. They could not choose their own mates, but had to marry the people selected for them. Today, however, there is ample evidence of youthful irresponsibility and independence. Children no longer look always to their parents for approval, but are tending more and more to act as they please. Many of them now do their own courting, and infant betrothal, a recognized practice in old days, has almost entirely disappeared. Premarital sex relations, formerly severely condemned, have become almost

a matter of course, and many girls bear children out of wedlock.

These are only some of the changes that have occurred. But
even they are sufficient to suggest that there is a marked
difference between the modern Kgatla family and the family of,
say, fifty years ago. The difference, however, is not universal.
There are still families that are polygamous, or in which parents
arrange the marriages of their children, and there are very many
more, the great majority in fact, in which husband and wife do
not get married in church, and so do not come under the provisions of the civil law. Practices discarded by some continue to
be observed by others, so that there is apparently much more
variation than before. One of our problems, then, will be to see
how far there has actually been change. What traditional aspects
of the family have most readily succumbed and, on the other
hand, which are the features that have persisted? How widespread has been the acceptance of European traits, and to what
extent are they substitutions or merely additions? And why have
the changes occurred? Why have the people, or some of them,
accepted certain of the new usages and ideals brought to them by
Europeans, and why, again, have they rejected others?

Such problems are dictated by the nature of our material, by
the fact that we are dealing with a people whose culture has been
altered through contact with a more powerful civilization. Our
main task, however, is to investigate the nature of family life
itself among the Kgatla. We have to discover how and why
people get married, what obligations their marriage imposes
upon them, what relationship exists between marriage, sexual life
generally, and procreation, what is the form of the Kgatla family,
what social functions it performs, how stable it is as a unit, what
are the personal relations between husband and wife, and between parents and children, and what part the family plays in
tribal life as a whole. These are among the topics a study of
family life in any society must consider, and it is upon them that
we must concentrate if our work is to have any value for comparative purposes. And if in the course of our inquiry we are also

able to see whether cultural contact has tended either to strengthen or to disintegrate the bonds uniting the members of the family, we shall have data perhaps particularly relevant at a time when the family in Western society is notoriously being weakened by the emergence of new economic and social forces.

THE TRANSFORMATION OF KGATLA LIFE

A knowledge of recent tribal history is indispensable if we are to understand why the Kgatla family has altered so greatly. The changes it has undergone are the outcome of contact with Europeans extending for over a century. The BaKgatla baga-Kgafêla, to give them their full name, belong to the Tswana cluster of the Sotho group of southern Bantu peoples. They are by origin a junior branch of the BaKgatla bagaMosêtlha of central Transvaal, but have for the past two centuries and more been a completely separate tribe. At the beginning of the nineteenth century they were living in what is now the Rustenburg District of western Transvaal. Here, towards 1840, during the reign of their chief Pilane, they were encountered by the Voortrekkers, Boer (Dutch) emigrants from the Cape Colony. These Boers, dissatisfied with British rule, had moved away in search of independence, and they carried into their new homes the repressive principles of Native administration that, among other things, they felt had been betrayed in the Cape. They spread all over the country now known as the Transvaal, which they brought under their rule and named the South African Republic. They made its Native inhabitants their subjects, liable to taxation and forced labour, and divided the land up into huge farms for themselves, paying little regard to the rights of the local tribes.

Pilane died in 1848, and was succeeded by his son Kgamanyane. The new chief soon found the rule of the Dutch very irksome. They forced him to send men to work on their farms, and commandeered his warriors for use as auxiliaries in their campaigns against other Native tribes. The climax came in 1869, when the local Government representative (said to have been Paul Kruger himself) flogged Kgamanyane in front of the tribe for not producing enough men to serve him. Humiliated and angered by this insult, the chief trekked with the main body of his people into Bechuanaland, then still independent of European control. In 1871 he established himself at Mochudi, on the banks of the Ngotwane River. Before this, in 1864, a missionary of the Dutch Reformed Church had settled among the Kgatla, while they were still in the Transvaal, and soon after their entry into Bechuanaland another missionary of the same Church joined them there. He not only brought them a new religion, but established schools where converts were taught to read and to write.

The land in which the Kgatla had settled was at that time part of the territory belonging to the Kwena, one of the most powerful tribes in Bechuanaland. The Kwena chief claimed from them the tribute customarily given by subjects to an overlord. It was refused both by Kgamanyane and, after his death in 1875, by his son and successor Lentswe. The Kwena thereupon attacked Mochudi, but were repulsed. For the next few years a state of war prevailed, reflected mainly in sporadic raids on cattle-posts and fields. The Kgatla successfully held their own, and defeated all attempts to expel them. Hostilities finally ceased about 1882, with the Kgatla acknowledged masters of the land they had occupied.

In 1885 the British, who during the past year or two had been negotiating with the principal chiefs of Bechuanaland, established a Protectorate over the whole country, in order to check a Boer encroachment threatening to cut off the road to the north. The new Administration applied itself to defining carefully the boundaries of the different tribes, and a Proclamation of 1899 confirmed the claim of the Kgatla to the land they inhabited, henceforth known after them as the Kgatla Reserve. Several important changes preceded this. In 1891 the laws of the Cape of Good Hope were applied to the Protectorate. They limited in certain ways the powers of the chiefs, and imposed various new obligations upon the people. In 1892 Lentswe was converted to Christianity, which now became the official religion of the tribe. In 1896 the construction was begun of the railway line to the new territory of Southern Rhodesia farther north. The railway passed close to Mochudi, and made it more easily accessible to the outside world. In 1899, again, the Administration imposed special taxation upon the Native inhabitants of the Territory, thereby greatly influencing their economic life. The early years of the Protectorate saw also the establishment in the Reserve of the first trading stores, another powerful instrument in the diffusion of Western civilization. During this time, too, the numbers of the tribe increased considerably owing to the accession of small groups of foreigners, and of various Kgatla headmen who had not originally accompanied Kgamanyane from the Transvaal. Many of the newcomers were placed by Lentswe along the borders of his Reserve, so that a number of small villages came into existence outside Mochudi.

Towards the end of 1899 war broke out between the Dutch Republics of South Africa and the English. Lentswe, through no fault of his own, found himself involved, and, after fighting two small engagements against the Dutch, managed to loot many cattle from their farms in the Transvaal while the owners were campaigning elsewhere. The years immediately following the war, which ended in 1902, were not particularly noteworthy in incident. But during this time the European influences already at work among the Kgatla gradually consolidated their position. Christianity, in particular, penetrated more and more into the life of the people. A large church was built in Mochudi, educational work was extended, and many of the ancient tribal rites were abandoned in deference to the wishes of the missionaries. The Administration, on the other hand, interfered very little with the traditional forms of government and jurisdiction, its general policy being 'to preserve the tribal authority of the chiefs and the laws and customs of the people'. But its official dealings with the tribe steadily increased, while in 1914, when the First World War broke out, it induced Lentswe and other Protectorate chiefs to send men to join the African Labour Corps which accompanied the South African troops to German South-West Africa and subsequently to France. In the same year the chief suffered a great personal bereavement through the death of his eldest son and heir Kgafêla. He never really recovered from the loss, and in 1920 himself became so ill that the conduct of tribal affairs was entrusted to his second son Isang, who was to act as regent until Kgafêla's son Molefi came of age. Lentswe lingered on a few more years, but took no further active part in the government of the tribe. He died in 1924, greatly lamented by all his people.

Isang, who ruled until 1929, contributed much to the spread of European culture. He strongly encouraged economic development, and brought education under the direct control of a tribal committee. The beginning of his regency coincided roughly with new Administrative intervention in the life of the people. In 1919 official machinery was provided for the first time to regulate the hearing of appeals by European magistrates from the verdicts of the chiefs. The following year a Native Fund, financed by additional Native taxation, was created to subsidize education and economic development, and a Native Advisory Council of chiefs and other tribal representatives was set up for the whole Territory. With contributions from the Native Fund education expanded rapidly in the Reserve, while at meetings of the Advisory Council Isang always took a prominent part in urging upon the Administration the economic needs of the Kgatla and other tribes. It was largely due to him, too, that the Bechuanaland Protectorate Native Marriages Proclamation of 1926 was promulgated, which restored to the chiefs partial jurisdiction over the matrimonial affairs of tribesmen married under civil law.

About the same time there was an important change in Mission policy. The Church had previously aimed at developing a European type of Christianity, stripped of everything pertaining to heathenism. It had accordingly forbidden converts to practise such patently 'uncivilized' usages as the initiation ceremonies, polygamy, *bogadi* (the giving of cattle for wives) and the inheritance of widows. But under the Rev. J. Reyneke (1923–35), the policy, as he described it to me, was 'to give the tribe a form of national religion, based on the principles of Christianity, but adjusted as far as possible to Kgatla beliefs and aspirations. *Bogadi,* for instance, is now recognized as an essen-

tial part of Christian marriage; the initiation ceremonies for boys
are no longer frowned upon, but an attempt is made to control
and direct them; and national Church festivals have been instituted.' The Mission, moreover, now that it no longer controlled
education, diverted its energies and resources to the medical
needs of the people. A qualified European nurse, and shortly
afterwards a European doctor, were added to its staff, and a
dispensary and later a small hospital were built in Mochudi.

In 1929 Isang formally handed over the chieftainship to his
nephew Molefi, then a youth of twenty. The accession of the new
chief marked another turning point in Kgatla history. In 1930
the Administration itself took over the control of education
throughout the Protectorate. The following year an agricultural
show, the first of its kind in the Territory, was held in Mochudi,
and soon afterwards a Native agricultural demonstrator was appointed to the tribe. For the first time, also, a Government representative was now stationed at Mochudi itself. Previously the
local Administrative centre had been at Gaberones, outside the
Kgatla Reserve and some thirty miles from Mochudi. At the end
of 1934, finally, the Administration issued two Proclamations
regulating and modifying considerably the duties and powers of
chiefs and tribal courts. On the strength of these Proclamations,
Molefi was in 1936 suspended from exercising the powers of
chief, and soon afterwards he was banished from the Reserve.
His place was taken by his younger brother Mmusi.

This drastic action was the culmination of a period of internal
strife and misrule that had greatly affected the general progress
of the tribe. At first Molefi and Isang promised to work together
well, but it was not long before relations between them became
exceedingly strained, threatening at one stage, in 1932, to lead to
bloodshed. The Administration intervened time after time, but
with little success. Finally, at the end of 1934, it held a big public
inquiry at Mochudi. Here it was found that Isang had been
continuously guilty of despising and ignoring the chief. He was
fined £350, and ordered to remain for six months at his cattle-
post thirty miles from Mochudi. Succeeding events showed that
the feud between him and Molefi was not the sole cause of the

trouble. Molefi, although of attractive personality and good intelligence, was a drunkard, and frequently neglected his duties as
chief. A series of incidents in which he flouted the authority of
the Administration and violated the goodwill of the tribe led to a
further inquiry into his conduct, as the result of which he was
suspended.

THE MODERN TRIBAL CULTURE

The developments summarized above brought much that was
new to Kgatla culture. They also modified or destroyed many
traditional customs and beliefs, but left many more virtually
intact. The culture of the people therefore now embodies elements of both Bantu and European origin. This fact must obviously be taken into account in our study of marriage and the
family, if we desire to understand their present organization
and functions in tribal life. But before I proceed to discuss them
more fully, it will be as well to review briefly the main features of
modern Kgatla culture as a whole, so that we may have some
knowledge of the background against which domestic institutions must be considered.

The Kgatla Reserve covers an area of approximately 2,800
square miles, situated in the south-east of Bechuanaland Protectorate. It is completely surrounded either by European-owned
farms or by other Native Reserves, but although so essentially
rural in location it is easily accessible by rail and by motor. Its
resident Native population was returned in the 1936 census as
nearly 14,000, and its European population as only fifty. In addition, some 1,900 other Kgatla were absent at the time, almost
all in the Transvaal and other European centres of employment.
About three fifths of the people live round the chief in the large
central town of Mochudi (actual population in 1936 approximately 8,600). The rest are distributed over nine much smaller
villages from six to thirty miles away. Mathubudukwane, the
largest village, has approximately 1,000 inhabitants, and Rasesa,
the smallest, approximately 250. Some distance beyond each
settlement, and extending in large blocks for many miles across

country, are the fields used for cultivation. Much farther away, and dotted about thickly in suitable areas, are the grazing-posts where the people keep their cattle and other livestock. As a result of this territorial arrangement, the bigger settlements are fully occupied during the dry season only, from about July to November. As soon as the first rains fall, the inhabitants scatter to their fields, where they remain right through the agricultural season until the harvest is reaped in June or July. The cattle-posts, again, are looked after all the year round by herd-boys, whose contacts with village life are usually sporadic and brief.

For subsistence the people still rely mainly upon the traditional pursuits of agriculture, animal husbandry, and hunting. Each family has its own fields, and usually also its own domestic animals (cattle, goats, sheep, fowls, and pigs). The principal crop is Kafir corn, supplemented to a minor extent by maize, millet, melons, pumpkins, sweet cane and beans. The corn is converted into porridge or into a mild and much-relished beer; the other crops are eaten either raw or as prepared dishes of various kinds. The cattle and more rarely the goats supply food in the form of milk, drunk both fresh and sour. They are seldom slaughtered, save by wealthy owners or on ceremonial occasions, but all dying of disease or other causes are eaten. Meat is also obtained by hunting, for, despite extensive destruction of game, the Reserve is still fairly well stocked, especially with smaller buck.

In addition to providing its own food supply, each family formerly built its own huts and made most of its own clothing and domestic utensils. Additional labour, when necessary, was obtained from neighbours and kinsmen, to whom similar services were rendered in return. There were also sporadic exchanges of food and other commodities between closer relatives, who thus helped one another to make good any immediate deficiencies. A few craftsmen supplemented their income from farming by making and bartering certain implements and utensils, but production and trade of this description were not systematically organized. Each household further paid tribute in various forms to the chief, who in turn was expected to provide for his poorer subjects.

Today the tribe is no longer economically self-contained and self-sufficient. New commodities of many kinds have been introduced, most of which can be obtained only from white traders, while the taxes imposed by the Administration and the levies occasionally raised by the chief have made the acquisition of money a universal necessity. To satisfy these new wants, the Kgatla have taken to selling their produce to the traders. But although methods of cultivation and animal husbandry have improved under European guidance, the people cannot from this source alone meet all their modern requirements. Many have therefore engaged in new forms of occupation, including above all temporary wage-labour in European industrial and farming areas. About 40 per cent of the men are away at work every year, and their absence from home has reacted in various ways upon domestic life and other aspects of tribal culture. In the Reserve itself the range of specialized occupations has been considerably extended, although every family still relies primarily upon farming for its food supply.

Politically all the Native inhabitants of the Reserve are under the authority of the chief, whose position is hereditary from father to son. It is primarily through allegiance to him that the members of the tribe express their unity, and the chieftainship is therefore an institution of paramount importance in the life of the people. The chief is not only their representative and spokesman to the outer world. Formerly he was also the head of the tribal government; he administered and laid down the law, adjudicating over all serious crimes and civil disputes; he was the principal magician and priest, and often the leader in war; he regulated the distribution of land, and controlled many other economic activities; he received tribute from his subjects in various forms, and had the right to claim free labour from them at any time for both public and private purposes; and generally speaking he watched over their interests and kept himself informed of local happenings.

In administering the affairs of the tribe, the chief was assisted firstly by a few selected relatives and other confidential advisers, whom he consulted on all matters of policy. He also had a wider, more formal, council, comprising the hereditary headmen of all the wards, whom as a rule he summoned only in times of emergency, when he was anxious to ascertain beforehand the trend of public opinion. All important matters were dealt with finally before a general assembly of the men. Free debate was here allowed on the matter in hand, and no chief dared go against the wishes of the majority, unless he were willing to risk personal disaster.

The right to attend a general political assembly was restricted to men already enrolled in an age-regiment. These groups were formed at irregular intervals several years apart, when all the older adolescent boys were simultaneously subjected to elaborate initiation ceremonies, the most conspicuous feature of which was circumcision. Each regiment was headed by a brother or son of the chief. Once initiated, its members as a group could be called upon at any time by the chief to work for him or to perform other duties. In time of war the younger regiments also formed the tribal army. Girls were initiated into corresponding regiments, under the leadership of the chief's sisters and daughters. They too could then be summoned to work for him.

This system of administration has not altered markedly, for the tribe has on the whole been allowed to retain its own forms of government and law. The chief is still its ruler and judge, and, with the aid of his traditional councils, continues to exercise many of his former powers and privileges. But his religious and magical functions have largely vanished since the introduction of Christianity, and the missionary has in effect succeeded him as tribal priest. His use of regimental labour has also been restricted, while most of the income formerly accruing to and controlled by him as head of the tribe is now paid into a separate fund, from which he receives a fixed annual salary. He must carry out the orders and instructions of the Administration, he is responsible for the collection of hut-tax, and he must cooperate with the District Commissioner and other officials in all sorts of developmental schemes and activities. His formerly undivided control over every aspect of tribal life has thus been diffused through various Government Departments with superior authority. Finally, the Administration has the power to punish him by fine, suspension, or deposal, if he does not carry out his duties properly, and it can also vary the succession if it considers the rightful heir unsuitable for the chieftainship. The tribal courts are still allowed to adjudicate according to Native law, but their constitution and functions have been formally defined; their jurisdiction, especially over crimes, has been greatly curtailed; provision has been made for recording cases tried before them; and safeguards, including the right of appeal to the District Commissioner's Court, have been instituted for the due administration of justice.

The principal administrative and social units in the tribe are the wards, whose structure and functions have been but little affected. A ward is a collection of households occupying their own well-defined portion of a village under the authority of an hereditary headman. The ward-head, assisted by his paternal relatives and the heads of other prominent families, administers justice to and presides over political meetings of his people. He provides them with land for their various needs, can demand free labour from them for public purposes, and is responsible for maintaining order over them and seeing that they carry out the chief's commands. Each ward has its own name and traditions, and sometimes also differs from the rest in origin and customs; while in the age-regiments, and occasionally also at feasts and tribal assemblies, its members are grouped apart.

There are in all sixty-eight recognized wards in the tribe. Each contains on the average between 150 and 250 people, although there is a wide range of variation. Most of the families belonging to a ward are related to their head through descent in the male line from a common ancestor, and as a rule a man belongs to the ward of his father, and continues to reside in the same settlement. But almost every ward also contains affiliated members. These are sometimes newcomers to the tribe, who, being too few to form their own ward, have been placed by the chief within one already existing. Sometimes they are people who have come from another ward as adopted children, or because of disagreement with their former neighbours. Members of the same ward are permitted to intermarry, but in most cases take outsiders as husbands or wives.

In each ward settlement the compounds or dwelling-enclosures of the various constituent households are generally built close together in the form of a rough circle, and face a large open space reserved for such activities as meetings, many forms of work, dances, and games. Apart from some trees left to provide shelter from the sun, this central space usually contains one or more cattle-kraals, in which any livestock temporarily in the village are kept at night. Close to each kraal is a windbreak of stout poles, where the men of the ward habitually foregather to sit round the fire, discuss their affairs and try cases, and perhaps even eat and work. This council-place is the centre of the ward's political and ceremonial life. Women and children must stay away from it, except when their attendance is specially required by the men.

The council-place of the chief's own ward, situated in the heart of Mochudi, is the seat of the tribal administration. It is a large open space surrounded by a circular fence, with a wooden shelter at one end and a visitors' hut at the other. Here the chief administers justice, receives visitors, interviews people, and presides over assemblies. The great cattle-kraal leading into it is also a place of political and ritual importance. The chief sometimes holds secret meetings in it with his advisers and ward-heads; Lentswe is buried there, and in times of drought the women occasionally come to dance and sing round the site of his grave for rain.

Within the ward the outstanding social unit is the family or household. As I shall be dealing fully in later chapters with its structure and functions, I need merely refer to them here very sketchily. The household consists typically of a man with his wife or wives and dependent children, but often includes other people as well. It may be a simple biological family, or comprise two or more which are very closely related. Members of the same household associate together more intimately than the members of any other group in the tribe. They live, eat, work, and play, together, consult and help one another in all personal difficulties, and share in one another's good fortune. They produce the great bulk of their own food and other material wants; they form a distinct legal and administrative unit under their own head; they are the group within which children are born, reared and trained in conduct and methods of work; and they perform the ceremonies connected with birth, marriage, death and other ritual occasions. The self-contained character of the household appears most strongly perhaps at the fields, where for part of the year it lives as an isolated unit. In structure it tends to be of the patriarchal type, in that a wife normally lives with her husband among his paternal relatives, and, with her children, is legally under his authority, while succession, descent and inheritance of property, are all patrilineal.

Beyond the family are its relatives either by birth or by marriage. The Kgatla attach considerable importance to kinship ties, upon which, as we shall see in due course, are based many social and economic institutions. The closer relatives of a man, especially his parents' brothers and sisters, enter intimately into the normal routine of his daily life. They and their families are bound to him by various social and ceremonial obligations, frequently help him in his domestic undertakings, and are the people from among whom his wife should be chosen. His paternal relatives normally live immediately around him, and families whose heads have a common grandfather or great-grandfather may form a well-defined body for administrative and legal purposes also. In many respects, indeed, the individual family is merged in this wider unit, which I shall call the 'family-group'.

The ties between kinsmen were formerly reinforced by religion. Each family-group worshipped the spirits of its dead ancestors, the man senior to the rest in line of birth acting as common priest, while within the individual family the father performed the same function for his immediate dependants. But there has been a great change. Christianity became adopted as the tribal religion when Chief Lentswe was baptized in 1892. Since then it has so firmly established itself that little active trace now remains of the old system of worship. Those men and women who do not belong to the Church – and they constitute about four fifths of the adult population – are for the most part simply indifferent to religion. Such vague beliefs as they hold are inspired largely by echoes of missionary teaching blended confusedly with memories of ancestor-worship. There is no organized cult at all outside Christianity.

Lentswe's acceptance of Christianity prevented that marked rift between converts and heathens found in some other South African tribes. It is true that church members are distinguished by their system of worship, and that they must also conform to the social and moral ideals preached by the Mission, and abstain from tribal customs regarded as incompatible with true Christianity. But they do not always live up to these standards, and, as we shall have frequent occasion to note, there is often little difference in conduct between them and the 'heathens'. As would be expected, however, the latter have on the whole more openly retained the beliefs and practices ostensibly abandoned by Christians.

The Church is partly responsible for the decay of polygamy and certain other marriage practices. It also persuaded Lentswe to abolish the ancient ceremonies connected with the initiation of an age-regiment. The regimental organization still flourishes, but the initiation rites have been so greatly modified that what was a powerful force for discipline in old Kgatla life has disappeared. But although the Church has destroyed, it added much that is new to Kgatla culture, apart from religious beliefs. It erected churches, introduced the vocations of evangelist and catechist, and established a local Church council; it instituted catechumen classes; it introduced baptism, confirmation, and communion ceremonies and the observance of the Sabbath and other religious holidays; it developed new forms of marriage and death ritual, and through its hymns provided a new form of music. It sought to impose a new system of morality conforming to Protestant ideals, and to this end introduced sanctions of various kinds regulating the lives of its members. It built schools and appointed teachers, so that converts could learn to read the Gospels and other religious works. It insisted that all Church members should wear European clothing, and taught women knitting and sewing. For the past fifteen years it has carried on medical work, and more recently it has published a small vernacular journal named *Lesedi la Sechaba* ('The Light of the Nation'), conducted a reading-room for teachers and others, and fostered 'youth' movements for boys and girls.

Nevertheless, the path of Christianity has been far from smooth. The monopoly given by Lentswe to the Dutch Reformed Church Mission deprived it of the stimulus that might have come from competition. The adoption of Christianity as the tribal religion meant that many people accepted it as a matter of course rather than from persuasion or conviction. The missionaries themselves, with few exceptions, were seldom able to win the confidence and trust of the people. On several occasions unfavourable criticism developed to such an extent that it was only with difficulty, and after the intervention of the central Mission authorities in Cape Town, that more friendly relations between them and the tribe could be restored. In 1937 part of the congregation actually broke away, under a Native minister who had fallen into disgrace. They established their own Church, independent of Mission control but adhering generally to the same doctrines. Shortly afterwards still another Church was formed, this time as a branch of one already existing in the Union under the name of the 'Zion Christian Church'. It is patronized mainly by partisans of the suspended Chief Molefi, and serves to some extent as a cloak for political activities previously declared subversive by the Administration. For convenience I shall henceforth speak of the Mission Church itself as 'the Church', and where it is necessary to distinguish the two others will refer to them as 'the separatist Churches'.

Christianity has also failed signally to stamp out magic and sorcery. The practice of magic still persists strongly, even among members of the Churches. Many a man who has long abandoned ancestor-worship in favour of the Gospels, or perhaps never even known the old tribal cult, yet feels it necessary to have himself and his family, his huts, his cattle and his fields, regularly 'doctored' to ensure good health and prosperity. The belief in sorcery is also vigorous. There is little Kgatla fear more than being be-witched, and should any misfortune befall them they will readily attribute it to the 'black magic' of their rivals or enemies. The Administration will no longer tolerate the killing of sorcerers, and in 1927 made it a penal offence to accuse people of be-witching others. Until very recently, however, cases did still occur where alleged sorcerers were prosecuted in the tribal courts, and if found guilty they were usually fined and thrashed. Poisoning, which is regarded as sorcery, is actually practised at times, but almost all the other reported forms of bewitching cannot possibly do any physical harm. Nevertheless, the belief in their existence is a disturbing factor in social life and the cause of much ill feeling and malicious gossip, and magical methods of counteracting or avenging them have increased considerably of late.

The persistence of these beliefs and practices, in contrast with the almost complete disappearance of ancestor-worship, may be due partly to the continued existence of the professional ma-gicians, who have not been restrained from carrying on their activities. The chiefs themselves, although ostensibly Christians, believe firmly in magic, and Isang, during his regency, actually insisted on the performance of certain magical rites connected with mourning. Lentswe too, despite his enthusiasm for Chris-tianity, considered it his duty to continue practising certain rain-making ceremonies in secret. His successors followed his example more openly, and thus set a lead which the people generally have been happy to follow. Magic plays a part in tribal life that none of the new influences has so far been able to fill. It enters inti-mately into everyday activities and occupations, providing people with hope and confidence, and so enabling them to tide successfully over difficulties and disappointments. Christianity is for the average tribesman too remote from the realities of econ-omic and domestic life to be an acceptable substitute. Modern scientific teaching, again, is too recent an innovation, and reaches too few people, to have been able to make much headway against the traditional system of ideas underlying the belief in the efficacy of magic.

We now have the historical and cultural background for our study of Kgatla marriage and the family. They too have inevitably been affected by the process of civilization to which the tribe has been subjected. Some of the new influences impinged directly upon them. The Mission Church, bringing with it Protestant ideals of sex and family relationships, demanded from its members adherence to rules of conduct differing markedly from those traditionally observed. The Administration regards all Church marriages as valid under European civil law, with the result that the people concerned are bound together by mutual obligations, and have individual privileges, not known in the old tribal system. Christianity and education between them have introduced new conceptions of personal freedom running counter to the traditional insistence upon family solidarity and male dominance. Economic factors have disturbed the old division of labour, and diminished the self-sufficiency of the household. Migration to European centres of employment has weakened the social cohesion of the family, and created difficult problems of personal adjustment. Let us turn therefore to marriage, and see in more detail what has become of it as the result of these innovations.

2. The Choice of a Mate

The Kgatla consider marriage an essential step for every normal person to take. The adult who deliberately chooses to remain single is virtually unknown among them, and would be regarded as failing in his duty to provide for the increase of the tribe. Unmarried people are occasionally met, old enough to be referred to, somewhat contemptuously, as *mafetwa*, 'those who have been passed by'; but, in every instance that I investigated, their celibacy was due not to their own preference, but to some factor beyond their control, and few had abandoned all hope of ultimately marrying. The various genealogical records I collected show that in fact extremely few people, if any, fail to get married before reaching middle age. The only doubtful cases were men so long away that their marital history was unknown.

The common motives for marrying can readily be ascertained. Unmarried people are in tribal law always subject to the guardianship of their father, and are less highly respected than husbands and wives. Through marriage, therefore, they acquire enhanced social status. Marriage also enables them to indulge freely in sexual relations, undisturbed by fear of the trouble sometimes resulting from premarital intrigues. It permits a woman to bear children, without involving her in the disgrace that would ensue if she were unmarried; it entitles her husband to claim these children as his own, and so to rely upon them for support in his old age. It provides him also with a helpmate whose labour at home and in the fields is economically advantageous. The woman, again, will in time become the mistress of her own household, a position that she values highly. Finally marriage, through the comprehensive daily intimacy it permits, affords both husband and wife personal companionship of a kind otherwise unobtainable in Kgatla society.

Getting married, however, is accepted so much as a matter of course that people do not as a rule deliberately weigh its merits against those of remaining single. Their more urgent problem is not whether to marry, but whom to marry and when. In the old days even this was seldom a problem to those immediately concerned, for their marriages were arranged by their parents. They themselves, so it is said, were not consulted at all, and only after the customary negotiations had been successfully completed would they be informed of what had been decided. This procedure, however, was followed for a man's first wife only; any others he might take were chosen by himself.

The parents' task was probably made easier because unmarried people had few opportunities of associating together intimately and so developing strong attachments. Boys and girls, once they approached the age of puberty, were kept apart as much as possible. Boys spent most of their youth and early manhood at the cattle-posts out in the veld, while girls always remained under the direct control of their mother, even sharing the same hut with her at night until married. Meetings between young people were therefore restricted mainly to the rare occasions of a boy's visits home. Moreover, girls were sometimes betrothed in early childhood, or even pledged before they were born, so that their fate might be settled long before they could choose for themselves. As a result, refusal to marry the person selected is said to have very seldom occurred. When it did, the offending child was forced into the marriage, if necessary by appeal to the power of the chief, who invariably upheld the authority of the parents. The only escape for a couple crossed in love was elopement to some other tribe, but if caught before they could get away they were severely thrashed in public and sometimes even tortured.

Most people seem actually to have taken much trouble to find suitable mates for their children. The merits of possible brides were carefully debated, and only when unanimous approval had been reached were negotiations with the girl's parents formally opened. The boy's father and mother first discussed together the question of his marriage, and then consulted his maternal uncles and their wives. These uncles, especially the one 'linked' to the boy, had so important a say in the matter that their opinion was generally accepted as decisive. Once agreement had been reached with them, the views of the other relatives were ascertained, serious consideration being given to any adverse criticism of the girl and her family. More emphasis was laid upon her capacity for work than upon her good looks. As a local proverb vulgarly puts it: 'A pretty girl either steals or wets her bed,' i.e. she is more likely to be a nuisance than an asset to her husband and his people. Ideally, a bride should be industrious, meek and modest. Her parents, too, should be of good character and respectable ancestry, and, a point emphasized by all informants, free from any suspicion of practising sorcery. The girl's people were equally careful in assessing the claims of her suitor and his family, though it was always a powerful inducement if his father was wealthy or a man of some standing.

Informants state that it was largely because parents were so anxious to secure a satisfactory wife for their son that they preferred to marry him if possible to the daughter of some close relative or neighbour, with whose conduct and reputation they were themselves well acquainted. Like all other peoples, of course, the Kgatla forbade marriage between certain kinds of relatives; but, in contrast with the practice in most Bantu tribes, the restrictions were remarkably few. The only women a man might not marry were any ascendant or descendant, his sister or half-sister, his paternal or maternal aunt and his sister's daughter. Sexual intercourse with them, let alone marriage, was a punishable offence. But informants stoutly maintained that it never occurred. 'A sister stinks in her brother's nostrils as far as sexual relations are concerned,' one remarked forcefully if crudely; and another added, 'Even if she bends down and you see her naked thighs, they do not excite you.' The only case of incest I heard of was where a man unsuccessfully attempted to violate his own daughter. She reported the incident to her ward-head, who referred it to the chief. The offender was fined an ox, and warned that if he repeated the attempt he would be thrashed.

The Kgatla not only permitted marriage with a far wider range of relatives than is customary in most primitive and civilized societies; they also held that it was eminently desirable for a man to marry his first cousin. The marriage most preferred was with the *motswala* or cross-cousin, i.e. the daughter of a maternal uncle or paternal aunt. But, a very unusual phenomenon in Bantu society, marriage with the daughter of a paternal uncle or maternal aunt was also regarded with approval, even although she was commonly termed 'sister' (*kgaitsadi*). Cousin marriages, it was claimed, were most likely to succeed: the girl selected would be intimately known to the boy's people, and, as near relatives, both she and her husband would tend to be more tolerant of each other's conduct. 'Side by side with his cousin a man is always happy,' says the proverb. The marriage, moreover, would bind the two families together even more closely than before, and ensure increased harmony and cooperation – a factor of considerable importance in a society where people depended greatly upon their relatives for help in major household activities. Another inducement was that the cattle given at marriage by the boy's parents to the girl's would remain in the same family circle, and not pass into the hands of outsiders. 'Child of my paternal uncle, marry me,' says the relevant proverb, 'so that the cattle may return to our kraal.'

So much importance was attached to these marriages that a boy's parents almost invariably first sought him a wife among the daughters of their own brothers and sisters. Priority was given to the maternal uncles' daughters, and it was mostly with them that child betrothals occurred. A girl's cousin could generally obtain preference over any other suitor, while, if no one at all seemed anxious to marry her, her maternal uncles were expected to find her a husband among their sons. 'A cripple is looked after by his own people,' is the proverb quoted in this connexion. Moreover, if a man who already had several wives subsequently married his maternal uncle's daughter, she would rank higher than the others in status, and her eldest son would become his principal heir.

Nevertheless, the claims of relationship could be offset by the lack of other desirable qualities, and if either the girl or her parents failed to reach satisfactory standards of conduct and character, a wife would be sought somewhere else. Her own people, similarly, might refuse to hand her over to some cousin

of whom they disapproved, or with whose parents they had quarrelled. And, of course, it happened often enough that no cousin
was available at all. Genealogical records show that in fact
cousin-marriages were far less common than is suggested by the
stress informants laid upon them. In one genealogy I collected,
only seven men out of ninety-six had married first cousins: four
had married a maternal uncle's daughter, two a paternal aunt's
daughter, and one a maternal aunt's daughter. Another contained only three such marriages in a total of ninety, the wives
being the daughters of the husband's maternal uncle, paternal
uncle, and paternal aunt respectively. It will be noticed, however,
that each of the four possible types of cousin-marriage is represented in the two genealogies together.

If no suitable first cousin was available, a wife was sought
among the more remote relatives. Marriage with agnatic relatives
of this kind was fairly common, far more so, apparently, than
marriage with maternal relatives; but the explanation of this
seeming difference may possibly be that relationships through the
father are more clearly remembered than those through the
mother. The majority of marriages, however, took place between
people not actually related. But even here there was a measure of
preferential selection, for it was considered desirable that a man
should marry a woman of his own ward or at least of his own
village – once again, so informants maintained, because his
parents would be well acquainted with all the eligible girls, and
the two families concerned would always be at hand to help each
other. Marriage into a completely unknown family seldom occurred, and it was most unusual for a wife to be taken from some
other tribe, except by members of the royal family, who for political reasons often married daughters of neighbouring chiefs.

MODERN COURTSHIP

We have just seen that in the old days the parental choice of a
child's husband or wife was generally made with the object of
ensuring a congenial and stable marriage. It is still fairly
common for marriages to be arranged not by the children them-

selves, but by their parents. But it has become far more usual for
a son to take an active part in the preliminary family discussions
regarding whom he should marry, and his own preference is
always seriously considered. Frequently he selects his own wife,
and only when he has successfully wooed the girl does he ask his
parents to conduct the formal negotiations with her family, without which no marriage can be concluded under tribal law. Similarly, it is now customary for a girl's parents to consult her
whenever a proposal to marry her is received, and if she objects
strongly to her suitor they may reject him. Infant betrothal, too,
hardly ever occurs; at least, I failed to come across any recent
instances.

The factors responsible for this change will be discussed in the
chapter dealing with the general relationship between parents
and children. I need merely state in passing that the spread of
Western moral ideals, especially through Christianity, has led to
greater readiness on the part of parents to consider the wishes of
their children, while the possibility of getting married by
European civil law has provided a new means of circumventing
opposition to marriages of love. The abandonment of the old
initiation ceremonies has weakened parental control, and the introduction of schools has given children greater opportunities
and inducements to act on their own. The periodical migration
of young men to European centres of employment, where tribal
sanctions do not affect them so strongly, has likewise tended to
make them more intolerant of dictation, and affords them new
possibilities of escape if life at home becomes too oppressive.

> The heart eats what it desires,
> but rejects what is sought for it,

is the song of the modern young Kgatla.

One symptom of the new freedom, which bears considerably
upon the question of marriage, is the extent to which young
people now indulge in sexual relations. Formerly, as I have indicated, some attempt was made to keep unmarried girls chaste.
Not only were opportunities for love-making restricted, but
heavy penalties were inflicted upon a girl so unfortunate as to

become pregnant, and upon the boy responsible for her condition. She suffered numerous public humiliations making her an object of universal scorn, and her lover, apart from other punishment, was treated with special severity when being initiated into his age-regiment. Today, however, boys and girls mix together freely. The schools provide a new and favourable meeting-ground for adolescents; their elder brothers, temporarily home from work abroad, seldom go to the cattle-posts, as they should, but loaf through the village streets or about the trading-stores, where they get to know many girls apart from those with whom they have grown up; and the dances held on most rainless nights allow young people of all ages to develop and ripen new acquaintances. Most of the older children now have separate huts, in which they can entertain at home free from the presence of their parents, and calling on a girl has become an established part of modern courtship. Moreover, the decline of polygamy, and the absence of young men at labour centres, have deprived many women of the prospects of early marriage, and made them more willing to accept the advances of a lover. 'It is against nature,' as one informant put it, 'for them to remain chaste all the time.'

It is consequently taken for granted nowadays that boys and girls will acquire full sexual experience, and few Kgatla women, let alone men, are still virgins at marriage. The young people themselves deride their companions who are openly promiscuous, but they are equally contemptuous of those unsuccessful in the pursuit of love or remaining obstinately chaste. Parents sadly complain about the decay of morality, but feel unable to impose any effective check. It is only when pregnancy results that legal action can be taken. The girl's lover is then called upon either to marry her or to pay damages in cattle to her father, the standard amount being fixed at four head; but he can, and occasionally does, escape both alternatives by running away to seek work abroad. So many unmarried girls have borne children, in spite of *coitus interruptus* and other contraceptive practices, that the traditional penalties against them are no longer enforced. But they are not often regarded as desirable brides, except possibly by their lovers, and to avoid this additional handicap to their chances of marriage some try to procure an abortion if they conceive. I shall discuss later what happens to them then.

Sexual adventure not only enters largely into the lives of the young Kgatla, but strongly affects modern courtship. Youths always stress physical charm as among the qualities most desirable in the kind of girl they would like to marry. Individual preferences naturally vary, but the generally admired type is a light-skinned girl of somewhat heavy build, with prominent breasts and large, firm buttocks. The buttocks, especially, have a powerful erotic appeal, and evoke many compliments, while much of the love play before coitus consists in caressing them. Girls with slim backsides are seldom considered attractive; they are disparagingly said to have 'the bodies of boys'. Less interest is shown in facial beauty than in bodily proportions, but refined oval features, with shapely ears, large eyes, slender noses, and relatively thin lips, are more admired than others.

The enthusiasm that may be aroused by sexual relations with the right sort of girl is suggested in the following letter, written by a young man from Johannesburg to a recent mistress in Mochudi:

I still think of how we loved each other; I think of how you behaved to me, my wife; I did not lack anything that belonged to you. All things I did not buy, but I just got them, together with your body; you were too good to me, and you were very, very sweet, more than any other sweet things that I have ever had. We fitted each other beautifully. There was nothing wrong; you carried me well; I was not too heavy for you, nor too light, just as you were not too heavy for me nor too light; and our 'bloods' liked each other so much in our bodies.

It is hardly surprising, after this, that he concludes with the request: 'This letter contains secret matters, you must not lose it; if you don't want to keep it, burn it in the fire.'

I could not discover that girls made any special effort to enhance their perceptible physical attractions, apart from frequently smearing their faces and legs with vaseline and similar ointments. The few whom I questioned on the point asserted that the most important thing was to wash the genitals every day, 'to prevent them from stinking of sweat' and so putting off possible suitors. But there is one common practice directly correlated with sexual life. With the onset of puberty, sometimes a little later, most girls start pulling regularly at their *labia* in order to lengthen them. Sometimes a girl does so when sleeping alone, but two intimate friends often combine for the purpose, taking turns in working on each other. If the *labia* do not stretch quickly enough, magic is employed. The girls kill a bat, cut off and burn its wings, and grind the ashes to powder, which they mix with fat. Each then makes small cuts on the other's pubis and thighs right round the *labia*, and smears in the ointment they have prepared. 'In this way the *labia* will grow long like the wings of the bat.' The practice of stretching them is continued even after marriage. Its admitted object is the direct sexual gratification of both men and women. 'The *labia*,' explained a young wife, 'are there for the man to hold after having had intercourse with his wife, and then she also feels happy and at ease.' I shall return to this topic when discussing the sexual life of married people. For the moment it need only be said that since a girl will never allow a boy to see her naked genitals, even when they are sleeping together, the length of her *labia* is not an attraction observable in the early stages of courtship, though its subsequent erotic importance is stressed by all.

Nor is there much opportunity for girls to rely upon dress, since few can afford more than the standard costume of simple skirt and blouse, with one or two petticoats, locally made from purchased prints or art silks. But they always take care to wear their best when expecting male visitors or when going to church, which affords them a convenient occasion for displaying their attractions. Short skirts are regarded by older people as an index of loose morals, but evidently stimulate the boys, 'because', as Moeti remarked, 'you can then easily see the girl's thighs, and so you begin to wish for her'. Within recent years a few girls, newly home from Tiger Kloof or some other school abroad, have begun to appear in such relative luxuries as gaily-coloured frocks, high-heeled shoes, cotton stockings and hats. This enhances their appeal to the more educated youths, who in matters of fashion themselves tend to follow the European model; but the average young man considers such girls too fastidious for him, and prefers to court some one less elegant.

Physical charm is, however, in itself not always sufficient. The Kgatla youth prefers sexually attractive girls for his mistresses, but demands additional qualities in his future wife. Like his parents in the old days, he pays considerable attention to a girl's behaviour and character. He notes if she is cleanly in her person and keeps her hut neat and tidy; if she is polite and hospitable to visitors, respectful and obedient to her parents, and thought well of in her neighbourhood; if she is industrious or lazy, quiet or garrulous, good-tempered or quarrelsome. Chastity is not considered important, but a girl should be temperate and discreet in her love-affairs. As we have already seen, it is a drawback if she has been 'spoiled' by bearing a child to some one else – the main objection voiced by the young men being that she may continue, even after marriage, to bestow her favours upon him.

Girls likewise have their own standards by which a prospective lover or husband is judged. Bodily cleanliness, good manners and dress, and moderation in speech and drink, are all desirable qualities; industry and ability at work are highly valued; a father rich in cattle or prominent in tribal life is a decided asset; and popularity with other girls adds to the pleasures of conquest, although promiscuity in dispensing sexual favours is little attraction.

These ideals of beauty and conduct are important in determining the choice of a mate, but boys are obviously also influenced by opportunity and the willingness of the girl. Courtship tends to follow a fairly simple pattern. The boy may be acquainted with the girl from childhood, if they are relatives or neighbours, or he may get to know her through chance meetings. In either event, if she attracts him he asks if he may visit her. It is seldom that she refuses, unless she greatly dislikes him, for, as the proverb says, 'The [future] saviour of a person is not known,' and so prospective suitors must not be discouraged. The earlier visits are generally paid in the afternoon, the boy chatting with the girl and other members of her family in the open courtyard. It is considered a promising sign if she is always at home when he has arranged to call, and that she regards him as sufficiently distinguished to be given a chair to sit on. As they grow more friendly, he starts coming at night, after the evening meal, and sits with her either round the fire in the courtyard, or, if they wish to be alone, in her hut.

Should the girl's parents dislike the boy or fear his intentions, they will if possible never allow matters to reach the latter stage. They tell him openly that his visits are unwelcome, and may even ask his father to keep him away. If he is then found again in her hut late at night, and in theory he has no right to be there unless actually engaged to her, they are justified in forcing him out and thrashing him. The girl also will be scolded or whipped, and warned that she is heading for disaster. Few parents, however, dare go to such lengths, for other opportunities of meeting secretly now abound. In any case the father, who is usually stricter than the mother, is not always at home to see what is going on. And if no objections are raised the boy rightly assumes that his visits meet with tolerance, if nothing more, while often enough he is directly encouraged by the friendliness and hospitality with which he is received. I was told of one woman who actually slept out in the courtyard night after night, so that her daughter might remain undisturbed with a suitor in the only hut of the compound.

If the girl shows no sign of responding favourably to the boy's advances, he will try to win her over by means of little gifts, like the decorated spoons and porridge-stirrers made at the cattle-posts. Sometimes he asks his sisters to cultivate her and discreetly further his suit. He may try to prejudice her against his rivals by malicious gossip about them, although this more often involves him in a fight than brings him success. He may deliberately avoid her for some time, in the hope that she will miss him and therefore be more friendly in future. Or, alleged to be the best tactics of all, he may divert his attentions to other girls with the object of making her jealous.

Some boys also make use of love-medicines (*meratisô*), of which many varieties are commonly known. One of the most popular includes such diverse ingredients as the body and nest of two different birds, the web of a large spider, bits of vegetable matter, and the sweet-smelling leaves of a certain bush. These are roasted together in a potsherd, the boy bathing his face in the smoke and murmuring the name of the girl. He then grinds the ashes to powder, and mixes them with fat to make an ointment, with which he carefully smears his face and hair whenever he goes to visit her. He tries also to convey some of it surreptitiously on to her skirt or kerchief, and so leave its scent with her, or he may present her with some beads or a kerchief similarly anointed. Adolescents still fresh in their amorous career consider such medicines very effective, but few young men take them seriously enough to feel that they will bring success where everything else has failed.

Courtship is sometimes carried on with marriage directly in view, sometimes merely because the boy wants to make the girl his concubine. But even in the former event he almost invariably tries to persuade her to sleep with him. Once they have become sufficiently friendly, he starts protesting his love for her, and leads up, either crudely or with finesse, to the suggestion that she let him 'share her blankets'. A good tactician will refer frequently to the engagements and marriages of others, and so persuade her that he is himself contemplating marriage with her, but does not yet wish to say so openly. Then he will go on to hint that, before one gets engaged, one should 'taste' the girl to see what she is like. If educated, he is sometimes rash enough to state his desires in writing, with the result that if she becomes pregnant she has convincing evidence of his responsibility for her condition. Most girls, if they really like a boy, show little reluctance in complying with his wishes, although it is considered good form to refuse the first time of asking. If the girl hesitates too long he will threaten to seek satisfaction somewhere else, 'and then in many cases she will agree, because she is afraid of losing him'.

A young unmarried woman described to me how she was first seduced:

I slept for the first time with a boy when I was already big. It took him a long time to persuade me. I told him that I had heard it was sore, but he said, 'No, it is very nice.' And as I kept on refusing, I saw that he was getting sad, so I let him persuade me, and we slept together. When he started, it was so sore that I tried to push him away, but I could not do so. He put his penis into me, and the blood came out. I thought he had burst something in me, and it was not nice at all. But nowadays it is not sore, except sometimes at the very beginning, and as he keeps on working I feel like biting him, only we girls are cowards, and I feel like hugging his neck tightly, the sweetness is so great. But I don't like those boys who simply ejaculate quickly and then want to rest and sleep. Boys are snakes; when they beg for this, they implore, they even kneel down, and that is how they overcome us.

And the ease with which a girl can sometimes be won is well illustrated in the following little episode related to me by one of my more regular informants:

Last night I went to visit Gonntse Phokobye. We sat in her hut laughing and talking. Her brother was also there. I sat on a chair, not intending to sleep with her, and as we were talking her brother went away. We continued talking about school matters, and then I began to think of sleeping with her. She asked me if I had liked Johannesburg, and I said, 'Yes.' Then I told her: 'What I don't like about the girls here is that they have no manners,' and when she asked why, I told her what had happened to me last year with Mosodi, who said that I had got her into trouble. Then she said, 'Oh, then you people take no notice of us?' And she asked me if I had decided to stay away altogether from girls, but I said, 'Of course not.' She continued to say that boys and girls were not meant to stay without each other; and I said that even if I did think of it, there were no girls here with whom I could sleep, because none of them was any good. She said, 'Well, but you must use a girl.' I said, 'Yes, but even if I did think of it, it is no good, because you would not allow it.' 'Oh,' she replied, 'I did not mean myself, I meant other girls, because I have my own lover.' I said, 'No, you must, it is only fair.' I left my chair and went to sit beside her on the bed where she was sitting, and put my arm round her shoulders; and she said, 'Au! Why are you troubling me?' But I continued to say, 'No, you must help me, man.' She kept quiet, and I kept asking her, 'Do you want to do it or not?' But she did not answer me. Then I blew out the lamp and began taking off my shoes, and as I was doing so I heard her undressing, and then I knew that it was all right. I spoke to her several times in a low voice, but she would not reply.

Then she pulled back the blankets, breathing hard. I got in between them, and she followed. She turned her back on me, facing the wall; I pinched her back, she turned and chuckled and breathed very heavily; she put her arm under my neck, and then drew my hands on to her body; she shivered, and turned over on to her back, and then I got on top of her.

As this suggests, the girl herself may at times take the initiative. She pays the boy marked attention whenever she meets him, thus showing that he attracts her; she is obviously pleased and friendly when he visits her, and responds readily to all his advances. If she hopes to marry him, she may even resort to love-medicines to keep him by her side. A common prescription is the dirt and moisture from her thighs and genitals, which she puts in the porridge or beer given to him as a favoured guest. More reliance, however, is placed upon the medicines obtained from the 'doctors' (professional magicians). Natale, a doctor who was one of my principal informants, described with great gusto how among his clients were two Church evangelists, whose daughters seemed likely to remain on the shelf. And he remarked with evident gratification upon the success that followed his treatment. The ingredients of his medicine include the heart of the honey-bird, 'because this bird never deceives a hunter, and so the boy will speak the truth', and the fat of the hedgehog, 'because this animal does not move about much, and so the boy will keep hanging around the girl's home'. Some of the medicine is burned in a potsherd, the girl bathing her face in the smoke and calling on the boy by name; the rest she smears on her face whenever he visits her, or puts into the food she gives him.

Once the girl has accepted the boy as a lover he visits her fairly often, and whenever possible spends the whole or part of the night alone with her in her hut or in some other suitable place. They may remain attached for several months or even a year or two, and then drift apart. This sometimes happens if one is openly unfaithful to the other. Many a boy has several mistresses simultaneously, which, unless he is discreet, may arouse such jealousy that the girls fight one another, or on the other hand decide to have nothing more to do with him. The girl also may be impartial in her favours, with somewhat similar results. Or she may keep urging the boy to marry her, and either frighten him off by her persistence, or give him up herself when she realizes that his intentions are not sufficiently honourable. Often enough, however, their mutual affection steadily deepens and they ultimately agree to marry, particularly if she first bears him a child. On the other hand, her pregnancy is sometimes the cause of their separation, for, much as he likes her, he may not be keen enough to take her in marriage, and he must now either do that or get out of the scrape as best he can. Many a love-affair has come to an untimely end when the boy receives a communication like the following, which was written to one of my informants:

I let you know that I am still here at the cattle-post, but, my friend, I repeat what I told you when I was at home, I am really speaking the truth: from the beginning of August, and right through September, I have been missing my periods, and now it is the beginning of October. And, my friend, I have now given up hope of having them again; I let you know this so that you must realize what you have done to me. There is not the slightest doubt, I am pregnant, and that is why I am telling you this. I have no more to say, but wait to see what you will do.

But, as is so often also the case elsewhere, a girl abandoned by her lover sometimes continues, in vain, to cherish an affection for him. The same young gentleman whose correspondence I have just quoted received the following pathetic letter, from a different girl, while he was working in the European town to which he had fled:

Receive my letter, here it is, so that you may know that I am still living and well. Truly, *my dear** Phoko, I wonder what wrong I have done you, that you no longer write to me, my love. And the child is still growing nicely, he even speaks. My friend Phoko, when will you come back to see him? When I ask him where his *papa* is, he says, 'He is far away.' I send you a *foto* [*sic*], here it is, although it is bad; he did not want to stand nicely but clutched me, because he is afraid of people, except me. I shall stop here with greetings, and the child also says he greets you very much. Oh, my friend, how intelligent your

* The words in italics were written in English.

child is! You would think he is already a big person. He greets you very much. Please let me have a letter soon, my friend. The writer is Fagare. *Good-bye, Dear*. He was crying and did not want to stand; that is why he is not standing nicely.

PARENTAL OPPOSITION

The freedom now permitted to young people does not necessarily mean that their choice always meets with parental approval. If the girl is a relative, or the daughter of a friend, the boy's parents are usually pleased, and do what they can to further his suit. But if they regard her family as unsuitable, or feel that her own manners leave much to be desired, they will object to the marriage he proposes. This is particularly so when the girl's people are strangers to them, for although the traditional restrictions and preferences still prevail, the growth of the villages and the increased facilities for travel have tended to make marriages with outsiders far more common. It will be remembered that Sedimo, whom we met at the beginning of Chapter 1, had intended at one time to marry a Mafeking girl, and several of the men working in Johannesburg have actually brought back wives who are foreigners. The vast majority of marriages, however, are still within the tribe, but the possibilities of choice have widened so greatly that the boy's parents are not always acquainted with the girl and her family. Christian parents, too, prefer that their children should marry other communicants, although the Church itself, which first introduced the rule, no longer insists upon it.

Should the boy's people dislike his choice, they may press him to give up his idea of marrying her. If they are sufficiently persistent, they may succeed in gaining their wish. But if he is really attached to the girl, and her own parents also favour him, he will not yield so readily, and many a painful family conflict has resulted from such a situation. In the long run, however, the boy has the upper hand. He can make his home with the girl's parents, or go abroad to work and get her to follow him there, or marry her by civil law in the District Commissioner's office. But he need seldom exercise any of these alternatives. Under modern conditions he has acquired new importance as a wage-earner, and in order to retain his support his parents will finally submit, however reluctantly. His marriage, however, may result in much distress if they continue to harbour resentment against him and his wife.

A case that took place many years ago illustrates the transition from the old parental compulsion to the modern possibilities of escape. Lesilo wished to marry a young widow to whom his parents objected, mainly because she had not borne her former husband any children, and was therefore considered sterile. He insisted on having her, and, failing to gain his father's approval, ultimately ran away with her. His father pursued and overtook them, and brought them before the chief. They were tried and severely thrashed for their disobedience, and were ordered to stay apart. Lesilo then went to live in a small town in the Transvaal, where the woman soon afterwards managed to join him. They were married by European civil rites, and stayed there until the death of Lesilo's father. Then they came home. They are still living together, but the marriage has remained childless, a fact to which people often point as showing the greater wisdom of parents in choosing wives for their sons.

In another instance, much more recent, the boy's parents objected to the girl because she was notoriously promiscuous, and they feared therefore that she would become sterile. They offered to find him some one else, but he said he wanted only her. Since they would not give way, he started sleeping regularly with her and spending most of his time at her home, her mother not objecting. The upshot was that, even although the girl did not become pregnant, the boy's parents finally agreed to his marrying her, and went through the formal betrothal negotiations on his behalf.

Girls have more difficulty in marrying against the wishes of their parents. Where the main objection is to her lover or his family, the girl may ultimately persuade her people to withdraw their opposition, if no other suitor appears whom they regard with greater favour. This happened, for instance, with Dikeledi, who, after becoming the mistress of Modise, wished to marry

him. Her parents, however, refused to agree, saying that
Modise's people were not Church members like themselves, and
also had the reputation of being sorcerers. She appealed to an
influential friend, who interceded on her behalf. Her parents said
that their objection was not so much to Modise as to his family,
but after a good deal of argument and hesitation they were finally
induced to give their consent.

But when the girl's parents have their own chosen husband for
her, they sometimes succeed in parting her from her lover and
bullying her into an unwelcome and distasteful marriage. Several
such cases have occurred within recent years, for parental
authority, although weakened, has by no means completely disappeared. Mokgethi, for instance, had for over two years been
the mistress of a youth whom she wished to marry; but when
another suitor appeared, closely allied to the royal family, her
parents forced her into what they considered the more desirable
union. She remained with her husband for only a few months,
and then, finding him intolerable, returned home and refused to
go back to him. There is a well-known girls' song expressing
forcibly the contempt they sometimes have for a husband thus
selected by their parents:

> I heard it said that I was engaged,
> and one afternoon when I was at home,
> as I was sitting I saw a fool coming;
> he came dragging his coat on the ground,
> and his trousers were made of khaki;
> I said to him, 'Fool, where do you come from?'
> And he replied, 'I am your fiancé.'
> I gave the dog a chair, and his tail hung down.

The only possible escape a girl has in such a situation, apart
from running away and joining her lover abroad, is to bear him a
child. Some parents will even then withhold their consent, but
the majority, aware that her prospects of marriage to some one
else have now been diminished, accept the situation with as much
grace as they can. This happened with Motlapele, who, after
being engaged by her parents to a man whom she disliked intensely, succeeded in becoming pregnant by the one she really

loved. Her fiancé thereupon broke the engagement, and her parents, having no alternative, had to agree to the marriage she desired. They are now very pleased that they did so, for their son-in-law helps them considerably both financially and at work.

I must emphasize again that love matches, on the one hand, and forced marriages, on the other, are two opposite extremes. Often enough boys and girls have no particular preferences of their own, and accept willingly enough any reasonably suitable mate chosen by their parents. It is in fact by no means unusual for a boy, when he wishes to get married, to leave the selection of a wife largely in the hands of his parents, for he is not always anxious to marry his mistress. Traditional usage is therefore still strong enough for arranged marriages to be common, although much greater scope is given nowadays to personal choice by the young people themselves.

Two recent instances may help to illustrate this. In 1932 Pule's parents suggested his marrying a certain girl. He refused, saying that he was not anxious to marry yet, and despite many heated discussions he would not give way. He then went abroad to a technical school. While there he received many letters from home urging the match upon him, for his parents were fond of the girl, and feared that some one else might marry her first. He himself also liked her, but not sufficiently to want her as a wife. His parents kept pressing him, and at last he wrote back saying they could do as they liked. They accordingly approached the girl's parents, only to meet with an immediate refusal. When Pule came home he was told what had happened. Since his parents had given him so much trouble, he asked them to try again. They sent a couple of times, but with no greater success. He then told them to drop the idea. They asked him what he now wanted to do, and he mentioned the name of the girl, one of his mistresses, whom he really wished to marry. His parents replied that they preferred her younger sister, but he insisted that as they had formerly had their way he now should have his. They ultimately consented and, the girl's people also being agreeable, the marriage was duly arranged.

In the other instance, the boy had no say at all in the matter. Morena's mother, a widow, thought him old enough to get married, and consulted her brother about a suitable bride. They selected one, the grand-daughter of their elder sister, but she refused to accept him. One of his aunts then suggested another girl, and his uncle, after inquiring about her, said that she would do. Morena himself had not yet met her, but agreed to whatever was done, and the betrothal was duly arranged in accordance with custom. Only then was he taken, also in accordance with custom, to be introduced to her parents. She herself was not present at the time, and he returned home without yet having seen her. The next day he went alone to her home, but found nobody there. He came again the following day, and, seeing a girl of about seventeen in the courtyard, asked where her elder sister was. She replied that she had no elder sister. 'I mean Nayang,' he said. 'Oh, that's me,' she replied. 'Goodness!' he remarked, 'I had no idea that you were so young.' But he liked her well enough, and became so fond of her that, to his mother's disgust, he began spending most of his time at her home by day as well as by night.

BETROTHAL CEREMONIES

The examples just given have shown that, once a suitable bride has been chosen, her family's consent to the marriage must still be obtained. This involves a series of formal approaches, collectively known as 'to seek'. They can never be made directly by the boy himself, but must be undertaken on his behalf by his relatives. No form of cohabitation that has not been preceded by this 'seeking' is considered a true marriage in tribal law. To the Kgatla, as we shall constantly see, marriage is still a process linking together two families rather than merely the couple directly concerned, and failure to seek or obtain formal sanction for a union shows that it is not acceptable to one family or the other. Occasionally, as when a man marries abroad, it is impossible for his parents to negotiate his betrothal, but inside the Reserve it is still considered correct that they should do so. This means in effect that they could prevent his marrying some one whom they dislike, for if he cohabits with her before she has been 'sought' for him she is considered to be merely his concubine. But, as I have shown above, it is now possible for him to get round this difficulty in various ways if he is really determined to marry her.

Tradition lays down broadly each step of the relevant procedure. Nowadays this is often curtailed when the families concerned are fairly intimate, but occasionally the old ritual is carried on through all its stages. Before any formal step is taken, the boy's parents may themselves privately sound the girl's, if well known to them, or they may ask him to ascertain from her the prospects of acceptance. This is done merely by way of precaution, but unless a promising reply is received the matter may be dropped at this stage, to avoid the shame of a public refusal.

The subsequent negotiations are carried on through intermediaries ('the seekers'). A paternal uncle or some similarly close relative, with another member of the boy's family as witness, is sent to the girl's father 'to beg for a calabash of water', this being the formula conventionally employed in speaking to him. He, whatever his own attitude may be, must as conventionally make some non-committal reply, to the effect that he must first consult 'the owners of the girl' (her other relatives). When the messengers have gone, he discusses their proposal with his wife, and then with her brothers (the girl's maternal uncles). The girl herself may also be asked at this stage if she knows the boy and wants to marry him. Should the general opinion favour refusal, the intermediaries will be told so when they next come. The boy's father may send them back to try again, or may decide to seek some other wife for his son. Failing a definite refusal, they come every few weeks or so to learn how matters stand. It is good etiquette to prolong the discussions, and several months may elapse before a definite answer is given. The girl's parents meanwhile consult their other relatives also, carefully weighing up the merits and demerits of the boy and his family, and, if little is known about them, make discreet inquiries in the village about their standing and reputation.

When at last agreement has been reached, the intermediaries are told to come on a certain day for their answer. They are received not only by the girl's father, whom alone they have been seeing all this time, but by most of her other relatives, including especially her maternal uncles, whose presence is essential. Then, if the decision is favourable, as it is almost certain to be if matters have been allowed to reach this stage, they are conventionally told: 'Here is the child, you can take her; take her living, and if you return her, return her still alive,' i.e. if you become tired of her in future, send her back unharmed.

Sometimes the giving of the answer is preceded by the request that the boy's parents should 'send the women'. Shortly afterwards his paternal aunt, or some similarly close relative, comes with another woman to see the girl's mother. They repeat the proposal made by the men, and, after perhaps another call or two, are told to return on an appointed day for their answer. They come with the male intermediaries and some of the boy's other relatives. Formal consent to the engagement is then given in the manner already mentioned. Elderly informants state that the use of female intermediaries at this stage is an innovation. The traditional practice was that the women did not visit the girl's mother until after the proposal had been formally accepted, their mission then being to confirm it and to thank her for her consent. 'This is done to show that the girl is being taken not to the council-place (where men habitually sit), but to the compound (which is a woman's proper domain).' Occasionally, women are employed from the beginning as intermediaries if the girl's father is dead and her mother must therefore be approached directly. This also is an innovation, as formerly the girl's guardian (usually a paternal uncle) would have been the right person to see first, and this could be done only by men.

Several days after the proposal has been accepted, the female intermediaries go again to the girl's home, bringing her the gifts made to seal the betrothal. These gifts, known as 'the goods brought', consisted formerly of skin clothing, beads, and other ornaments. Nowadays they generally comprise one pound in cash, a white blanket with red stripes, a red shawl, a kerchief, and two lengths of dress material, costing in all between three and four pounds. They are bought by the boy's parents soon after the negotiations have begun, or, if he is working abroad, he may get them himself and send them home. They are handed to the girl's mother before some relatives as witnesses. The girl is later called to see them, and is told by her mother: 'Here is your debt' – implying that henceforth she is bound to the boy and must watch her conduct. She may not begin to use them until two or three weeks have passed, lest she be accused of unbecoming anxiety to get married soon.

With the delivery and acceptance of the gifts the betrothal becomes legally binding. Two more rites remain, however, before the 'seeking' is finally concluded. The boy, while the negotiations are in progress, should not visit the girl's home openly. Formerly he would in any case have been unable to do so, since he was usually stationed at the cattle-post while they were going on. Today, as we have seen, many boys do their own courting before any further steps are taken about the marriage. In such cases, although the boy is not forbidden to see the girl at all during the period of 'seeking', he should at least avoid consorting with her publicly. However, once the betrothal has been sealed, he is for- mally taken to her home one evening by the original inter- mediary, and is presented to her parents as their 'son-in-law'. They entertain him and his uncle, and tell him that from now on, whenever he is hungry, thirsty, or tired, he can always come to them for food or for rest. He is then free to visit their home alone whenever he likes.

For the last ceremony of all, the girl's parents make beer, which they invite the boy's people to come and drink. This beer- drink is known as 'the sandals', because of the many visits paid by the intermediaries, or as 'inspection of the compound', be- cause the boy's relatives in general are now officially introduced to those of the girl. He himself is seldom present; the occasion serves mainly to acquaint the two sets of people with one another, and to cement the union that will henceforth prevail between them. Sometimes his parents also do not attend, but come alone the following evening to drink a pot of beer specially reserved for them. This pot is termed 'What one lies waiting for'. 'It refers to the time when a woman lies on her back waiting for her husband to sleep with her, or for her child to be born; the boy's parents must therefore realize that when the girl herself was conceived and born, her mother sweated and suffered, and so cannot now part lightly with her.' And the boy's parents must come alone because procreation is the act of two people only.

3. Getting Married

Once the betrothal ceremonies have concluded, a considerable time usually elapses before the wedding itself. This does not seem to have happened formerly, except with child betrothals, for otherwise there was nothing to prevent the couple from getting married as soon as their parents wished. Today, however, a boy, once he is engaged, usually goes abroad to work for money, and, except for occasional brief visits home, his absence is often prolonged. Most engagements last two or three years, some as many as four or five. But from the moment the betrothal gifts have been made the couple are referred to as 'husband' and 'wife', and their families speak of each other as 'relatives-in-law'. Associated with this new terminology are reciprocal observances laid down by law and custom.

The parents of the engaged couple exchange visits from time to time, help one another when additional labour is required for some task, and occasionally send one another presents of meat, beer, or thick milk. They invite one another to their feasts and other celebrations, and in general try to be as friendly as possible. The boy's parents are especially attentive to the girl and her people, to show that they still approve of the match. They give her additional presents now and then, like dress material, pots and baskets, and may send her to their cattle-post to grow fat on the milk of their cows. They must be informed about any matter affecting her welfare, particularly when she is sick or in trouble, and she can never be doctored except with their knowledge and permission. 'But,' Sofonia commented sardonically, 'each family will keep secrets from the other. If the girl is syphilitic, or has had an abortion, or is caught sleeping with some other boy, her

parents do not tell her fiancé's people; and the latter, if their son
does something wrong, likewise conceal it.'

The girl during all this time, however delighted she may be
about her engagement, is required by convention to act very de-
murely. She should of course cease to have affairs with other
young men, and, if her fiancé is in the village, must remain home
at night in case he comes to visit her. Whenever she encounters
him in public, away from her home, she talks to him with
diffidence and reserve, and sometimes goes so far as to avoid him
completely if she can. She is still meeker when with his parents or
older relatives; her general conduct is under close observation,
and if she misbehaves they may break the engagement. If she
meets them in the street, she simply greets them and passes on,
without stopping to talk unless they do so first; and she may not
visit their home at all, except on the rare occasions when she is
specially invited there to work or to attend a feast. 'She must
have shame,' as the Kgatla put it, and avoid any hint of what
would be considered undue familiarity. Even if others talk to her
about her engagement, she pretends to be indifferent, reserving
her enthusiastic confidences for her closest friends only. All this,
the Kgatla say, she must do lest people comment disparagingly
that she is 'throwing herself' at the boy's people because she is
anxious for an early marriage.

The boy, on the other hand, may visit his fiancée's home
freely, and is expected to do so frequently whenever he is in the
village. He is treated there with marked respect and cordiality,
for, as the proverb says, 'A son-in-law is the food of his wife's
parents', and so they take great care of him. Porridge is set aside
for him daily in a special bowl, whether he comes to eat it or not,
and such delicacies as fowls may be served in his honour. He can
remain alone with the girl in her hut at night, and it has become
common for them to sleep together – if they have not already
been doing so – without meeting any objection from her parents.
But public demonstrations of affection are considered most unbecoming, and are in fact seldom seen, owing partly to the behaviour demanded from the girl. It is only when they are alone,

or writing to each other, that any display is given to their mutual attachment.

'When they sit together like this,' said an informant, 'they talk about their life, what they are doing, how they are keeping, how they long for each other, and about their mutual love. The girl asks the boy how he came to love her, and after telling her he asks, "Do you love me as much as you love yourself, or do you love others also, do they attract you?" And the girl will say, "Why do you annoy me with such silly questions?" She too asks him about the quality of his love, saying that she saw him paying attention to another girl. This is just to tease him, but he will feel uneasy, and say, "I have no time for other girls, I regard them as leaves blown past by the wind." Then the girl, to comfort him, will say, "No, just do as you like." And he will reply "One day when I ask you the same question, you must not be angry for it has hurt me greatly." '

During this time also the boy, when at home, should occasionally help the girl's parents, e.g. by bringing them loads of firewood or earth, building fences at their fields, or ploughing with them. Considerable store is set by any such services he volunteers to do, and people will say of him approvingly: 'He is a good son-in-law, he has manners.' Normally, however, he goes abroad to work soon after getting engaged, for he is nowadays expected to earn the money with which to buy his own and the girl's wedding outfits. While away he writes to her or gets some literate friend to do so for him, and he may occasionally send her a blanket, a shawl, or some cash, these gifts being as usual transmitted through his own parents. Failure to seek employment abroad often leads to complaints that he is a shirker who will be unable to provide properly for his wife and children, and this may be an important factor in wrecking the engagement.

In the old days, the death of an engaged person did not necessarily break the bond between the two families. If the girl died her parents were expected to give her fiancé a younger sister or some other relative to marry instead; if the boy died, the girl would be married to his younger brother, and the children she bore him were considered the legal offspring of her original fiancé. The parents on either side might refuse to sanction such marriages if

the first engagement had been a failure, but the children themselves are said to have had no choice in the matter. Today both
customs are still practised at times, but only if the children also
wish it. Thus, in 1933, Setimela died two days before his wedding was to have taken place, and, after a brief interval for
mourning, his fiancée was married to his younger brother
Morake. Similarly, Maganelo, the announcement of whose wedding we read in Chapter 1, had for several years courted Isang's
eldest daughter Dikolo, and it was only after her death that he
became engaged to her younger sister Mamorema. Whether such
a marriage takes place or not, the bereaved person is always
brought to the deceased's home as soon as possible after the
death, in order to condole formally. If the couple have had a
child, the survivor may be doctored for 'mourning sickness', but
there are no other special mourning observances.

Engagements may also be ended through disagreement. This is
in fact fairly common. The boy may refuse to marry his fiancée if
he becomes attached to some one else, or, on the other hand, if
she herself openly ignores him whenever he comes to visit her, or
is unfaithful to him, or, most frequent cause of all, is made
pregnant by another lover. Considering how long most engagements are, and the time spent abroad by men at work, it is
not surprising that a girl frequently succumbs to temptation
during the absence of her fiancé. Sometimes he is willing to go on
with the marriage all the same, but generally he refuses to do so. I
have already mentioned the case of Motlapele, whose engagement was broken because she became pregnant by a rival
lover, and I know of many others like it.

To avoid such a contingency the girl sometimes tries to procure an abortion, hoping thereby to prevent her fiancé from discovering her infidelity. Dikeledi, the story of whose engagement I
told in the last chapter, carried on with several lovers while her
fiancé was working in Johannesburg. She at last became pregnant, and, fearing the consequences, successively tried croton oil,
washing blue, epsom salts, castor oil, and several local herbs as
abortifacients. When all these had failed, she fled into the Transvaal. Her parents informed her fiancé's mother, who burst out

crying and said, 'I feel hurt about this, because when I betrothed my son to your daughter, people murmured, "How can Dikeledi, the daughter of a respectable Christian family, be married to the son of a witch?" Now I am surprised that she has done such a thing and run away. For myself, I can still accept her as a daughter-in-law, but I doubt if my son will agree, because even before this he had been complaining about her loose behaviour.' The son, however, wrote back in due course that he would nevertheless marry Dikeledi, as he loved her greatly; and, after giving birth to her child in the Transvaal, she returned home to await his arrival for the wedding.

The girl and her parents, similarly, may break the engagement if her fiancé takes no further interest in her, turns out to be a worthless loafer, or neglects her for some one else. Mosetha, for instance, broke with Nthithane because he made no attempt to seek work abroad, yet seldom came to visit her. 'How can I marry a man like this?' she said. 'I am much better than he is, because I once went to the Transvaal to work for myself, while he remains here in his loin-skin' (i.e. without decent clothes, which he could have got by seeking employment like others). And Mmaphefo, after being long engaged to a man who seldom came near her, found another lover by whom she became pregnant. Her fiancé's people were informed, but they did nothing at all. She waited a year, and as no word had yet come from them, she agreed to marry the father of her child. Preparations for the wedding had already been started, when the first man's parents suddenly demanded that she carry out her obligation of marrying their son. Her people refused to let her do so, complaining that her fiancé, after avoiding her for so long and taking not the slightest interest in her welfare, now wanted her just because she was getting married to some one else. The matter ultimately came to the chief, who decided that Mmaphefo was not to blame. 'She could not wait in darkness all this time without any word from the boy.' She was therefore allowed to marry her second suitor, while the first had to forfeit his betrothal gifts because of his conduct.

As this case shows, the dissolution of an engagement is first discussed privately by the two families concerned. If they cannot reach a settlement, the matter is referred to the court of the ward-head, or, if it proves too difficult for him, to that of the chief. If the person wishing to break the engagement is not supported by his own people, the court may insist upon the marriage taking place. This is particularly so when the boy has himself impregnated the girl and now refuses to marry her. But if the families concerned side with their respective children, the engagement is always dissolved. The girl's people, if to blame, must then return the equivalent of all the gifts made to her; if the boy is to blame, he and his people forfeit their goods. The offending party may in addition have to pay damages to the other.

The following case, for instance, came before the chief's court in 1938. Koti, a widower, became engaged to Matsau, and, with the permission of her parents, lived with her in her hut. She went to his fields to help him plough, and stayed with him all the season. Then she left him, and he afterwards found her consorting with other lovers. He complained to her parents. When the usual family discussion was held, she said that she no longer wanted him. He therefore sued her, through her father, for the return of the various gifts he had made to her. She and her parents put up as defence the story that Koti had driven her away. The chief, however, accepted his evidence, and ordered the girl's people to pay him not only the value of his gifts but also an ox, since they were obviously trying to cheat him out of the marriage. The goods concerned, incidentally, consisted of two bags of corn, and the following other articles, valued in all at £5 16s.: a shawl, two dress-lengths of print, two kerchiefs, a reel of cotton, two rugs, a pillow, a bucket, two blouse-lengths of print, soap, a blanket, two fowls, four jars of vaseline, a goat and a pair of sandals. This illustrates the kinds of present a man makes to his fiancée at and after the betrothal, and shows also the meticulous care with which every item is remembered.

In another case, heard before the same court in 1937, the parents of Mmamothusi sued her fiancé Ramosukwana for breach of promise. He had seduced her and, having no cattle with which to pay the usual damages, had promised to marry her. His father initiated the betrothal negotiations, and soon after their conclusion the child was born. Ramosukwana then began to live with her regularly at her home, and two years later they had another child. Soon afterwards, however, he refused to go through with the marriage, saying that she had been unfaithful to him. But the evidence showed that her maternal uncle wished him to marry another niece instead, and that he himself was more than willing. He was therefore ordered to pay Mmamothusi's father six head of cattle as damages before he could marry the second girl, while the uncle, for causing all the trouble, was fined an ox.

WEDDING CEREMONIES

As we have just seen, an engaged couple may live together and even have children. But although commonly referred to as 'husband' and 'wife', they are not considered married until the wedding festivities have taken place and the cattle known as *bogadi* have been given by the boy's parents to the girl's father. The festivities are normally held when the girl, with the consent of her parents, goes to live at the boy's home and so is received into his family. But until the *bogadi* cattle have been given, the marriage is not considered fully valid in Kgatla law, and the children born of it belong to their mother's people and not to their father's. Getting married is therefore a process that may extend over many years after the engagement has been concluded and the couple have begun to cohabit.

In the old days people could not get married until they had been initiated into membership of an age-regiment. This generally took place when they were on the average probably from eighteen to twenty years old. Today, boys still cannot marry until their age-regiment has been formed, unless they obtain special permission from the chief. Girls, however, are no longer bound to wait. Nevertheless, it is seldom that people get married really young. Among the 211 women, other than widows, married in church during the years 1920–29, 18 per cent were aged twenty or less, the youngest being seventeen; 64 per cent were aged from twenty-one to twenty-five; 16 per cent from twenty-six to thirty;

and 2 per cent over thirty. Of the 194 men, excluding widowers, 18 per cent were aged twenty-five or less, the youngest being twenty-one; 54 per cent were from twenty-six to thirty; 20 per cent from thirty-one to thirty-five; and 8 per cent over thirty-five. People married outside church may on the average have been a little younger, but I have no reason to consider that the age limits just given are abnormally high for the tribe as a whole. Many of my unmarried informants, whether Church members or not, were in their twenties when I first got to know them, and in several instances, although seven or eight years have since elapsed, they are still single and not even engaged.

Unlike betrothal ceremonies, which appear to have suffered little change, wedding ceremonies have altered greatly, for the introduction of Christianity brought with it European marriage rites and observances. Church marriages are actually comparatively few – in the period 1901–38 they averaged just under thirty a year, with no marked tendency to increase – but they thirty a year, with no marked tendency to increase – but they have set the tone for many of the rest, and led to the widespread incorporation of elements directly attributable to European first the traditional and then the modern ceremonies.

Formerly, when the boy's people thought it was time for his marriage to take place, they asked the girl's parents to let him 'enter her hut'. This having been agreed to, a day was appointed for the ceremony. In the morning the boy's people sent a goat to the girl's home to be slaughtered for the coming feast. In the afternoon he and some male companions of about the same age went to the girl's home with a few older people, preferably the original intermediaries. The boys were shown into a separate hut, where they were joined by the girl and an equal number of female companions. They were given meat, porridge, and beer, each boy being waited upon by one of the girls. After eating and drinking, they went out into the courtyard, where the girl's other relatives and friends were feasting. The peritoneum of the slaughtered goat was cut into thin strips and hung round the necks of the girls; and after this ceremonial indication that the couple were now considered married, the people continued to feast, sing, dance and play games. When it was dark the boys and girls went back into their hut, and slept there together all night, pairing off as before. The next morning the boy and his companions returned to their homes.

The boy after this came every night to sleep with the girl in a small hut set aside for them, but returned home in the morning to eat and attend to his normal duties there. This form of cohabitation continued sometimes for only a few days, sometimes until the girl was already pregnant. The boy's parents then sent to ask that she come to take up her proper domicile amongst them. The usual formal discussions followed, after which a day was fixed and preparations were taken in hand for the ensuing festivities. The girl was kept in seclusion for several days or weeks beforehand, 'in order to grow fat and beautiful'. On the morning of the appointed day the boy and some of his relatives went to her home, where a feast had been prepared. If the *bogadi* cattle had already been given, the girl's 'linked' maternal uncle slaughtered one of his own beasts 'to feed the *bogadi*'; its peritoneum was cut in two and hung round the necks of the couple, as a sign that they were now fully married. But if, as was frequently the case, the cattle had not yet been given, this particular rite was postponed until they were. Feasting continued all day until late in the afternoon. The boy's people then formally asked leave to take the girl home. Her older female relatives first lectured her on the behaviour henceforth expected of her, and also warned the boy's people to look after her properly. The bridal party then went in procession to the boy's home, where another feast had been prepared, which was held on the following day. These feasts marked the conclusion of the wedding. Once they had been held the newly married couple resided with the boy's parents in a hut of their own.

Today there are two main types of wedding ceremony. In what are considered 'proper' weddings, whether celebrated in church or not, the traditional 'entering of the girl's hut' has ostensibly been discarded, and the boy is supposed to bring her to his own home before beginning to live with her. The associated festivities consist mainly of elaborate feasts similar to those traditionally observed. Actually, as we have seen, it is common enough for the boy to sleep with the girl during the period of betrothal, or even before; but this is done secretly, and not by public arrangement, and if she is pregnant or already a mother by the time the wedding takes place, the festivities are greatly curtailed. The second type of wedding is a modified form of the ancient one. Its distinguishing characteristic is that the boy openly cohabits with the girl at her parents' home before bringing her to live among his own people. There is also much less festivity associated with it.

I shall describe the 'proper' wedding first. The date of the ceremony is fixed by the two families in consultation. As soon as it has been finally decided, the couple go to a trading-store to buy the bride's wedding outfit. The bridegroom's own outfit – a dark suit, hat, shirt, shoes, and gloves – he has usually bought already in the town where he was working; if he has never been away, it is also obtained locally. The bride is accompanied by her appointed 'supporter', generally the daughter of a maternal uncle or aunt, and the bridegroom by his 'supporter', generally the son of a maternal uncle. Two older women, probably the wives of maternal uncles on each side, complete the party. The bride retains her air of marked bashfulness throughout, indicating her preferences merely by nods of the head, and the actual purchasing is done mainly by the aunts and 'supporters'. The goods bought vary according to the wealth and status of the boy's parents, who pay for them all. Normally they should include at least two lengths of dress material, a hat, a pair of shoes, stockings, material for underwear, laces, and ribbons, ear-rings, a kerchief, gloves, a white sunshade for the wedding procession, and a veil. The last is considered indispensable for this kind of wedding, which is often known after it as 'the wedding of the veil'. The day after the goods have been bought the bride is taken to a dressmaker to be fitted. The cost of making up her costume is also borne by the boy's people.

Then, if the wedding is to take place in church, and this can only happen if at least one of the couple is a communicant, they go with their fathers or guardians to see the missionary. He asks them all individually if they agree to the marriage, and if arrangements have been made for giving the *bogadi*. If the replies are satisfactory, he notes down the names and ages of the couple, and tells them to be in church the following Sunday when he publishes the banns for the first time. If the marriage is to be in the District Commissioner's office, similar notice must be given there to allow for the publication of the banns. Until recently such marriages were extremely uncommon, as before 1932 the local Administrative centre was at Gaberones, outside the Kgatla Reserve. It is really only since the separatist Churches came into being in 1937 that a few couples, who would otherwise have got married in church, have gone to the District Commissioner instead, for the leaders of these Churches are not legally recognized as marriage officers.

Preparations for the festivities are now taken in hand. All relatives and friends on both sides must be formally notified and invited, or great offence will be taken, and, as has happened on several occasions, the wedding may be marred by family dissensions. The bride's eldest brother is made responsible for inviting the umarried youths, and her 'supporter' for inviting the girls; her maternal and paternal aunts invite the married women on their respective sides of the family, and her father and maternal uncle the married men. The same procedure is followed at the bridegroom's home. All the married women invited start making beer for the feasts and contribute corn to be stamped, and come themselves or send their daughters to help repair and smear the walls and floors of the huts and courtyards. In the evening the girls rehearse songs and dances for the coming celebrations, many of the songs having European tunes and even English words. The young men on the bridegroom's side, under the supervision of his 'supporter', fetch loads of earth and firewood for use at both homes, and erect the shelters in which privileged guests will be accommodated. If the wedding is to be celebrated in church, the bridegroom's father also starts collecting the *bogadi* cattle for delivery to the bride's home a day or two before the ceremony. It is not essential to give them so soon in the other types of wedding.

The bride, from the time the banns are first read, or, in

heathen marriages, two or three weeks before her wedding-day, goes into seclusion in her hut. She does not leave it except to relieve herself, and is then always accompanied by another girl and wears a heavy disguise. While in the hut she keeps her face covered to the eyes with a kerchief, which she wears also when sleeping. 'This is done to acquire a white complexion, and to look nice under the veil.' She lives upon milk, soft porridge, and, if possible, meat, 'so as to become fat', and washes herself frequently, afterwards smearing her face with vaseline or cream, 'in order to look beautiful'. She spends most of her time sewing and chatting with her 'supporter' and the other girls waiting upon her, one or two of whom sleep with her every night. No one but these girls and older female relatives may come in to see her without the special permission of her 'supporter'.

The day before the wedding, or sometimes on the wedding-morn itself, the bride and bridegroom are both doctored to protect them from witchcraft and other evils. The doctoring, which is a traditional ceremony, is usually done even if they are both members of the Church. Occasionally the bridegroom is brought to the bride's hut and they are doctored together; the general practice, however, is for them to be treated separately. The ritual varies with the doctor, but generally consists in rubbing a medicinal paste into small cuts made on the wrists and various other joints. The person doctored may also be given a little of the paste to eat. The doctor finally smears all the cooking-pots with the same paste, and sprinkles other medicines over the entrances to the compound. These additional rites serve to counteract any attempt at bewitching that may be made during the course of the feast.

Most weddings start on a Thursday, the day conventionally set aside by the Church for this purpose, and now used also by heathens. Early in the morning the married female guests start going to the bride's home with the beer they have made. As they walk through the streets they trill loudly and frequently as a sign of joy. They remain to help make porridge and tea, while the men slaughter oxen, sheep, and goats, and cook the meat.

The bride and her companions, with a few older relatives, go a little later to the dressmaker's home, where she puts on her wedding costume, which is invariably white. Her parents in the meantime send a pot of beer 'to summon their son-in-law to the feast'. On its arrival, he and his companions, with some older relatives, go to the place where the bride has been dressed. If it is not a Church wedding, her maternal uncle or some other senior relative tells the couple to link arms, and the procession, surrounded by a growing horde of interested spectators, returns to her home. At Christian weddings the party goes from the dressmaker's to the church, where the couple are married with the appropriate religious rites. This is the only essential difference in procedure between the church wedding and a 'proper' heathen wedding. After the ceremony, the party proceeds to the bride's home, the women and girls singing and trilling.

As the wedding procession approaches the compound, more and more people surround it. Women dance about and trill, children run around and get into everybody's way, men shout, curse and joke. The bride and bridegroom, meanwhile, look solemn and very self-conscious, and it is considered good form if she can manage to keep tears running down her face. On reaching the compound, she is sprinkled with handfuls of corn by the female guests, some of whom also dash in front of her and cut at the ground with hoes – all this symbolizing the future importance of agriculture in her life. Finally, she is picked up by her husband or his 'supporter' and carried over the threshold into the courtyard, a gun being fired at the same moment to announce her arrival.

The greater part of the day is spent in feasting at the bride's home. Meat, porridge, beer, thick milk, bread and tea have been provided as abundantly as her father and other relatives can afford. Her 'linked' maternal uncle, if the *bogadi* has already been given, must as in the old days slaughter an ox, but the rite of bedecking her and her husband with its peritoneum has long been discarded. It would spoil their beautiful clothes! All the food is distributed with due regard to precedence. The newly-wed couple, with their personal companions, sit in a separate hut, and are served before the rest; until the bride has begun to eat, no one else may do so. The other people from the bride-groom's home likewise have their own shelter or hut, where they are waited upon with special attention. His parents, however, never attend this feast: it is held primarily for the bride's relatives and friends. The female guests sit in small groups out in the courtyard, each group representing a separate branch of the family; the men sit together, or also in clusters, immediately outside the compound or at the local council-place. Each group has its attendant, more consideration being shown those who have contributed to the feast. Special portions of the meat are, according to ancient usage, given to each different class of rela-tives; the maternal uncles, for instance, receive the heads, and junior paternal uncles the forelegs, of all the animals slaughtered. Some meat and beer are also given to the uninvited people who always flock around hoping for a share in the feast. So persistent are these 'beggars' at times that a man is specially placed at the entrance of the compound to see that no one enters but those entitled to do so. A few ribs of beef and some pots of beer are further sent to the central council-place of the village, where they are distributed among the men usually sitting there. This tribute is a formal notification to the tribal authorities of the marriage that is taking place.

Feasting continues until late in the afternoon, to the ac-companiment of singing and dancing by the girls' choirs, and with occasional squabbles as people get drunk. Towards sunset the bridegroom's relatives formally ask permission to take the bride to their home. Before leaving, she is privately given some final advice by a few old relatives chosen for the purpose by her mother. They tell her to be obedient to her husband and to look after all his needs, to be respectful to her parents-in-law, to keep her home clean, to work hard in her fields and at her other duties, and to bear up bravely against the hardships and insults that she may receive where she is going. They tell her also to be ever ready to gratify her husband's sexual desires, and frequently add some instruction on the technique of intercourse. Then, to the accompaniment of blessings and other expressions of good-will, the bridal party proceeds to the husband's home. It is led by the choirs of girls singing, and as usual attracts excited public attention as it passes slowly through the streets. If, as sometimes happens, the husband lives in another village, he and the bride, with their companions, go there by wagon straight from her home, timing their departure to get in before dark.

On reaching its destination, the procession is welcomed with great jubilation, the women trilling while men shout out the praises of the bridegroom's family. He and his wife are shown into a hut, and she is given a young baby to hold as she enters – an obvious symbolization of the hopes now centred in her. They sit there a while, receiving privileged visitors, who congratulate them and welcome the bride to her new home. All the men then go out, while the women tell her not to fear her wedding night or disgrace herself 'in the blankets'. Her companions help her change her costume into something more informal, a few elderly women from her mother's home having come after the procession with the blankets and other goods she will require for the next day or two. She joins the gathering in the courtyard, where the younger people continue to sing, dance, and make merry, until it is late. Her own people then bid her farewell, and return to their homes. She and her husband retire to their hut, and, if he has not already anticipated the event, he is now expected to consummate the marriage. The old women next day privately question her about this, and if the husband has failed in his duty give forcible public expression to their disappointment and disapproval: 'He is not a man, our daughter is not married, she is lost!' If it is she who was reluctant, they violently scold her and threaten to beat her severely if she continues her stupid obstinacy.

In the morning the bride, after getting up, takes a broom and helps the other women sweep the courtyard clean. This task, the first she does in her new home, symbolizes her willingness and obligation to help her parents-in-law in their domestic activities. The bulk of the morning is spent in getting food ready for the feast to be held later in the day. Most of the guests are the people previously invited by the bridegroom's family, but there is also a party from the bride's home, her own parents, however, never being present. The feast is conducted like that of the day before, but the bride's relatives are now the honoured guests. In theory, although practice does not always correspond, the bridegroom's people should not kill cattle for this feast unless they have already given *bogadi*. The idea is to prevent them from disposing of animals that should have been put to the more proper use. But sheep, goats and pigs, will in any case provide sufficient meat.

The next day, finally, the newly-married couple and their companions go in the afternoon to the bride's home, where another small feast has been specially prepared for them. On departing they take the rest of her personal belongings, including the few presents that may have been given to her by her parents. She remains at her husband's place for a few days, and is then formally escorted by one of his aunts to spend an afternoon or evening at her parents' home. She is now free to visit them whenever she pleases.

The ceremonies just described are observed only when people are first married. When a man takes an additional wife, or a widowed person remarries, they are not nearly so elaborate. Beer is drunk at the woman's home, after which she is quietly taken away by her husband and the few relatives with him. Another beer-drink is held at his home the same evening or the next day, and if wealthy he may also slaughter an animal for meat. The same simplicity marks the marriage of a girl who is already pregnant or a mother. After a small feast at her own home, she is taken unostentatiously to her husband's residence, two or three relatives accompanying her with her few personal belongings. She may not wear the veil and white costume of an 'unspoiled' girl. Nor, if she is a Christian, can she get married in church unless she had been restored to communion, the ceremony being held instead in the missionary's office. Girls sometimes feel greatly humiliated if they have to get married in this way, for, like many of their European sisters, they prefer the glamour and excitement of the full-dress affair. One of my acquaintances, after becoming engaged to the boy whose concubine she had been, refused to let him sleep with her any longer, saying that she did not wish to become pregnant and so unable to get married in a veil!

There is still another type of wedding ceremony, the modern version of that traditionally observed. If the boy's family are too poor to provide an elaborate wedding feast, they ask the girl's people to let him 'enter her hut'. This being agreed to, he is taken to her home by the original intermediary, and henceforth sleeps there with her, but every morning he returns to eat and work with his own people. Sometimes he cohabits with her like this before obtaining formal permission from her parents, but so long as he shows that he still intends to marry her they seldom object. Occasionally he tends after a while to spend most of his time at her home, eating there and working with her people, and returning to his own home only when required for some special purpose. This continues until she has borne one or more children. Her husband's people then send some of their close female relatives to fetch her, her family having as usual been informed beforehand. A small beer-drink is held, and towards sunset she goes quietly with these women, and some of her own relatives and friends, to her new home, where more beer is drunk.

This form of marriage, although considered less fashionable and becoming than the 'proper' wedding, is nevertheless more commonly practised. Of 80 married men belonging to Makgophana and Rampedi wards in Mochudi, only 11 had been married in church, and 25 others outside it but with the full wedding festivities; 36 had brought their wives home pregnant or already mothers, and the remaining 8, all fairly young, were still cohabiting with their 'wives' at the homes of the latters' parents. In more than half of these cases, therefore, the man had 'entered the woman's hut', and not married her according to the new fashion set by the Church, and now accepted as correct by people considering themselves more 'civilized' than their fellows.

MARRIAGE GIFTS AND PAYMENTS

We saw above that among the features involved in betrothal and wedding ceremonies is the presentation of gifts by one family to the other. These gifts require more detailed consideration than I have yet given them, for they play an extremely important part in the Kgatla laws relating to marriage. Among them are the articles of clothing given to the girl to seal her betrothal, and the goods occasionally sent to her afterwards as an indication of continued interest on the part of the boy and his family. As we have seen, careful note is kept of them all, for in case the engagement is dissolved the boy's parents may be entitled to reclaim them. They impose an obligation, as it were, upon the girl to become his wife, and, as we have noted, once the initial gift has been sent and accepted, he may be allowed to anticipate some of the privileges of married life. Her own people do not make him similar presents, but should at least be very hospitable to him and his parents. Here the emphasis lies mainly upon the expression of goodwill and mutual attachment, which is further reflected in the occasional exchanges of food and services between the two families. That much importance is attached to the latter is evidenced by the possibility that if they are neglected steps may be taken to break the engagement.

By far the most important such exchange, however, consists of what the Kgatla term *bogadi*, i.e. the livestock that should normally be given by the boy's people to the girl's father at the time when she is brought to live at their home. No matter what other ceremonies may have been observed, no form of cohabitation between the couple is ever considered a true marriage until these animals have been given. In matrimonial disputes coming before the tribal courts, the two points about which inquiry is always made are, firstly, whether the families on both sides have formally agreed to the union, and, secondly, whether *bogadi* has yet been given. If it is still outstanding, the couple are held to have been living in concubinage.

Kgatla themselves say that *bogadi* is a thanksgiving to the wife's parents for having raised her, and a token of gratitude for their kindness is now letting her husband marry her. Some add that it is compensation for the loss of her services. Others, influenced by European ideas, term it a 'registration' of the marriage. Still others stress the point that it creates a special bond between the two families, just as the transfer of cattle in other contexts – say from chief to subject, or from owner to herdsman – imposes reciprocal obligations upon the people involved. In Kgatla law, however, the main effect of *bogadi* is to give the husband and his people a valid claim to any children the woman may bear. No matter who the real father of these children may be, they belong to the man in whose name *bogadi* was given for their mother, and, if no *bogadi* has yet been given, they belong to her own family, and not to that of the man with whom she is living. In practice, as we shall see, this second principle is interpreted according to the circumstances of the union, but in theory it is inflexible.

The nature of *bogadi,* the fact that it is a transfer of property, has led many European observers to conclude that it is simply a purchase of the woman, subjecting her to many humiliating obligations towards her husband and his people. It is true that a woman for whom *bogadi* has been given is in law more closely bound to her husband than she would otherwise be, and that if she leaves him, except with very good reason, her parents will usually send her back. It is also true that in the old days she passed after the death of her husband into the care of his younger brother, whose right and duty it was to cohabit with her. On the other hand, she is more highly honoured in the tribe than is a woman for whom no *bogadi* has been given, and if neglected or deserted by her husband she is entitled to protection and assistance from the tribal authorities, remedies not available to a concubine. Moreover, the number of cattle given as *bogadi* is determined by the husband's people alone, the wife's father very seldom having any say in the matter. This in itself shows that the payment does not arise from any bargaining over the value of the woman. And, as we shall see when discussing divorce, *bogadi* once given can never be recovered if the wife parts from her husband, unless she is barren, and even then her own conduct must be responsible for the breach. This is hardly consistent with the view that *bogadi* is a purely commercial transaction by which a woman's people sell her to her husband.

This view, nevertheless, was responsible for the temporary abandonment of *bogadi* during the reign of Chief Lentswe. The early missionaries regarded the giving of *bogadi* as undisguised wife-purchase, and forbade Church members to practise it. In 1892 Lentswe himself joined the Church, and his acceptance of the Mission attitude towards *bogadi* was probably facilitated by the great rinderpest epidemic of 1896, which decimated the herds of his people, and would in any case have made it difficult for the old custom to be strictly observed. For the next fifteen years or so the giving of *bogadi* was completely forbidden. By that time, however, Lentswe had found that the prohibition was leading to confusion and dissatisfaction, and tending to make marriages unstable, in that husbands and wives parted on relatively flimsy grounds. Since the tribe had again become rich in cattle, he therefore allowed the people to revert to the custom, leaving it to the Christians to do as they pleased. Isang, on becoming regent, revived *bogadi* more strongly, and even enforced it as far as the heathens were concerned. He used to insist that the cattle should be displayed at his council-place the day before a wedding, so that people might know what marriage was taking place and how many animals had been given. On several occasions he actually punished men for taking women to their homes without having given *bogadi*. He further persuaded the Mission authorities to investigate the possibility of allowing Church members also to revert to the practice. After prolonged discussions extending over several years, the Church about 1927 accepted the view that *bogadi* was primarily a registration of marriage, and agreed to recognize it as consistent with Christian morality.

Mr Reyneke, the missionary under whom the change came about, described as follows his reasons for consenting to it:*

* *De Kerkbode* (the official organ of the Dutch Reformed Church), 31 October 1928, p. 647. I translate from the original Afrikaans.

Lobola* is well-nigh universally condemned by missionaries of our Church as the root of almost all evil. In Mochudi it was formerly also forbidden, but nevertheless it still flourished in secret. It is so integral a portion of Native law and custom, in many respects the foundation of the whole tribal system, that it is difficult to remove it without disturbing the whole native social organization. The Church at Mochudi therefore decided, after consultation with the Chief, to permit *lobola*, but to combat the evils attaching to it. The Chief for his part also undertook to work against everything in it which was repugnant to Christian feeling, provided that the Church recognized what was good in it, and undertook not to condemn it any further as a system. And now we are convinced that we have not sacrificed a principle, but that we have acted wisely. We can now read with a smile the arguments that are generally advanced against *lobola*, for here they simply do not apply any more. *Lobola* is at Mochudi virtually nothing more than a thanksgiving and a pledge of fidelity. When it has served its purpose, it will die a natural death, but never will the people be able to say to the Church: 'You have robbed us of one of the oldest features of our family life, which we have always regarded as one of the most outstanding aids to morality.' Nothing is demanded by the bride's family from the bridegroom. He gives voluntarily what he can, as an indication of his honesty and good intentions.

The giving of *bogadi* is therefore once more an essential part of marriage, for both Christians and heathens, and even those men who got married during the time of its suspension have since been held liable for it. *Bogadi* almost invariably consists of large cattle. Sheep may be given instead or as well, although this appears to be very rare, but goats can never be given, 'because of their destructive tendencies'. Money payments, now common in some other parts of South Africa, where they have degraded the custom by introducing a direct mercenary element, have apparently not yet become acceptable alternatives among the Kgatla. The cattle given as *bogadi* should always include one or more females, to allow for further increase. Heifers and young oxen

*Lobola is the Nguni word for what the Kgatla and other Tswana term *bogadi*. It has now become the general South African name for the custom of giving cattle to a woman's family in consideration of her going to live with a man as his wife.

are preferred, but a cow accompanied by a sucking calf is also accepted, the calf counting as an additional animal. Bulls, however young, may never be given: any suggestion of doing so is considered highly insulting, for they are 'warriors', and would cause the marriage to end in disastrous quarrels.

The number of cattle given as *bogadi* is not standardized. Theoretically, it should always be even, 'each animal with its mate, to show that two people are being bound together', but odd numbers are frequently accepted, with the exception of seven, this number being considered unlucky. The amount is never discussed beforehand between the two families; there is none of that preliminary bargaining, found among the Nguni tribes of South-East Africa, which is mainly responsible for the view that *bogadi* is a mercenary transaction. The husband's people give as many cattle as they wish or can assemble; the wife's father must accept the number given, and cannot reject it as insufficient, or claim more at court. Should he feel that it is ludicrously small, considering his own or the husband's social standing, he may protest. More may then be added, but as a favour, and not as a right. In one instance the husband's father, a fairly wealthy man of some authority, proposed to give only one heifer and four sheep as *bogadi*; the wife's people expressed loud indignation, so he gave them three heifers instead. Actually, as this shows, the number given is usually fairly small – much too small, on the average, to arouse special complaints. In 27 cases of marriage by commoners, I found that 10 men had each given two head of cattle as *bogadi* for their wives, 9 had given three each, 7 four each, and the remaining one six. A *bogadi* gift of six head or more is considered large, and is usually exceeded only by men of both rank and wealth. Komane, a son of Chief Pilane in the second house, gave only five head of cattle for his own wife, and four for his son's; but Kgari, a more remote though influential member of the royal family, gave ten for his wife, while Chief Isang gave thirty, and Chief Molefi forty.

The *bogadi* cattle for a man's first wife come from his father or guardian and various other relatives. In theory, his 'linked' maternal uncle, paternal uncle, and paternal aunt, are each expected to contribute; so are his brothers and mother, and he himself, if they have cattle of their own. But there is no compulsion, and any one unable to afford it will not be blamed for failing to assist. In practice, as the following few instances show, a good deal of variation occurs. Komane's *bogadi* payment (five head of cattle) included two from himself, one each from two of his elder brothers, and one from the son of his deceased eldest brother; Molefi's (four head) included two from his father, one from his mother, and one from his elder brother; Chief Isang's (thirty head) included fifteen from his father, ten from himself, three from his maternal uncle, and two from a paternal uncle; Mokgere's (three head) included two from his father and one from his maternal uncle; Thebe's (three head) included one from himself, one from his maternal uncle, and one from the son of his father's maternal uncle; and Rantsho's (also three head) included one from his father, one from his maternal uncle, and one from his maternal uncle's son. It is evident, even from this, that the giving of *bogadi* is a kinship obligation and not merely a private family affair. The husband's father, who is in charge, informs all his relatives that the necessary cattle are being collected, and each contributes if he wishes and can. If the husband afterwards marries again, he must provide the *bogadi* out of his own resources. His father is not responsible for it, nor are other relatives expected to assist.

All the cattle collected must be given simultaneously to the wife's father or guardian. There is no instalment system like those found in many other Bantu tribes. In theory the cattle should be given immediately before the wife is taken to live at her husband's home. During the time of Mr Reyneke, this was insisted upon in a church marriage, failing which he would refuse to perform the ceremony. Isang, as we have noted, also attempted for a while to enforce it in the tribe generally. But in practice *bogadi* is seldom given until children have been born of the marriage. Even then it may be delayed many years. Thus, in a group of fifty-two married men of Makgophana and Rampedi wards, I found that no fewer than twenty-five had not yet given *bogadi* for their wives. Sixteen of the debtors belonged to the two junior age-regiments of the tribe, and could therefore be regarded as newly married, but at least two of the others had been living with their wives for over thirty years. The temporary abandonment of *bogadi* during Lentswe's reign must obviously have contributed to this state of affairs, although informants maintain that it was not unusual even before.

Nevertheless, however long the delay in giving *bogadi*, the wife's father seldom ventures to sue her husband for it. It is even maintained by some that no *bogadi* at all is due if the marriage proves barren, or if either husband or wife dies childless, unless arrangements are then made, by the special customs that will be described in due course, for the procreation of children by a substitute. Where a marriage is fruitful, and *bogadi* has not yet been given, the wife's people are protected by the knowledge that her children are legally theirs, and can be claimed at any time. The mere threat of making such a claim would be sufficient to hasten payment, although this form of pressure is apparently seldom if ever exercised: it was mentioned to me as a theoretical possibility only. Moreover, although the children of such 'incomplete' marriages do not yet legally belong to their fathers, they are never regarded as 'bastards'. It is only the offspring of casual and unsanctioned liaisons who suffer that reproach. Where the union has taken place with the approval of both families, the husband's custody of his children is normally not disturbed, except in case of divorce. He can ultimately obtain full legal control over them when his first daughter gets married. The *bogadi* he receives for her he must pass on to his wife's people. It is regarded as replacing the cattle he should have given in the first instance for his wife, and should he refuse to hand it over he can be forced to do so by the courts. What generally happens, however, is that as soon as his daughter is about to get married, he himself hurriedly gives *bogadi* for his wife – in the hope of receiving more from his son-in-law. To this extent, and to this extent only, can there now be said to be any mercenary element in *bogadi*.

The *bogadi* cattle, after being received by the wife's father, may be distributed at once. Generally, however, he keeps them together for years until they have bred enough. He then divides the animals among those entitled to shares. His daughter's 'linked' maternal and paternal uncles, her paternal aunt, and her mother, are said to have preferential claims in addition to himself, and should receive at least one animal each, if the *bogadi* and their offspring are numerous enough. The remainder he keeps for himself, or may allocate in part to one or more additional relatives. The woman's 'linked' brother also has a recognized claim, and on the death of their father inherits all the cattle retained by him from her *bogadi*. If the father is dead when the *bogadi* is given, this brother in any case takes the balance of the cattle after the claims of the various other relatives have been satisfied.

This brief statement represents the ideal system of distribution. In practice, variations occur according to the composition of the kinship group, the number of cattle, and the time when they are divided. I was unable to obtain much concrete information on this point, the usual answer to my inquiries being that the cattle had not yet been distributed. In the few cases I did come across, the *bogadi* seems to have been divided mainly between the wife's father and her maternal uncle. Thus, Segale received five head of cattle as *bogadi* for his daughter; he gave two to her maternal uncle, and kept the others himself. Modise, who received three, handed them all to his brother-in-law (not having yet given *bogadi* for his own wife), and received one back for himself. Mathee's *bogadi*, received many years after her marriage and when her father was already dead, was divided by her only brother, who took two head himself, and gave her two sisters one each. Manyama's *bogadi* was shared between her father, who kept two head, and her maternal uncle, who received the other one.

It is evident from all this that *bogadi*, both in its collection and in its distribution, helps to ensure that not merely the parents but also the other relatives on both sides take an active interest in a marriage. We have already seen how the kinsfolk generally participate in the betrothal and wedding negotiations and feasts, and shall find in due course still more evidence that no marriage is ever considered a union merely between husband and wife. It remains the concern of their relatives as well, upon whose help they depend for carrying on their major tasks and for smoothing out their personal difficulties.

The extent to which husband and wife are economically bound up with their kinsfolk may explain the comparative insignificance of the settlements made upon them at marriage. The wife's parents, when she goes to live with her husband, generally give her a few domestic utensils. Thus, Masobana received a sleeping-mat, a food-bowl, a blanket, 10s. in cash, a hoe, and some seed corn; Dikhukhu received only a blanket, a food-bowl, and some seed; while Mmajosefa was given a blanket, a cooking-pot, a basket, and a food-bowl. More than this a woman seldom receives, unless her father is fairly wealthy. He may then give her one or more heifers or cows, and occasionally also a field, which remain her personal property and cannot be alienated by her husband without her consent. A newly-married man, again, must be provided by his father with a field and perhaps also one or more heifers to start his own herd, unless, as is customary, he had already received during his youth an animal to breed for him. This represents the great bulk of the private property, other than personal possessions, with which the couple commence their new life together. A home of their own they do not yet need, for they live with the husband's parents, or, occasionally, the wife's.

4. The Setting of Married Life

With marriage, the conduct of both husband and wife must alter. They are now required to share the same residence, daily life and economic interests, to have sexual intercourse together, and to care for and help each other in many other ways. The husband is further linked to his wife's people, as she is to his, by reciprocal obligations of various kinds. All these forms of conduct are socially prescribed. Tribal law and custom lay down that husband and wife have certain rights and duties in regard to each other and to their respective kinsfolk and relatives-in-law, and means are available to enforce these rights and duties if need be.

I propose to outline in this chapter those rules of conduct that provide what may be termed the social setting of married life – that define formally the relationship that should exist between husband and wife, and between them and their relatives by blood and by marriage. It need hardly be said that, in spite of the superficial uniformity that such rules aim and tend to produce, no two married couples lead exactly the same sort of life. Personal idiosyncrasies, desires, and conflicts, feature as prominently among the Kgatla as anywhere else, and a study of marriage must in fact resolve itself very largely into a discussion of the way in which two human beings of opposite sex and with their own peculiar characteristics adjust themselves to living together in conformity with socially prescribed standards of behaviour. With this problem, however, I shall deal in later chapters, when analysing more fully the different aspects of Kgatla marriage. Here we are concerned mainly with married life as laid down in tribal law and custom – with the conventional standards, that is, against which individual variations must be con-

sidered and without a knowledge of which they cannot be rightly
understood.

THE COMPOSITION OF THE HOUSEHOLD

Most Kgatla couples start married life as members of a larger
household. The reason usually given is that the wife must first be
taught how to run a home of her own. Moreover, even when
labour is available, it usually takes several months to build a
completely new dwelling-enclosure or 'compound', and the work
is sometimes spread over a much longer period. Where they have
been 'properly' married, the couple spend their first years
together in the home of the husband's parents, to which the wife
is brought immediately after the wedding. In the other forms of
marriage, she usually stays on with her own parents, her husband
coming nightly to sleep with her. This frequently continues, in
either case, until the couple have one or more children. They
may then build a separate compound for themselves whenever
they wish. They need not do so at any particular time, except
that when they are with the husbands' people they should normally move out to make room for his younger brother when the
latter also marries. But they sometimes continue to live there for
years, especially if too lazy to build their own home. A youngest
son, in any case, generally stays on permanently, for he will
inherit his parents' compound after their death. If both parents
are dead when a marriage takes place, the couple stay with a
married brother or sister in the same ward, and then usually
build their own home as soon as they can.

The new compound is generally built next to that of the husband's parents or brothers, if sufficient land is available on the
plot originally allocated to the family by the ward-head. Failing
this, the ward-head will give them a suitable site somewhere else
on the area under his control, for every married man is entitled to
a free grant of land for residential purposes. If there is no room
at all in the ward holding – a most unusual event, for ample
provision is always made for future needs when a village is founded and residential land portioned out among the wards – the

ward-head obtains from the chief or village headman a new holding on which to settle his people henceforth. The members of a ward are all expected to remain together in their own part of the village, and, since the ward is patrilineal, the great majority of couples therefore live in the immediate vicinity of the husband's paternal kin. It is only exceptionally that a man will be allowed or ordered to build his home somewhere else, as when he is always quarrelling with his neighbours or suspects them of bewitching him. He then generally attaches himself either to his maternal relatives or to his wife's people, if neither of these groups belongs to his own ward. But a man going to live permanently at his wife's home is greatly despised, and it is scornfully said of him: 'He has been married by his wife,' or, 'He has been drawn away by her apron-strings' (lit., 'by the girdle of her skirt').

Once they have obtained their land, husband and wife, assisted by their relatives, clear it of the weeds and rubbish with which it is covered. A magician is next called to doctor it by burying charmed pegs in each of its corners and sprinkling the site as a whole with other 'medicines'. This is done to protect its future occupants from sorcery and other evils. The women then start building the mud wall of the main hut. As soon as it is finished, and before the roof is put on, the magician comes again to doctor it. It is customary also for husband and wife at this stage to sleep together one night inside the wall, 'to break the hut in', and so prevent illicit lovers, who might use it as a convenient rendezvous, from anticipating them and thereby depriving them of their procreative power. Meanwhile the men have been busy cutting and shaping rafters, posts and beams, for the framework of the roof, which they now proceed to erect. It is then thatched by the women. In the better types of modern hut, however, the erection and thatching of the roof is done by a male specialist hired for the purpose. The women finally lay down the floor, and plaster the wall both inside and out. The hut is then doctored for the last time, and its owners, if they have not already done so, 'break it in' as described above. As a rule only one hut is built when the compound is being established; others are added later as need arises. The walls and floors of the surrounding courtyard are the last to be made, this also being the work of the women.

The compound when complete consists of one or more detached huts and granaries situated in a courtyard surrounded by a low rectangular wall of dried mud. The vast majority of huts are of the traditional Tswana type, consisting essentially of a circular wall of dried mud surmounted by a conical thatched roof with protruding eaves. But they vary considerably in size and finish, some of the more elaborate being carefully thatched in the European manner and provided with good wooden doors and glass windows. Progressive people often have rectangular houses of the European type, usually made of mud and thatch, but occasionally, if the owners can afford it, of brick and corrugated iron roofing. The huts are used principally as bedrooms and stores, most activities taking place in the open courtyard, except in wet weather. The front yard, facing the street, is kept scrupulously clean and free from unnecessary encumbrances; it is the place where all visitors are received, and if untidy is sure to arouse adverse comment. All the rough housework is done in the backyard, a much less presentable spot often littered with utensils of various kinds, one or more granaries, stacks of spare rafters, bundles of thatching-grass, fowl roosts and other odds and ends, including occasionally a small kitchen garden. The walls of the huts and courtyards, although regularly plastered with fresh coatings of mud and cow-dung, are often left undecorated, the drab grey-brown of the natural dried mud; but a woman proud of her home will smear them both inside and out with coloured earths to produce the geometrical designs in black, white and terracotta red that make some Kgatla dwellings look really attractive.

It is very seldom indeed that any but extremely close relatives live together under the same roof. For all practical purposes, we may say that the inhabitants of a compound consist basically of the members of a simple family (husband, wife, and unmarried children), frequently supplemented, however, by married children and their families, and by the husband's unmarried or married brothers and sisters. Adopted grandchildren, nephews, or nieces, are also included at times.

A survey I made in 1929 of Sikwane village showed that, of the 130 compounds then in it, there were 63 each occupied by husband, wife and their own unmarried children; 5 occupied by husband, wife and their adopted children; 5 by husband and wife alone; 26 by widows and their unmarried children; 4 by widowers and their unmarried children; 2 by widows alone; and 1 by a widower alone. These 106 compounds were therefore each inhabited solely by the members of a simple family. Seventeen others also contained married children: in 8 there were sons, in 5 daughters, and in 4 both sons and daughters, with their respective spouses and children. The remaining 7 compounds included unmarried or married brothers or sisters of either husband or wife, and in one case also a completely unrelated couple living in a hut temporarily borrowed while their own home was being built.

The average number of people in each compound was between five and six. But there was a considerable range of variation: three compounds had only one occupant each, and thirteen had two each, while on the other hand one had fourteen, and still another sixteen. The number of huts in each compound was usually two or three, and seldom more than four. Every married couple had its hut, shared in some cases with its younger children or grandchildren. Adolescent children of both sexes lived together in another hut, or shared one with an older female relative, while unmarried adults had separate huts, one for the people of each sex.

The occupants of each compound usually form a single household under the immediate authority of the husband and father of the main family. He is entitled to the respect, obedience and services, of all his dependants; he keeps order over them, and deals with any disputes or quarrels arising among them; and he is responsible for their conduct in matters affecting outsiders, watches their interests when they come before the tribal courts, and can be held liable for their debts and misdeeds. After his death his eldest son, if old enough, succeeds him as head of the household, and takes over the corresponding duties and responsibilities, rights and privileges. Failing a son old enough, a younger brother living in the same compound is recognized as its temporary head. But where, as sometimes happens, there is no suitable man in the compound, its inhabitants come under the guardianship of their nearest male relative in the same ward, and for the time being form part of his household. Kgatla law insists that every household must have a recognized male head to act as its protector and public representative, so that a widow and her young children living in their own compound can never be legally independent.

It is seldom nowadays that the household comprises a polygamous family. Even in the old days, judging from genealogical records, most men had only one wife at a time, and few commoners more than two or in exceptional instances three. Of 74 men in my genealogies who belonged to age-regiments formed in 1880 or earlier, 46 were monogamous, 20 were bigamous, 7 had three wives each, and 1 had four. The percentage of polygamists in this little group is 38.* Households of four wives or more were found as a rule only among members of the royal family and other prominent or wealthy people. The biggest establishment known among the Kgatla was that of Chief Kgamanyane (ruled 1848–75), who had forty-six wives. Chief Lentswe, in the seventeen years before he became a Christian, had married only three wives, two of whom he put away on joining the Church. Since then, nearly fifty years ago, polygamy has become far less common. This is due mainly to the spread of Christianity, for the Mission from the first forbade converts to have more than one wife. The Administration, too, levies an additional tax upon polygamists, while educational progress, the general diffusion of

* Some interesting and valuable figures for comparative purposes were collected by Dr Livingstone about 1850 among the BaKaa, another Tswana tribe. He found that of 278 married men, 157 were monogamists, 94 had two wives each, 25 three wives each, and 2 four wives each. The percentage of polygamists was 43. (Quoted by J. J. Freeman, *A Tour in South Africa*, London, 1851, p. 280.)

European ideals and the example of the chiefs themselves have presumably also contributed to the widespread abandonment of the practice.

Polygamy is still a recognized institution, and has not been explicitly forbidden either by the tribal authorities or by the Administration, except (by the latter) to men married under civil law. But there is on the whole little desire to indulge in it nowadays, save perhaps when a wife is barren. Its economic advantages are no longer so great as formerly, the cost of maintaining and paying tax for additional wives being considered a bigger burden than is offset by their labour in the fields; the cattle that at one time could best be used as *bogadi* for new wives are now required for ploughing and transport, or for sale in order to procure various wants; and further sexual satisfaction can easily be obtained from concubines, who do not need to be supported in the same way as a wife. In 1930 only seventy-three taxpayers in the whole tribe (roughly 3 per cent of those married) were registered as having more than one wife, and of these all but four had two wives each. These figures may not have been altogether reliable, for it is highly probable that in order to evade paying the extra tax some men may not have listed all their wives. But they do at least suggest that the proportion of polygamists to other married men is very small. In Sikwane village, in 1929, I found that only seven husbands out of ninety-eight were polygamists, and they each had only two wives, while in Makgophana and Rampedi wards in Mochudi none of the seventy-four married men (1932) had more than one. The percentage of polygamists in these three groups together is 3.6.

Each wife in a polygamous household has her own 'house' or establishment, comprising herself, her children and any other people inhabiting her compound. The compounds of the co-wives should normally be next to one another or even joined together. But the actual arrangement seems to depend largely upon the wishes of the husband, and often enough the wives are placed some distance apart, although almost invariably within the same ward settlement. In Sikwane, however, the junior wives in three polygamous marriages were still in their mothers' homes, and in only one of the four other cases were the two wives living next to each other.

The diagram on p. 90 illustrates the composition of a polygamous household occupying three adjoining compounds, and shows also how huts are allocated for residence.

HUSBAND AND WIFE IN TRIBAL LAW

In describing the household I mentioned a fact of outstanding importance: few couples ever live away from the immediate environment of their relatives. As a rule they start married life in the home of either the husband's parents or the wife's, and even after they have built their own compound they are normally still surrounded by the husband's paternal kin. This is shown clearly by an analysis I made of Rampedi ward in Mochudi. Of the sixteen households belonging to this ward, and so forming a separate local group, the heads of twelve were all patrilineal descendants of Rampedi, its founder and eponym. Each of these twelve households was therefore genealogically allied to the rest. In three instances they were further connected by recent intermarriage. Of the four remaining households, the heads of two were also related to the majority, for although not born into the ward they had come there to live among their mothers' people. There were only two households whose members were not actually part of the kinship group; both were families of strangers lately affiliated to the ward.

This close proximity of their kin means that husband and wife are seldom free from the persistent influence of people entitled to make many demands upon their services and property, and if necessary to interfere with the manner in which they run their home or behave towards each other. Similar kinship rights exist, of course, in most other societies also; but amongst Europeans, for instance, it is unusual for relatives to enter so intimately and so continuously into the life of a married couple, and convention certainly does not demand it by insisting upon adjacency of residence. But before I proceed to show how married life among the Kgatla is affected by kinship ties, let us first see what are the

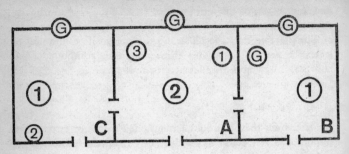

A. (*compound of MmaDikeledi, first wife of Diphale Kgosi, head of the household*):

(1) Diphale Kgosi and MmaDikeledi; they share the hut with a young girl and two small boys (children of their daughter Ntheleng, a widow who has come back to live with her parents).

(2) Pheto (son of Diphale and MmaDikeledi) and his wife Dikeledi; newly married.

(3) Ntheleng (daughter) with her baby son, and Khutsafalo, an unmarried woman, daughter of Diphale's sister's daughter.

(G) Granary.

B. (*compound of Mokhute, Diphale's second wife, now dead*):

(1) Molefe (son of Diphale and Mokhute) and his wife Mamabusa. (Their children, a boy and a girl, stay with Mamabusa's mother in another part of the town.)

(G) Granaries.

C. (*compound of Modiegi, formerly a widow, and now Diphale's third wife*):

(1) Modiegi, with the small children (a boy and a girl) of her eldest daughter (deceased) by her former husband. (The two other children of this daughter, an adolescent girl and a young boy, are at their father's home in another part of the town.)

(2) Tsholofelo (daughter of Diphale and Modiegi); unmarried, but has an infant son.

(G) Granary.

accepted standards of conduct between husband and wife. Here, I must again emphasize, we are concerned with the formal code only, reserving for later chapters the discussion of how the relationship actually works out in practice.

Where the couple form part of a larger household, their behaviour towards each other is governed by the fact that they are both still subject to its head. As long as the wife lives in her parents' home, she remains under the immediate authority of her father, to whom she must answer for her conduct. She works together with the other women of her home, and has little to do with her relatives-in-law. Her husband generally comes merely to sleep with her, and so cannot control her by day; but even if he spends most of his time with her, and by helping his parents-in-law contributes to her keep, any attempt on his part to bully her is immediately resisted by them. They are actually entitled to claim an ox or goat from him as damages if he thrashes her while she is still under their roof. In a patrilocal marriage his authority is greater, for she is more directly under his supervision and protection. But he is himself still dependent upon his father, whom he must inform of all his movements and consult in all his business affairs; and should he neglect or ill-treat her, his parents will at once rebuke and correct him. A wife's lot, nevertheless, is notoriously difficult while she is living with her parents-in-law; she must attend humbly and submissively upon them, is given all the more unpleasant or monotonous tasks to do, and becomes in effect the general servant of the household. She must prove that she is a worthy addition to the family – and the standards set can sometimes be very exacting.

It is not until they have moved into their own compound that the relationship between husband and wife appears in its proper perspective. The change is reflected mainly in their respective legal positions. The husband is now for all practical purposes his own master. Although still tied to his father or eldest brother by obligations of deference, obedience and service, he has far greater freedom in running his home and managing his other affairs. He has attained to the dignified status of head of his own household, and with it becomes not only responsible for all his own actions, but also the full guardian of his wife and children. The wife is always legally dependent upon her husband. She cannot as a rule resort to the tribal courts except through him as her representative, and if she does wrong or falls into debt he is liable for any payments that must be made. She cannot bind herself to any contracts without his approval, she must live wherever he chooses to build his home, and she must obey all his commands. In spite of her legal subjection, however, her status too is improved by the establishment of their own household, for she now becomes its mistress and acquires a new authority in domestic affairs. She is responsible for the care of the compound, she can entertain friends and visitors more freely than ever before, and in time she will have her children and other dependants to work under her own supervision.

Both husband and wife contribute to the economic maintenance of their household. The wife must see to the building and care of the compound itself, the preparation of food and other forms of housework, and the cultivation of the fields; the husband helps in the building and ploughing, but his principal activities are to supervise the care of the livestock and to hunt. As long as they are dependent members of another household, they work with the rest for the common benefit. But once they have established their own home, the burden of maintaining it falls largely upon themselves alone. The husband, especially, is obliged to provide his wife with a dwelling, clothing, food and similar forms of support; he must clear one or more fields for her to cultivate, and procure cattle and other livestock to furnish her and her children with milk and occasionally meat. Nowadays, when the range of goods considered essential to every decent home has increased so greatly through contact with Europeans, he must also, if necessary, and if young enough, go abroad to work for the money with which to purchase them. As he grows older, he relies upon his sons to do so instead.

Property a husband sets aside for the use of his wife he cannot afterwards alienate without her consent, and when she dies it is normally inherited by her own children. She looks after the huts, the produce from her fields, the fowls and all the ordinary household utensils and implements; she decides how they are to be used and she can at her discretion sell some of the crops, fowls and common utensils, in order to supply other wants. In case of divorce she is entitled not only to her personal belongings, such as clothes, but to most of the household utensils and to half the corn in her granaries. She cannot however, dispose of her husband's personal belongings, guns, wagons, and similar objects used exclusively by men, and the produce of any fields not specially assigned to her. So, too, the cattle and fields allotted to her by her husband remain under his authority, subject to the qualification noted above, and if she is divorced she has no claim over them. Church and other civil marriages, dissoluble only in the District Commissioner's court, formerly involved European conceptions of property rights conflicting in this respect with Kgatla practice: the law held that if the wife was the innocent party in case of divorce, she could claim half of all the property in the joint estate, including cattle and fields. Isang succeeded in having this amended, however, so that now, after the couple are divorced, any questions of property are referred back to the chief's court, where they are settled in accordance with ordinary tribal law.

In a polygamous household each 'house' has its own property, consisting of a compound, livestock, fields and domestic utensils. These are inherited by the children of the woman concerned. But the 'great wife', normally the woman first married, usually has more property assigned to her 'house' than have the others, her fields are ploughed first, and she is given precedence in various other ways. Her eldest son succeeds the father as head of the household, and inherits not only the property of her own 'house', but all other property not previously assigned to any special 'house' or person. Similarly, a widower, if he marries again, must provide his new wife with her own fields, cattle, etc. The property he assigned to his former wife is the inheritance of her children.

A wife may also have property in her own right. As we have

seen, her parents at marriage give her a few household utensils, and occasionally also a field and a heifer or two. She may afterwards acquire property as part of the *bogadi* received when her daughters get married, or by outright gift from her husband, or by inheritance from her mother and nowadays also from her father. Moreover, she can earn money by making and selling beer, pots, baskets and similar commodities, or by the practice of dressmaking or magic. Her earnings are at her own disposal, but a good wife will share them with her husband. Any property a woman thus possesses at marriage, or subsequently acquires, is never looked upon as part of her husband's estate; he cannot use it without her authority, it cannot be attached to pay his debts, and, in case of divorce, she takes it away with her.

In addition to all this, marriage imposes sexual obligations upon husband and wife. She must always be ready to gratify his sexual desires, except on the occasions when intercourse between them is specially prohibited. Moreover, she is expected to be faithful to him. If she commits adultery, he can beat or otherwise punish her, and can claim damages from her lover; but he will not usually divorce her, unless she persists in this conduct. He himself, on the other hand, is not required to be as faithful to her. Even if he has no other wives with whom she must share his attentions, he frequently has concubines, and normally she can take no action against them at court. It is only in Christian marriages that the ideal of a husband's fidelity is now sometimes met, and here, too, adultery by either spouse is accepted in court as a ground for divorce. Usually, however, a wife does not complain about her husband's love-affairs, so long as he cohabits with her regularly, and so gives her a reasonable opportunity of bearing him children. No marriage is considered really complete unless it produces offspring; and a barren woman is regarded with some contempt by her neighbours, and with scarce-concealed disappointment and even hostility by her husband's relatives. Under tribal law he is entitled to divorce her merely for this and to recover his *bogadi*, although she may instead bring another woman from her home to bear him children in her place. The children of a marriage always belong to the husband and his people, once *bogadi* has been paid. They never go with their mother in case of divorce, unless they are still young, when she may receive custody of them until they are old enough to return to their father.

The wife's inferior status, evident enough from what has already been said, is further reflected in the behaviour demanded of her in everyday life. She should pay formal deference to her husband, speaking to him respectfully, waiting upon him, serving him first with food, walking before him in the street, and not going about, especially at night, without his knowledge and permission; she sits on the floor, whereas he has his stool or chair; and if strangers come to the compound she must refer them to him and wait in the background while they are talking together. But despite these and many other discriminations against her, her position is by no means humiliating. She and her husband often eat together, speak to each other by their personal names or by the conventional terms 'father' and 'mother' used between all adults, sit together when entertaining visitors, go about together to beer-drinks and other festivities, and, above all, consult together in matters of domestic importance. She has her recognized place in the wider family councils, and is particularly influential when the marriages of her children are being considered.

NEIGHBOURS AND KINSMEN

So far I have been discussing husband and wife mainly in relation to each other. But, as we saw in Chapter 1, the Kgatla for at least part of the year live together in large settlements each containing several hundred people, and in the case of Mochudi as many as eight thousand. This means that every household, except perhaps when at the fields, is always closely surrounded by others, which impinge upon its life in various ways. Mochudi itself is so big a settlement that many of its inhabitants do not even know one another by sight, let alone as friends or acquaintances, and it is only at tribal meetings and similar public functions that they ever act collectively as one body. In the smaller villages contacts between the inhabitants are more intimate. They know one another and, either directly or through gossip, what goes on in most homes, and they come together fairly often, not only at public meetings or at church, but at work, at feasts and at funerals.

Even the village, however, is normally too big to enable all its inhabitants to feature prominently in the everyday life of their fellow-citizens. Here, and more markedly still in Mochudi, most of a man's interests and activities are linked up primarily with the members of his own ward. They are his nearest neighbours, and know him and his affairs very intimately. Whether actually related to him or not, they work with him and relax with him, help him in his troubles and share in his rejoicings. They are his trusted friends and sometimes also his enemies, for the close proximity in which they live inevitably breeds jealousies and quarrels as well as strong mutual attachments. It is they who constitute the public opinion that most directly affects him. So long as he is popular and respected, his life at home can be harmonious and pleasant; but their adverse criticism or open condemnation when he offends may cause him acute discomfort, and deprive him of friendly attentions and other services with which he can ill afford to dispense. So far as his married life is concerned, the ever-present interest they take in all he does is a force compelling him and his wife to adhere fairly closely to the conventional standards of good conduct.

Among the members of his ward, his own near relatives are of primary importance. They are linked to him by special rights and privileges, duties and obligations, which his other neighbours cannot command or be called upon to satisfy. Among the Kgatla, as everywhere else, relationship by blood or by marriage forms the basis of many social institutions. People are expected, merely because they are related, to behave towards one another in certain ways. They are not only forbidden or desired to intermarry, according to the nature of their relationship; they must also help one another at work or with gifts of property, stand by one another in times of trouble, and, on ceremonial or other formal domestic occasions, play clearly specified roles of various kinds to which much importance is attached. Kinship serves therefore to establish greater social cohesion within the tribe, and integrates the activities of its members into a wider cooperation than obtains within the restricted limits of the household alone.

Kgatla carry recognition of relationship much further than is common in European society. Everybody with whom genealogical connection can be established, no matter in how remote a degree, is included within the circle of kin; and as genealogies are often remembered in great detail, itself an indication of the importance of kinship, the number of known relatives may at times be very large indeed. These people a man groups into classes according to their sex and to their relative age and line of descent or affinity in regard to himself. Thus, he distinguishes between his paternal and maternal uncles, his paternal and maternal aunts, his brothers' children and his sisters' children, his elder and younger brothers, and his senior and junior paternal uncles (going by their status in regard to his father). In principle every class of relatives is bound to him by a different set of reciprocal obligations. In practice, the more remote relatives are merged into a somewhat amorphous body, and are not clearly differentiated from one another in behaviour. Only those more immediately connected have particular roles assigned to them, usually in connection with such formal occasions as marriage and death ceremonies; their obligations in everyday life are also general rather than specific.

The importance of close relatives is reflected particularly in the system of 'linked' relationships featuring so prominently in Kgatla society. In almost every family of any size the parents usually pair the children together – elder brother with younger brother, brother with sister, elder sister with younger sister. Those of the same sex are paired together alternately (first and third, second and fourth, and so on), those of opposite sex go in relative order of birth (eldest brother with eldest sister, second brother with second sister, and so on). Moreover, a man's linked sister is also the linked paternal aunt of his children, just as he is the linked maternal uncle of hers, while linked brothers are the linked senior and junior paternal uncles respectively of each other's children. Among his immediate relatives, therefore, every man may have one of each class to whom he is specially attached, and with whom he is said 'to work together for life'. It is with them that he is most closely associated in kinship obligations, and it is they who on all formal occasions should carry out the roles traditionally assigned to relatives of their class.

The formal pattern may however be distorted according to circumstances. A man's relatives are often widely scattered through the tribe, and as a result of intermarriage may even include people of other tribes. Some he never meets at all, or perhaps very seldom, owing to the distance at which they live from him. In consequence, it is generally only those fairly close by who matter a good deal in his life; they are the ones with whom he comes into most frequent contact, and who therefore have more occasion and opportunity for behaving in the manner prescribed. A remote uncle or cousin living in the same ward is thus likely to be more immediately important than a linked uncle or brother in some other village, although on all momentous occasions the latter will be specially sent for to carry out his traditional duties.

We have already noticed the part played by close relatives in betrothal and wedding ceremonies, and shall have occasion, throughout the rest of our survey, to cite many other specific instances of intervention by kin. It may be as well, however, to summarize briefly the more conspicuous aspects of their behaviour in relation to husband and wife. At the outset reference must be made to the dominating importance of the paternal kin. Most Kgatla social institutions are patrilineal in character. Tribal, totemic, ward and lineage affiliations are determined in the first instance by descent through the father; a man's surname is usually the given name of his paternal grandfather, and his second name that of his own father; property and social position normally pass from father to son, or, failing a son, to the nearest male paternal kinsman; and in the old days the spirits of its deceased paternal ancestors were the main gods of a family. In genealogies, too, the father's relatives are invariably remembered further back and in greater detail than the mother's.

Apart from all this, paternal kinsmen tend to live together in the same ward settlement, and generally side by side in adjacent compounds. Many exceptions are found in individual instances, but, as I have already shown in the case of Rampedi ward, the great majority of a man's neighbours are also his close paternal relatives. This community of residence reinforces the legal principles noted above. It renders possible cooperation in activities requiring more labour than is available within a household, it enables people to help one another readily in times of need, and it facilitates the handling of such domestic affairs as marriage negotiations, the organization of feasts, the conduct of funerals and the disposal of widows – matters all regarded as concerning not the family alone, but its kinsmen as well. As far as the household is concerned, these obligations mean that it has around it people who not only take a neighbourly interest in its affairs, but are required by virtue of their relationship to intervene actively on many occasions.

Relations between paternal kinsmen are, however, coloured by the emphasis laid on the maintenance of discipline and authority. The head of each household, as we have seen, controls the conduct of all his dependants, to whose unfailing obedience and respect he is entitled. Among brothers, similarly, the elder always governs the younger, whose services he can freely command, even after they are both married. This pattern is extended to paternal uncles, those older than one's father having greater authority than even he, while his younger brothers are considered junior in status to his children, and, allowing for differences in age, should normally defer to him. In everyday life the hierarchy of age and seniority tends to be relaxed, although never completely, but on formal occasions or when disagreements arise it is rigidly enforced. The man senior to all the rest in line of descent is their 'elder', the head of their lineage or 'family-group', and exercises considerable authority over them. Assisted by the other adults, he deals with all serious disputes arising among his people, and only if he is unable to effect a settlement can the matter be referred to the official tribal courts. His primary concern is not so much to administer justice as to bring about a reconciliation. To this end he appeals to family sentiment rather than to strict legal principles, but if rights of seniority have been violated he can impose punishment upon the offender. It is to this family council that all matrimonial disputes of any gravity must come in the first instance, so that, once again, the fate of a marriage may depend upon what the relatives decide.

Maternal kinsmen, on the other hand, usually display greater cordiality and goodwill towards one another, for they are not subject to the jealousies and conflicts that often arise between paternal kinsmen owing to arbitrary exercise of authority and rival claims to property or position. Just as a mother is normally more sympathetic and indulgent to her children than is a father, so her own relatives tend to be more benevolent and friendly. Children when small are sometimes sent to live for a while at the home of their mother's father or brother, and are in any case encouraged to visit it frequently. They always have many privileges there, especially if their mother's *bogadi* has already been paid: they can count on a warm welcome and cordial hospitality, receive ungrudging help in their domestic affairs, take precedence over their cousins in ceremonies involving recognition of rank, and carry great weight in the local family councils. 'A child is important in the home of his mother's people,' says the proverb, and practice generally bears this out.

The relationship between people and their linked maternal uncle is particularly intimate. The uncle must be consulted on all matters specially affecting his sister's children; his opinion is so important when their marriages are being arranged that his veto is often decisive; he contributes towards the *bogadi* given for the wives of his nephews, and shares in the *bogadi* received for his nieces; he helps with food and clothes when they are born, initiated, confirmed into church membership, or married; he takes a leading part in their funerals, being charged with the duty of preparing their corpses for burial, and receiving as his portion of their estate their clothes and other personal belongings; and exchanges of property are frequent between him and his nephews. It is to his maternal uncle perhaps more than any one else that a man tends to look for disinterested advice and for aid in times of necessity; and when disputes arise between father and son, or brother and brother, it is often the maternal uncle also who brings about the reconciliation, or with whom the oppressed child or younger brother goes to live if no amicable settlement can be reached.

When a man marries one of his relatives, his original kinship ties with her family usually dominate over the new relationship. A father-in-law who is also a maternal or paternal uncle continues to be treated along the same lines as before, although the interest he takes in the welfare of his daughter may at times prove embarrassing. But since most men marry women who are not actually their kinsmen, a new series of relationships is thereby created. In the main, the behaviour already described for the betrothal period persists after marriage. There is little of that formal restraint between a man and his parents-in-law reported of other Bantu tribes, and when I told my Kgatla friends of the famous 'mother-in-law taboo' they were invariably amused to find how 'stupid' other peoples could be. If the man's parents-in-law live in the same ward or close by, he continues to see much of them; if they are some distance away, he should make a point of visiting them from time to time. Their attitude towards him, however, is now to some extent coloured by the question of *bogadi*. If he has already given *bogadi*, they generally welcome him at their home, help him at work and in his personal difficulties, and reprimand or even punish their daughter if she does not make him a good wife. If on the other hand *bogadi* is still outstanding, they are seldom so ready to show him respect, and should he quarrel with his wife they are more apt to side readily with her. However, if he comes to stay with them permanently, as occasionally happens, they may treat him with greater consideration, mainly because he can now help them more often at work.

A daughter-in-law, as we have seen, has a difficult time when she first goes to live with her husband's people. This is true even if she is closely related to them, for in her case any kinship tie that may exist is definitely subordinated to the new role she has to play in their household. But apart from having to work hard and conduct herself with becoming meekness, she is not subjected to any restrictions similar to the special taboos found in other tribes, and in most cases, so long as she does not deliberately offend, she encounters little real trouble. She has a much easier time on the whole when she moves with her husband into their own compound. Most women manage then to settle down comfortably enough and to live on friendly terms with their relatives-in-law. They help one another at work, share their food, look after one another's children and generally function as a close-knit social and economic group. The young wife is treated by her parents-in-law as a daughter; they take her part if her husband neglects or ill-treats her, while she in turn looks to them for advice and support in her domestic problems. She continues also to see much of her own relatives, especially if they are in the same ward or village. She visits them often and gets their help in work; if she does not begin married life in their home, she must in any case go back there for her first confinement; they must be notified of any matter specially affecting her welfare, e.g. if she is to be doctored or has become involved in a court case; and she can generally count on their support in case of trouble with her husband or his family, unless she is obviously in the wrong.

It is evident from all this that the success or failure of a marriage is determined not merely by the personal relations between the couple themselves. We have seen that the choice of a wife or husband is usually a matter of careful consideration and lengthy negotiation between their respective families and other kinsmen. So, too, their married life is always a matter of deep interest to their near relatives and neighbours, upon whose help they also depend for additional labour and food, and whose intervention may go a long way towards ensuring stability in case of disagreement. On the other hand, these relatives, if not treated with what they consider becoming respect, may assert their rights so strongly as to produce friction between husband and wife. The behaviour of the latter towards each other is therefore governed not merely by their personal dispositions, but also by regard for the opinions of their neighbours and kinsmen.

5. Making a Living

Now that we have learned something about the social environment in which husband and wife live together, and about the rules governing their mutual conduct, we may begin our more detailed study of the relationship between them by discussing how they procure their food and other material wants. This aspect of domestic life is here given preference not merely because it is always of outstanding importance, but because among the Kgatla it has changed markedly since the coming of the Europeans, and in doing so has affected the other aspects as well. The full extent of the change can best be appreciated if, before proceeding to discuss conditions as they are today, I describe rapidly how the household maintained itself formerly.

THE OLD ECONOMIC SYSTEM

The commodities with which the Kgatla were familiar in pre-European times, and to the acquisition of which they directed their efforts, were neither very numerous nor very varied. Each family needed land for residence, cultivation, and grazing. It required a compound or at least a hut in which to live. Its food consisted mainly of Kafir-corn porridge and beer, supplemented by the milk of cattle and goats, the meat of wild and domestic animals, and vegetable dishes made from subsidiary crops and various wild plants. Its members wore clothing made chiefly of skins, and ornaments of beadwork, iron, copper and bone. For carrying on their daily work they used such implements as baskets, clay pots, iron-bladed hoes, spears, axes and knives, skin bags, mats and milk-sacks, wooden food-bowls, milk-pails, spoons and clubs, and calabash cups, scoops and bottles. All these goods were required in the first instance for maintaining the household itself. But every man owed certain forms of gifts and tribute to his kinsmen, neighbours, and chief, so that he worked to satisfy not only his own domestic needs but also his obligations to others.

Among these commodities land occupied a special place. The tribal territory and all its resources were administered by the chief through the headmen of villages and wards. It was their duty to see that every married man received, free of special charge, a site for his home, a plot to cultivate and facilities for grazing cattle. He was entitled only to what he and his children were themselves likely to use, and could never claim more. He could give away or lend out land he did not want at the moment, but he could neither sell it nor hire it out. He therefore had no incentive to the acquisition of large holdings for speculative or renting purposes. The result was that everybody obtained land at no other cost than the obligation, common to all, of carrying out his tribal duties, and that holdings did not vary in size except in so far as households differed in magnitude. No private rights at all were recognized over game and other natural resources: anybody could hunt wherever he liked, or take wood, grass, clay, water, earth and wild edible plants, wherever he found them.

The demand for other commodities was not similarly regulated by law. They were not bestowed upon all by the tribal authorities, but had to be acquired by individual effort, nor was the quantity of each a man might possess limited in the same way as his claim to land. Variations in type and quality, however, were too few to create significant distinctions between the kinds of goods owned by one household and another. Generally speaking, all Kgatla, irrespective of rank, lived in the same sort of hut; apart from minor sex and totemic taboos, they ate the same foods; allowing for differences of sex and age, they wore similar clothing and ornaments; and they used the same implements, though magicians and smiths needed certain special apparatus. Wealthy people could indulge in utensils of better make, ornaments or karosses of greater value, or more frequent supplies of meat and beer; but, apart from a few such possibilities, there was little scope for developing or satisfying a variety of individual preferences. Most implements and ornaments, however, could be exchanged for other commodities, while food, in the form of meat, beer, thick milk and porridge, was widely used as payment for labour and to satisfy various social obligations towards kinsmen and neighbours. It was therefore advantageous to acquire surplus stocks of these goods.

Nevertheless, the goods just referred to had a very limited range of usefulness. Livestock were therefore the only form in which it was practicable to accumulate wealth. Cattle, goats and sheep, not merely furnished food and the raw materials for such industries as leatherwork and bone-carving. They were the principal mediums of exchange, and of sacrifice to the spirits of the dead. The more cattle a man had, the more wives he could marry. The labour of these women provided him with more corn, which, converted into porridge and beer, he could use to enhance his popularity by entertaining generously. The number of families to whom he was allied by marriage consolidated his standing in the tribe. By placing out his cattle on loan, he could also command the labour and allegiance of the holders for various purposes. Possession of wealth was accordingly reflected not so much in the wider range and superior quality of a man's clothing, huts and implements, as in the number of his cattle, and the size of the household and following he was consequently able to maintain.

One important reservation must, however, be made. In the Kgatla social system wealth was correlated with rank. The chief and his subordinate political authorities were entitled in varying degrees to tribute from their subjects in both labour and kind, and to the fines paid at their courts; the chief also kept many of the cattle looted in war, and all stray cattle whose owners could not be found. As a result, these men were always richer than any one else, the chief himself being by far the richest of all. Their wealth enabled them to attract additional labour, and so increase their possessions still further. Commoners could never command the same privileges, and therefore had less opportunity of acquiring many cattle or accumulating large stocks of food. The inheritance of livestock and other forms of property helped to maintain class distinctions by ensuring that men of rank generally started independent household life with greater riches than others.

Let us now see how people obtained the goods that they wanted. Each household, to start with, normally produced the great bulk of its domestic requirements. It got its food by cultivating Kafir corn and other crops, breeding live-stock, hunting, and collecting wild edible plants. Deficits were made good by gifts or loans from relatives or friends, or by exchange for some other commodity, but nobody ever obtained all or even most of his food in this way. Each household also built its own huts and granaries, and did its own housework. In all these activities everybody except the infants took part, men, women and children, having specified occupations according to sex and age. The women and girls tilled the fields, built and repaired the walls of the huts, granaries and courtyard, prepared food and made beer, looked after the fowls, fetched water, wood and earth, collected wild plants and did all the other housework. The men and boys herded the cattle and small stock, hunted, and did all the timber-work in building. Tasks that a household was too small to carry out for itself, or wished to complete more rapidly than was possible working alone, were generally done either with the aid of relatives, or by organizing a work-party and paying with meat, beer or some similar commodity, the neighbours coming to help. Poor people had no other means of getting sufficient labour for such big undertakings as clearing or weeding a field, threshing corn, or building a hut; and since they were accordingly all dependent upon one another, it was good policy to help others when invited. The only specialist doing work for which most households were not equipped was the magician, whose services had to be hired for the protective and beneficent doctoring of compounds, fields and cattle-posts. Occasionally, however, a man with no son or other suitable relative might also have to employ an outsider to look after his cattle.

Wealthy men placed out most of their cattle on loan. This both simplified the task of herding, and insured against the total loss that might result from disease, raids or some similar disaster, if the animals were all kept together. It was also a means of obtaining adherents, for the holder of 'loan-cattle' not only looked after them but frequently had to render various other services to their owner. In return, he could use the milk of the cows entrusted to him, and at some time usually also received the gift of a heifer to breed for him. This was the principal way in which poor people could acquire milk and cattle, and it was fairly commonly practised. The chief and other men of rank also kept hereditary servants, who did most of the menial work for their households. These servants were usually descendants of captives taken in war, or fugitives from other tribes. In return for their labour they were supported almost entirely by their master. The chief, moreover, could call upon his subjects at any time for official or domestic services, including warfare, hunting, destroying beasts of prey, rounding up stray cattle and building his huts or clearing his fields. Such labour was unpaid and compulsory, but it provided him with the means of fulfilling his own obligations to the tribe.

The members of each household also made the greater part of their own clothing, ornaments and implements, all from materials locally obtainable. A few articles, however, like food-bowls, karosses and especially clay pots and metal goods, were made by specialists who alone had the necessary skill, and from whom others therefore had to purchase what was required. But there was no systematic production for exchange, nor any organized system of trade. No craftsman ever devoted himself to one particular occupation as his sole means of livelihood. Like the magician, he carried on the same farming activities as the rest, and the special craft he also practised was a subsidiary, if occasionally important, source of income.

Apart from satisfying their own wants in the manner just described, people were expected to show hospitality to their kinsmen and neighbours. Generosity with food was a virtue regarded very highly, and a selfish or niggardly person was always despised. A man was also expected on occasion to make special gifts to his near relatives. He should, for instance, send them meat or beer whenever he slaughtered or brewed, contribute towards the *bogadi* for a wife, provide clothing and ornaments for a boy or girl just initiated, or help pay a fine or damages imposed at court. All members of the tribe, again, paid tribute in various forms to the chief. Each village or group of wards cultivated a special field for him, every woman sent him a basketful of corn after reaping, households that could afford it presented him with cattle on his accession, and successful hunters gave him specified portions of their gain. In return he fed the men at his council-place or working for him, looked after poor widows and orphans, rewarded the services of his warriors and councillors with gifts of cattle, and in times of famine provided the people with corn from his granaries. 'The chief is the wife of the tribe,' it was said, i.e. he saw to it that all had food; and again, 'The chief has nothing of his own, everything he possesses belongs to the tribe.'

The Kgatla were thus normally self-contained as regards economic organization. There were both poor and rich people among them, but the reciprocal obligations of gift and service between kinsmen and neighbours enabled households to make good any momentary wants, while the chief's use of his wealth still further ensured that no one should ever be completely destitute. It was only in times of great scarcity that food would be sought in some neighbouring tribe less sorely afflicted. Otherwise there seems to have been very little dependence upon outsiders for any special commodity, although raids on weaker neighbours were a favourite means of adding to the cattle already owned.

THE GROWTH OF NEW WANTS

The self-sufficiency just described no longer exists. Contact with Western civilization introduced new commodities of many different kinds, whose acceptance drew the Kgatla into an elaborate system of exchange through which they are linked up with and even dependent upon the markets of the world. The early Boers in the Transvaal revealed to them new forms of dress, housing, transport, weapons and other instruments, and by employing them as farm-hands gave them some knowledge of

European agricultural methods. From 1864 the missionaries introduced new forms of religion and education, and very many years later they started medical treatment as well. All these stimulated wants of a kind that formerly did not exist. The Administration in 1896 built a railway line through the Reserve, in 1899 imposed taxation in money, and in 1919 created a Native Fund to finance education and economic development, both of which it has since been promoting actively. The traders, again, have since they settled in the Reserve about 1890 continuously brought in more and more of the products of Eastern civilization.

These innovations have greatly extended the range of accessible commodities. Food habits remain substantially the same, but many people have acquired a taste for sweets, sugar and tea, and some also for bread, jam and tinned meats. The horse, pig and donkey, have been added to the list of domestic animals. Housing, as we have seen, has been affected mainly by the adoption of European doors, windows and methods of thatching, but many people also build rectangular dwellings, and use bricks, iron sheeting and other new materials. The change in dress has been very marked indeed, for, except among the babies and younger children, European clothing is now worn almost universally, although costumes vary widely in completeness. Imported beads, earrings and bangles, have almost completely displaced the old Native ornaments. Implements, finally, have become far more numerous, for, apart from those formerly known, the Kgatla can now procure the products of factories all over the world.

Apart from procuring such goods, people must nowadays find money for making certain cash payments. Since 1899 the Administration has demanded from every man over the 'apparent age' of eighteen an annual tax, at first fixed at ten shillings, but raised in 1909 to one pound, at which amount, after several changes, it still stands. Polygamists may have to pay two or three times the normal sum, according to the number of wives that they have. Failure to pay the tax within three months from the time it is due renders the offender liable to a fine or imprisonment, although in fact men are seldom prosecuted unless they are persistent defaulters. On the other hand, men able to satisfy the District Commissioner that they are too poor to pay the tax 'without being deprived of the means of their subsistence' may be exempted from the whole or part of it. In 1935, out of 3,645 registered taxpayers, 49 had been so exempted.

In addition to the regular Government tax, people must on occasion pay the levies raised by the chief, either to finance some big public undertaking, or to liquidate debts incurred by him personally or on behalf of the tribe. Sometimes the levies are imposed upon all registered taxpayers. Thus, in 1926, Isang ordered every man to contribute either a good ox, or its then prevailing cash equivalent of £6 10s., to meet the cost of an extensive water-boring scheme he had planned. In 1936, again, there was a levy of £1 10s. a man for the payment of tribal debts, and in 1937 and 1938 a 'national welfare levy' of five shillings a man. Previously levies sometimes took the form of sending the men of an age-regiment to seek work abroad for the money required by the chief. The Makuka regiment had to find five pounds each to pay for the church built in Mochudi in 1903, the Machechele five pounds each for the National School built in 1923, and the Mafatshwana four pounds each for the house built at the same time for the first principal of the school.

A few other forms of cash expenditure fall regularly upon many people. Women getting water from the tribal bore-holes in Mochudi, and men watering their cattle at the tribal bore-holes in the veld, each pay a small seasonal charge towards the cost of running and upkeep. Owners of small stock pay an annual dipping fee (2d. per animal). Money is also required for church dues (5s. per annum), school fees and books, medical treatment by the Mission doctor and work done on wagons and ploughs by the European blacksmiths. It is the only form in which payment can be made for goods imported directly from mail-order stores and other places outside the Reserve, for postage stamps, and for transport by rail or bus to the Transvaal and other centres of employment. For many other purposes, too, it is preferred to anything else, although it is not the only acceptable medium, e.g. for purchasing goods at the trading-store and beer or other commodities within the tribe, and for the initial payment (now standardized at one shilling) made to a diviner for 'throwing the bones'.

Money has therefore come to be indispensable. But to most Kgatla it becomes desirable only when required for some special purpose of immediate urgency. The idea of trying to accumulate it for possible future needs, to set something aside for a rainy day, is still foreign to them. There are, of course, some who have developed the habit of saving, or who, being in receipt of regular wages, occasionally have more money in hand than they require at the moment, and can therefore save part of it. But they are still a minority.

The introduction of new commodities, and the creation of wants formerly unknown, have led to greater differentiation in standards of living. Poor people on the whole still occupy the same kind of hut as before, eat the same foods, and keep the same domestic animals, with perhaps the addition of the pig. Here there has in the main been relatively little change. But almost all wear clothing of European type, especially the women, who insist on having their blankets and dresses. In addition, even the poorest household tries to provide itself with a plough, axes, knives and other hardware implements, salt, soap, matches, candles, paraffin and various patent medicines. Its men must also pay the annual tax to the Administration, and the levy imposed by the chief. These may therefore be regarded as universal wants. Many people, however, also acquire more and better clothes and implements, as well as sugar and tea, arms and ammunition, wagons, crockery of some kind, sewing machines, tables, and chairs and large empty petrol drums (which are used for transporting water to the fields). More progressive men likewise invest in superior ploughs, live-stock of good quality, horses, dwellings and furniture of European type, European foods of various kinds, and similar goods still considered luxuries by the rest.

Professing Christians must maintain 'respectable' standards of dress, purchase Bibles and other religious books, and pay various dues to the Church. Moreover, since the Church expects them to use beer in moderation, and to abstain from it altogether if possible, it is among them that the use of tea and sugar is most widespread. Parents of school children have special expenses in the form of fees, clothing, and books and stationery. The young men working abroad have acquired tastes in clothing, food and amusement not shared by their elders, and those who have been to educational institutions outside the reserve, at enhanced cost to their parents, are beginning to indulge in such extreme local luxuries as bicycles, newspapers and even gramophones and cameras.

Coupled with this is another important change. The goods used today are far more numerous and varied than before. The range of alternatives from which to choose has accordingly widened very considerably, and with it new criteria of wealth and social status have emerged. The number of his wives is no longer the most important index of a man's position in Kgatla society. Polygamy, as we saw in the last chapter, has declined so considerably as to be almost insignificant, and with very few exceptions the leading men of the tribe, including all those of the royal family, are monogamists. Cattle remain a symbol of wealth, but more perhaps for their trade value than for their traditional social desirability. Brick houses, complete outfits of European clothing, wagons, rifles, good ploughs, suites of furniture and a large and varied stock of hardware tools – these, and other objects like them, are today the visible indications of the man of property. Moreover, the development of wage-labour for Europeans had made it possible for even the lowest commoner to earn money with which to purchase such goods, and so has broken down the old correlation of rank and wealth, and given more scope for individual enterprise in the attainment of riches. The chief and his immediate relatives are still the wealthiest men in the tribe, but teachers and shop-assistants receiving regular cash wages are sometimes better off than influential ward-heads not so able to adapt themselves to modern conditions.

MODERN HOUSEHOLD PRODUCTION

Let us now see how people try today to satisfy their various wants. The methods traditionally employed were obviously too few and too standardized to provide them with all their modern requirements. They had therefore to embark upon one or more of three possible lines of development. They could take over from the Europeans and practise for themselves the techniques involved in producing the new commodities; they could increase the output of their traditional forms of production to provide a surplus to exchange for these commodities; or they could enter into new forms of occupation to obtain the means with which to purchase them. We shall first ascertain which of the many goods they use today they produce for themselves, and how far methods of production aim at providing for exchange as well as for domestic consumption. This will enable us to appreciate more fully in due course how desirable some alternative source of income has become.

For their food supply Kgatla still rely almost entirely upon farming; imports, save in times of famine, are with the exception of a few articles like sugar and tea confined to what most people still regard as luxuries. Methods of cultivation have in some instances become more efficient through the introduction of the plough, which has also enabled larger areas to be dealt with than was formerly possible. Whereas in the old days fields were seldom more than two or three acres in extent, today they are usually four or five, and often even bigger. Some men, again, have through work for European farmers acquired better knowledge of technique, and Isang has since about 1920 been preaching the use of good ploughs and seed. But in the main there has been little further change.

Apart from oranges, grown on a very small scale in many compound yards in Mochudi, no new crops have been introduced, and only a few enlightened men pay special attention to their seed. Ploughing is often done badly, a field is weeded only once, and then sometimes too late, and no rotation of crops is practised. The persistence of old magical rites, such as relying upon charms to clear a field infested with pests, is also a bar to progress. In 1931 the Administration stationed a Native agricultural demonstrator with the tribe in order to raise the standard of cultivation. As yet, however, his experiments of tilling several model plots, and, in conjunction with the Education Department, running small vegetable gardens at some of the schools, have met with little response from the people generally. Since 1931, also, agricultural shows have been organized sporadically by the Administration, but their influence has so far been relatively slight.

No statistics of crop production are available. But traders' returns since 1929 show that, except in times of drought, imports of corn are so very small as to be negligible, and are usually more than counterbalanced by exports. This indicates that the Kgatla can normally produce more than they use to feed themselves and to make into beer. The rainfall, however, is too uncertain to make agriculture a flourishing industry. In the period 1925–34 good crops were reaped only four times, while in 1926, 1927 and 1933 harvests failed owing to drought. The year 1933 was particularly bad, when quantities of Kafir corn and maize had to be imported not only by the stores but also by the Administration, which rationed them out among people employed on small relief works specially initiated.

Animal husbandry has made greater progress. The Reserve is richly stocked with grasses of high food value, which make it good ranching country, and as the cattle range freely over the pastures they generally thrive fairly well, even during the dry season. The exploitation of underground water supplies by means of wells and bore-holes, and the consequent opening up of tracts previously useless owing to lack of surface water, have greatly increased the carrying capacity of the land, and there is little evidence of overstocking, that great curse of so many Native areas in other parts of South Africa. In 1936, according to the latest census figures, the Kgatla possessed approximately 47,500 head of cattle. This gives an average of only 17.0 per square mile, which although higher than in the other big Native Reserves of the Protectorate is appreciably less than in most of the Union

Native Reserves. Nevertheless, much still remains to be done by way of providing watering facilities, for even now cattle must often be driven many miles from grazing to water, with injurious effects upon their condition. In years of prolonged drought they suffer greatly, and die in large numbers. It is estimated, for instance, that during the great drought of 1933 the tribe lost between 12,000 and 15,000 head of cattle.

Most people, however, still attach less importance to the quality than to the number of their cattle, and little attempt is made to prevent the propagation of inferior stock. Raids on European farms in the Transvaal during the Anglo–Boer War brought in many animals of improved breed, whose influence can be seen in present-day cattle, which are often of good shape and size. Several enlightened owners, alive to the importance of quality as a factor in trade, have also purchased better bulls. But each man's animals, no matter how few they are, are still herded separately, with insufficient segregation according to sex and age. Consequently, not only is labour wastefully employed, but mating is indiscriminate, and heifers calve at an early age. Failure to castrate young bulls soon enough contributes to the defects in breeding. The result is that most Kgatla cattle are of inferior quality and relatively low commercial value. The Government Veterinary Department has lately been making serious efforts to remedy this. It has met with fair success in persuading people to adopt scientific methods of combating stock diseases, but so far has effected little change in the traditional system of herding, which is the main bar to progress.

Of the newly-acquired domestic animals, the pig is the most important. It is eaten and its fat is converted into soap, it has begun to figure prominently in the list of exports, and it plays the subsidiary but essential role of scavenger, its usefulness in this respect being fully appreciated by the Kgatla themselves. Few people, however, pay special attention to the care of either their pigs or their fowls, of which almost every household has some. Both are looked after mainly by women, as part of the ordinary domestic routine, and have not yet given rise to separate industries.

Methods of hunting have been considerably improved by the introduction of the horse, the gun and the iron trap. Horses are owned by very few men, but guns are fairly common, and the Administration allows everybody possessing one to purchase fifty rounds of ammunition yearly. Kgatla are therefore able to hunt more easily than when they had to rely upon the spear and the axe. The result has been, however, that much of the game round the villages and cattle-posts has been killed off or scared away, so that this important source of fresh meat has become far less plentiful. In the early days of contact with Europeans, ivory, ostrich feathers and the skins of fur-bearing animals, were valuable trade commodities, and the efforts to obtain them were intensified. Today, however, elephants have long disappeared from the Reserve, the demand for ostrich feathers has fallen off and they are no longer sold, and wild animal skins have slumped greatly in price. Hunting is therefore carried on mainly to obtain food or to protect the livestock.

Each household continues in the main to procure its own food by the methods just mentioned. All Kgatla in the Reserve still regard themselves primarily as farmers, no matter in what other occupations they may also be engaged. Even teachers, shop-assistants and others, whose time is largely taken up with routine activities of a new kind, retain their attachment to the land, and on every available opportunity will go off to inspect their fields and cattle-posts. The chief himself, with all his political duties and other preoccupations, is keenly interested in farming for himself. Time and again I heard old men at the tribal council-place complain that Molefi was away at his cattle-posts instead of attending to official business, while Isang has long been known as the most progressive farmer in the tribe, setting the lead in almost every new development that has taken place.

Not every household, however, manages to produce sufficient food to meet its wants. The considerable amount of internal trade in Kafir corn indicates that some at least depend partly upon the efforts of others. Of thirty-seven women about whose harvests I got information for the 1933-34 season, which, however, was disastrously affected by locusts, no fewer than twelve admitted that they would have to buy corn to supplement what they had reaped. Nine, on the other hand, had been able to produce much more than they required for themselves, and looked forward to disposing of their surplus by trade. Similarly, not every household has its own cattle. An inquiry I made in 1932 among eighty married men of Makgophana ward showed that, while three had very large herds, thirteen had no cattle at all, but mostly obtained milk and oxen for ploughing by serving others under the 'loan' system. Households like these indicate that, although the tribe as a whole is normally self-supporting in regard to food, some people do not produce all they require, and seek other methods of making up the deficit.

Each household generally still builds its own huts and granaries, and does all its own housework. Here, as in cultivating the fields, additional labour is normally obtained from relatives or neighbours by the traditional methods of reciprocal service or work-parties. Various changes, however, can be noticed in the domestic allocation of tasks. The introduction of the plough has forced men to participate more than formerly in agriculture, and ploughing is now done mainly by them. They also use animal transport for work originally done by women, like conveying corn home from the fields, and occasionally for what are still the typically feminine activities of fetching water, wood and earth. Women have acquired the new responsibility of looking after pigs. They are also no longer debarred from handling cattle, and are often seen helping in ploughing and driving. They do not as yet herd or milk, although occasional exceptions are found even to this. On the other hand, the spread of Christianity has caused many to stop making beer, which has therefore become a more specialized occupation.

More important still, there have been far-reaching changes in the domestic supply of labour. The decline of polygamy has reduced the average size of the household, and consequently the number of people available for carrying on its work. Labour migration, now the principal source of money income, means that many men are seldom at home to attend to the routine tasks in which they formerly engaged, and that a greater burden has been thrown upon those remaining behind. To some extent it has even led to retrogression in agriculture. Although some men still contrive to return in time to plough, others, especially those in the towns, stay away for several years without coming back at all. Formerly a man's relatives would plough for his wife during his absence, and even today this is often done, but it is becoming more difficult now that the number away for long periods is increasing. In any case, help is given only after the relatives have ploughed for themselves, so that the wife often loses the benefit of the early rains and her fields suffer accordingly. And failing such help, the ploughing must be done by the women and boys, with the result that it is usually still less efficient.

Similarly, complaints are nowadays often heard that, owing to the lengthening absence of the men abroad, herd-boys at the cattle-posts are left without supervision for much longer periods than formerly. They tend consequently to feel neglected, their occasional visits home are cut short because there is no one to relieve them, and they become slack and careless. Some even grow tired of remaining continuously with the cattle, and run away into the Transvaal to look for more exciting forms of work. Although this is not at all frequent, it is a symptom about which the Kgatla are particularly concerned. Moreover, the young men who in the old days would have taken charge at the cattle-posts are now mostly away in the towns, and on their return are said to take little interest in herding, preferring apparently to swagger about among the girls in the villages. The general result of these tendencies, according to local opinion, is that less care is nowadays given to the cattle, so that losses due to straying and neglect are more numerous than they used to be.

Education has also affected the working capacity of the household. Children going to school are for the greater part of the year unable to take as much part in domestic activities as the rest. Many parents actually complain at the loss of their services, and may remove them from school after only a year or two. So far as household economy is concerned, education means that still more work is being thrust upon those staying at home, and that keeping children at school involves not merely new expenditure, but also a sacrifice of labour resources.

The result of all this has been that in some cases additional help must be obtained from outsiders to perform tasks for which members of the household are not available. Thus, it is now fairly common for people to hire others to clear a new field for them, bring in a load of firewood, dig a well, or cut rafters and thatching-grass for use in building the roof of a hut. Cases are even known where men have been specially engaged to plough for some one else. The development of new skills in the more common methods of production has likewise led to increasing dependence upon others. This is most clearly seen in building, where the erection and thatching of a roof in the European manner is the work of male specialists, who must be hired for the purpose. Payment in all these cases is usually in either livestock or money, the household thus making good its labour shortage by its income from other sources.

Still another strain upon household labour resources may be imposed by the use the chief makes of the free tribal services to which he is entitled. He generally mobilizes one or more age-regiments for work, but occasionally summons all the inhabitants of his town. Formerly, as we have seen, the tasks they performed were directly beneficial either to himself or to the tribe as a whole. Since the coming of the Europeans, new tasks have been added. Some, like making dams or roads, or clearing sites for churches or schools and helping to build them, are likewise for the common good. But when regiments were sent abroad to earn money with which to finance building and other operations, the lengthy absence of the men concerned obviously affected adversely their own household activities. More recently, too, several tasks were ordered which people felt served European interests rather than their own. In 1931 all the able-bodied men and women of Mochudi had to make an agricultural show-ground few of them wanted, and in 1934 two regiments cleared the site for an aerodrome. In both instances a good deal of dissatisfaction was openly expressed, especially as the time spent on the work was more than two months. Moreover, since many men were abroad working for themselves, these tasks fell as a much greater burden upon those remaining behind, who could not but regard their lot as comparatively unfavourable. At the end of 1934 the Administration restricted by law the chief's right to employ compulsory tribal labour. But the system, although shorn of its abuses, still prevails: and a regiment at work can usually be recognized by the lackadaisical manner in which the task is being performed, the number of men hanging about in apparent idleness, and the marked lack of enthusiasm for what is being done.

While in the main each household, subject to the reservations noted above, continues to produce its own food and build its own huts, it has become far more dependent than before upon others for clothing and household utensils. New forms of domestic industry, it is true, have been introduced. Most men make for themselves the wooden sledges used by those who cannot afford to purchase wagons. Similarly, women directly under Mission or school influence have for the past thirty years and more been taught knitting and sewing; they can therefore make dresses and woollen caps for themselves and their daughters, and shirts for their husbands and sons, although the materials with which they work must be bought in the stores. Several more specialized occupations have also come into being. Some women are noted for their skill in dressmaking, and so are usually entrusted with such tasks as making up a bride's wedding costume. A few men make tables, chairs and similar articles; others manufacture whips and wooden yokes for the cattle, or buy ornamental wire in the stores and twist it into bangles which they hawk around. For goods like these the average household relies upon the products of others.

On the whole, however, the spreading use of imported goods has adversely affected domestic arts and crafts, and so deprived many people of occupations in which they formerly engaged. The art of working iron and copper is virtually extinct. The metal goods formerly made, like axes, hoes, knives and ornaments, are now obtained solely from the traders, and spears, more recently wrought from imported steel rods, are giving place to the gun. Leatherwork has decreased: much of the clothing now worn is bought in the stores, imported grain bags are far more common than those locally sewn of skin, milk-sacks are now generally made of canvas, while shields and bellows are no longer used at all, and are in fact unprocurable even as ethnographical specimens. Pot-making, basketwork and woodwork are all becoming more restricted, their products, although still often seen, being less widely used than before. Iron pots and empty petrol tins are replacing the more fragile cooking-pots and water-pots of clay, enamel basins and plates are used by many instead of Native-made baskets and wooden food-bowls, and hardware buckets and cans are preferred to wooden milk-pails. The widespread acceptance of these and other imported goods, many of which had no counterpart in old Kgatla life, has relegated local products to a minor place among the implements in common use. In this respect not only the average household, but the tribe as a whole, is no longer self-supporting.

MAKING ENDS MEET

Our survey of Kgatla industry has established the following facts. With some exceptions, each household produces its own food and builds its own home. Many people, however, cannot devote sufficient time to these pursuits, or, as in the case of hut-building, have not mastered the new techniques. They must therefore employ others to help them. Some, again, have no cattle of their own, or fail to grow enough corn for their needs. They also must look to others for relief. Many households can likewise make part of their own clothing and implements. But most of the goods now in use are acquired from other people, and, since very few are locally produced, they must almost all be imported into the Reserve. Finally, money has become established as the principal medium of exchange, and the imposition of taxes has made its acquisition a universal necessity. The cost of churches and schools, boring for water, and similar public works, has placed a further burden upon the resources of the people, and made it essential for them to find some additional source of income. Taking only the more conspicuous forms of expenditure – on imported goods, taxes and levies, medical expenses, church dues, dipping fees, school fees and railway fares – the amount of money that has been found by the tribe since 1929 has averaged approximately £15,000 per annum, or roughly £5 per household. Of this, traders' imports accounted for about £10,000, hut-tax for £2,500 and tribal levies for £650.

We must now see how the household manages to procure all the goods (including money) that it does not produce for itself. Formerly, as I have shown, occasional help was obtained in the form of hospitality from kinsmen and neighbours, and of gifts from certain relatives. This system of mutual aid is still a fairly notable feature of Kgatla life. It has even taken on new manifestations. Thus, a man may contribute towards the hut-tax of an uncle or brother, pay for the education of a nephew or niece, or buy dress material for a sister or aunt. It is said, however, that relatives sometimes show less readiness to help one another than they formerly did. Now that new opportunities of making a living have developed, the bonds of kinship are no longer so advantageous to all, and may even be found a burden by men whose occupations make them a suitable mark for the importunities of the needy. In any case, help of this sort merely provides momentary relief, and can never be a major source of income.

The chief also continues to carry out to some extent his traditional obligations of helping poor people and playing host to the tribe generally. Both Isang and Molefi have often provided paupers with food and clothing, lent wagons, oxen and ploughs, to men in need, and subsidized the education of several promising youths, and during the famine of 1933 they also imported corn for general distribution as seed. But, with the growth of new wants, the chief now maintains a relatively expensive personal standard of living which eats considerably into his means. Moreover, since the establishment in 1933 of the Tribal Fund, to which the revenue from levies, tax commission, court fines and similar sources, has been diverted, his official income has been limited to the annual salary (£300, with an allowance of £60 for entertainment and travelling) paid to him out of the Fund. The result is that he can no longer provide for his people on the scale

reported of Lentswe, of whose lavish generosity many tales are
still told. On the other hand, the Tribal Fund itself can now be
used for public relief when necessary. Previously, the Mission in
times of famine often helped the people with food, while during
the depression of 1929–32 the Administration reduced the rate of
tax, and in 1933 it also imported corn into the Reserve for the use
of the tribe. Once again, however, assistance of this sort, while it
may tide the household over a period of great distress, cannot
enable it to procure regular supplies of money and other
goods.

The principal methods, therefore, of satisfying wants, other
than by direct production, are to sell surplus produce and to seek
remunerative employment. In pre-European times, as already
mentioned, there was little systematic production of commodities
for exchange, although makers of pots, metal goods and certain
skin or wooden objects, could rely upon their specialized crafts to
supplement their income from farming. Smithing, one of the
most lucrative occupations of the past, has now disappeared
completely. All metal goods are imported, while such work as
repairing wagons and ploughs is done exclusively by European
blacksmiths resident in the Reserve. Workers in wood, leather,
clay and grass, can still earn a little by making and selling objects
like food-bowls, stamping-blocks, yokes, whips, sandals, pots and
baskets. These forms of production, however, do not at any time
constitute an important source of income, the demand being too
small and irregular.

The vast majority of Kgatla rely upon the sale of commodities
produced by almost all. There is a good deal of internal trade in
livestock, meat, corn and other forms of food, which enables
people to acquire money or other goods from time to time. Many
women, especially widows, earn an odd shilling or two now and
then by selling beer; and when, in July 1932, the chief temporarily prohibited beer-drinking, the effect was immediately noticed by the storekeepers, who complained that women were
spending much less money than before. Trade of this description, however, is wholly sporadic; there are no tribal markets of
any kind where goods are regularly offered for sale. Anybody

wanting to sell or purchase food or some other object inquires among his neighbours and acquaintances until he finds one with whom he can deal, and the transaction is concluded directly between them. Occasionally people also come from other tribes to purchase corn in times of need, but here again there is no organized system of trade.

The principal market for local produce is presented by the traders' stores, which purchase livestock, crops, hides and skins, and various other commodities. Almost all this produce is exported to the Union of South Africa and elsewhere; it is only occasionally, and to a very minor extent, that Natives themselves buy such goods from the traders. There are only four stores in the Reserve (two in Mochudi, one at Pilane Station, and one in Sikwane), but a fair amount of business is also done with those at Kopong, Gaberones and Derdepoort, just over the tribal boundaries. Many transactions take the form of barter, people exchanging fowls, eggs, skins, etc., over the counter for the goods they require. Cattle and other livestock, frequently sold as a means of obtaining money for tax, are paid for as a rule partly in goods, and partly in cash. People are beginning to realize that the prices given by traders are generally less than could be obtained by direct export, and requests to the Administration to open up new markets are nowadays often heard at meetings of the Native Advisory Council. For a long time to come, however, the local stores must remain the clearing-house for almost all exports. Few people produce enough to enable them to send direct to other markets, and cooperative selling is still completely unknown.

There is no restriction at all upon the sale of hides and skins, pigs, fowls and eggs. Kafir corn, on the other hand, may not be sold to traders without the written permission of the chief, given as a rule only after a very good harvest has been reaped. Violation of this tribal law is punished by a fine. Its avowed object is to ensure that people will always have enough corn in hand to enable them to tide over a bad year. In this respect, as experience has shown, it is highly desirable, although it has sometimes had the effect of preventing more cultivation than is absolutely necessary, people tending to take things fairly easily during the year following a season of good crops. Maize and beans are not subject to the same restriction, but are not grown sufficiently to make them important. Kafir corn, too, perhaps owing to the ban on its sale, is raised primarily for domestic consumption, and seldom in quantities leaving a large surplus for disposal. Nevertheless, in some years it figures prominently among the list of exports, and at other times always finds a ready market among the people at home.

Cattle and small stock also may not be sold without the written permission of the chief. But this measure is designed mainly to facilitate inquiry in case of stock-theft, and its application is usually a mere formality. Before 1923 cattle bought by the traders could be sent freely into the Union, after undergoing a period of quarantine. In that year, however, the Union authorities prohibited imports from the Protectorate for the open market, and in 1924 they imposed restrictions regarding the weight and condition of cattle imported for slaughter. These embargoes reduced the legal export of Kgatla cattle very considerably, most animals failing to reach the specified weights. But a new trade was developed with stock-dealers, who bought up scrub cattle which they smuggled into the Union. From the end of 1932 until the latter half of 1934 an outbreak of foot-and-mouth disease in the Protectorate led to the prohibition of all exports into the Union. Since then the cattle trade has resumed fairly normal proportions (of the post-embargo period), while smuggling, according to local reports, is more rife than ever. Small stock have never been an important item for export, but during the past few years pigs have been sold in increasing quantities.

The total value of produce exported by traders from the Reserve since 1929 has averaged about £2,250 per annum, or less than £1 per household. Of this amount, hides and skins accounted for roughly £650, cattle and small stock for £500, pigs for £420, and Kafir corn for £460. These figures, however, do not reflect the total value of cattle exported, since the majority are sold to dealers, or smuggled into the Transvaal and sold there to farmers and other Europeans. It has been estimated that this brings in well over £2,000 a year. Making as much allowance as possible for it, and for sales of other produce to stores outside the Reserve, it is evident that exports are not nearly sufficient in value to cover the cost of imports alone, apart from taxes and other forms of expenditure. It must also be remembered in this connection that not every man has cattle or corn of which he can dispose if the need arises. As we have seen, some actually have to purchase corn to make good their own deficits, while others have no cattle at all, or so few that they cannot afford to sell a beast every year to meet their tax and other cash obligations.

The income derived from the sale of produce is therefore supplemented by the sale of labour. Working for others was formerly restricted in the main to herding cattle under the 'loan' system, or to serving in a menial capacity in the household of some man of rank. Both systems still prevail, with the added advantage that the cattle-holder or servant can now, after ploughing for his employer, use the latter's oxen and plough to cultivate his own field as well. Sometimes a master also buys clothes for his household servants and pays their tax, apart from providing them with food; but there is no regular payment of wages. Nevertheless, many people manage in this way to satisfy their more essential wants. Magic, the only independent occupation formerly practised, is still a fairly lucrative source of income for the more famous doctors. Today some people also work for themselves as dressmakers, thatchers, or carpenters, or, as we have seen, do odd jobs for others. But their earnings, while at times relatively large (a thatcher gets paid up to five pounds per hut), are not regular enough to be a steady source of income.

The presence of Europeans in the Reserve has created other opportunities for remunerative employment. Men and women work in European households as domestic servants, or for traders as shop-assistants, 'yard boys', and cattle-herds. Education has provided openings for teachers; the Mission employs evangelists and catechists, hospital nurses and orderlies; and the Administration an agricultural demonstrator, a few police and various other functionaries. The needs of tribal administration have led to the creation of an office staff including a tribal secretary, an

assistant tax-collector and messengers, and to the paid remuner-
ation of the chief, his councillors, and the ward-heads presiding
over junior tribunals. All these people receive regular wages or
salaries in cash, and are therefore in a relatively good position
compared to the rest. Teachers get paid on the average about £5
a month, shop-assistants from £2 to £4, domestic servants from
£1 to £3 and food, 'yard boys' from £1 to £1 10s., cattle-herds
from 10s. to £1, evangelists £3 10s. and catechists £1, the tribal
secretary £10, his assistant tax-collector £5, and presidents of
junior tribunals £2.

But the smallness of the local European population, and of the
staffs they maintain, means that only a few Kgatla, probably not
more than about a hundred in all, can find paid employment
inside the Reserve. The rest must go out to seek work in the
Transvaal and other European industrial and farming areas.
This practice is of very long standing, dating back to before
1880, but within recent years, as standards of living have risen, it
has become increasingly important as a source of income. The
depression of 1929–32, followed by the temporary prohibition of
all exports owing to foot-and-mouth disease, greatly reduced the
value of local produce, and consequently stimulated the search
for work outside the Reserve. There are no accurate statistics of
labour migration. The 1921 census gave the number of absentees
as 842 out of a total population of 12,246; at the time of the 1936
census, the number had risen to 1,909 out of a total population of
15,775. These figures cannot be taken too seriously, owing to the
somewhat crude methods by which they were obtained, but they
do suggest a marked increase in the proportion of people away
from home, although of course not all had necessarily gone out
to work. A more reliable index is afforded by the tax registers.
When these were revised in 1937, it was found that, out of 3,933
registered payers, no fewer than 1,743 (44 per cent) were employed or resident outside the Reserve. It is evident from this
how markedly the Kgatla have become dependent upon the sale
of their labour.

The need for money is not the only motive for labour migration. Men are beginning to resent the chief's right to call upon

their services at any time, and rather than work for him compulsorily and for nothing they prefer to go where they will be paid. Some have become disgusted with the disturbances at home since Molefi took over the chieftainship, while others dislike being under the control of their parents, desire adventure and change and wish to experience for themselves the attractions of the Transvaal, about which they hear so much from those who have come back. The marked preference shown by girls for youths who have been abroad is also a fairly important stimulus. But that the financial motive is usually by far the strongest is reflected not only in popular opinion, but in the letters sent home by men out of work. The following series (freely translated from the vernacular) were all written to his wife by Hulara Megano, a young man working in a Johannesburg gold mine. As will be seen, they refer almost exclusively to economic matters.

(1). First receive my letter, my wife. I greet you, I ask how you are; myself I am well in the hands of the Lord. I have heard your news when you said that you will build a new wall [hut], so that when I come back I must find it ready. It is difficult to build a hut, as a hut calls for a person who is strong, and I don't know how you can build up your wall when I am not there. I wonder who is going to help you and show you how to build the hut? I am not objecting, but I see you will have difficulty. My wife, I wished to buy a 'tank' [a drum for carrying water], so that even if I don't manage to get other things I shall at least have got a receptacle for water. Or should I buy a sewing-machine before this? I don't know. Tell me which you want, machine or the 'tank'. Greet my child [an infant daughter] and Poifo [the baby's young nurse], and greet for me Kgosi [a friend] and his wife. I have heard that their mother is dead. Greet also for me Monna and Rapula [two other friends], and all those who know me.

(2). First receive my letter. I greet you and ask how you are. I have got a sore shoulder, I don't use its hand. All this time I have not been writing to you because I heard you say that you were going to the cattle-post. Now just lately Rampa came here and told me that you are still at home. I let you know that I sent a shawl with Seloma when he left here to go home; I don't know whether he has given it to you. I have heard your word when you say that a plough is also needed. My wife, there you have spoken the truth; but I don't know whether we can manage in one year all the things that we lack, for I am still thinking that when I come home I must bring with me some shillings with which we can help ourselves. And now the winter is coming, and it is going to be cold; there are no good blankets for the night. I will try to send you a blanket, because I have stopped using one of the blankets, the white one which was already getting old. Even Poifo [their baby's nurse], I think her blanket is already gone, I'll try to get a cotton blanket for her, so that while I work for other things you must [at least] have got blankets, because when there are no blankets it is shameful. I have heard that Poifo's mother came to see you, and I have heard your remark that you have given her a full bag [of corn]; I have nothing to say against this, it is all right, because we should also help her. I also let you know that I always forget about my tax-receipt. You must ask Morena [her brother] to send it. If you can go to Mosanteng [where he formerly lived in Mochudi], get me a little yellow paper, it is [a pass] for work, it is in the big yellow book, and put it into your letter. I want to get this paper because I want to show it to people when I look for work. As I haven't bought anything for myself, I shall come home in summer. Greet all your people and my children [another daughter had been born in the meantime].

(3). First receive my letter. I greet you and ask about your welfare. Ourselves we are well in the hands of the Lord. I want to tell you that I have heard when you said that you are at the cattle-post. What makes me sad is that you report sickness [she had had a bad spell of bleeding from the nose], but I don't know who can cure that sickness of yours. I have bought you a big cotton blanket, so that you can always put it inside the big blankets, as it is warm, and a shawl, it is a nice one. I have done this so that you must always keep the child warm. I have not yet sent them, but I will let you know when I do so. I am still waiting to buy Poifo's blanket, so that I can send them together. I thought of getting you a big travelling-rug, but I prefer to buy you dress material instead. I shall buy this later on, and not be in a hurry. Even if I can't buy many blankets, when we are at home we can use your blankets as well as mine. I have bought myself a very nice travelling blanket. Greet all my people at home, Pheli [his wife's younger brother], and my children. I have heard when you say that poverty has no end, but I must also think of coming back. The mine in which I am working [Crown Mines] is quite good, but I shall only work for two months, just to obtain provisions. My wife, I greet you. God be with you. I have finished.

(4). I let you know that I have sent you a parcel. You must hurry to get it from Pilane [station], otherwise you will have to pay money. I am enclosing here the receipt for it. I sent those blankets and also Poifo's blanket. If God helps me, I shall leave this place soon, only two weeks are left. If you have got those things, write quickly and let me know. If I don't get work here, I'll work my way home.

These letters are in a sense pathetic. The writer is not at all interested in describing his impressions of Johannesburg, or of life at the mines; he is concerned above all with the pressing economic problems of the moment. He left home to earn money with which to buy the goods that have become indispensable to every Kgatla household, and it is obvious that he is a poor man anxiously speculating how best to lay out his wages. There is nothing in what he says to afford us amusement. We are led rather to sympathize with his difficulties, and to admire the careful way in which he tries to make provision for what is essential. We must notice, too, the evidence he gives of genuine regard for his wife, and the way in which he consults her about his purchases. The Kgatla as revealed in these letters is not the idle, superstitious savage of popular fancy, but an honest, hard-working husband beset with the same economic perplexities as confront the poorer classes of our own European society.

The men go out as a rule in the first four months of the year, and many contrive to come back in October or November in time to plough. But there is now a marked tendency for more and more to remain away for longer periods at a time. In Makgophana ward, no fewer than 43 of the 82 men who had worked for Europeans had, at some time in the course of their employment, remained away for two or more years successively, and of these more than half had been away for three years or more. Similarly, in a group of 42 men working in Johannesburg, I found that 20 had been there for more than three years each, except for an occasional visit home seldom lasting more than a month. We have already observed the serious effects this may have upon production in the Reserve, and shall have cause later on to see also how it has affected married life generally. Sometimes men stay away for so long that they can be regarded as lost to the tribe. They marry foreign women in the towns, or bring out their wives from the Reserve, raise their families where they work, and although still keeping in touch with their relatives at home consider themselves permanent urban dwellers. To guard against losses of this kind, the chiefs make frequent visits to the towns, and the Kgatla in Johannesburg itself have formed a mutual aid society that keeps most of them together. Nevertheless, the few figures I have suggest that about one man in twenty of those going out to work never returns again.

The majority of the men ultimately find employment on the Rand or in other urban areas of the Transvaal, mainly as unskilled labourers for municipal engineering works, on the railways, in smelting works, breweries, power stations, etc., or as delivery 'boys', store and hotel 'boys', etc. The gold mines do not attract more than about a third; they generally dislike the work, and fear the dangers involved. The chiefs, too, in the past discouraged them from going there, except when it was urgently necessary to earn money to pay their tax, and preferred them to engage in some more 'educative' occupation. Isang, for instance, would urge them to go to the farms or engage in such work as road-making, where the knowledge gained could afterwards be applied at home. It is symptomatic of the attitude towards employment in the mines that, until the last year or so, no labour recruiter had ever been allowed to operate in the Reserve. A fair number of men go also to the tobacco farms and orange orchards of the Rustenburg District, while others have been as far afield as Natal, Cape Town, South West Africa and Southern Rhodesia. During the Great War of 1914–18 two regiments actually went to Flanders as part of the African Labour Corps accompanying the South African troops.

This wide dispersal, and the great variety of occupations in which men are engaged, make it difficult to generalize about the wages they receive. The average wages of Natives employed in the gold mines are about £2 17s. 6d. per month, in addition to housing, food and medical and other services. Those engaged in other occupations in the towns receive amounts varying from about £2 to £6 a month, according to the nature of their work and the length of their experience. In a group of forty-two Kgatla – unskilled labourers, messengers, etc. – working in Johannesburg in 1935, thirty-one were being paid from three pounds to four pounds a month, a figure which, judging from investigations on Native urban wages generally, may be regarded as fairly typical. Out of this amount, the man has to meet the cost of his housing, food, clothing, transport, recreation and other expenses incidental to life in an environment where he must pay for everything he wants. The result is that his savings are generally very small indeed, and, as we saw from the letters quoted above, they are frequently devoted to purchases for the people at home. Railway records, too, show that a large and varied assortment of goods is consigned to the Reserve every year by men working abroad. Some during their stay in the towns manage to accumulate a little money in the post-office savings-banks, but others either have more pressing wants, or else are more reckless in their spending. Consequently, few of them come back with much in the way of cash. Savings of this kind are sometimes invested in cattle, after other immediate expenses have been met; but it is seldom that enough is available even for this purpose, now that in comparison with earlier times more money is being spent in the towns.

An illustration of the way in which a town labourer manages his savings is provided by the case of Mokgere. The first year that he was in Johannesburg, as an unmarried man, he sent his father a coat and two pounds in cash, of which one pound was for tax. He also sent home two suits for himself, and when he arrived brought five pounds in cash and the betrothal goods to be given to his fiancée. Of the five pounds, he kept two pounds for himself, and gave the rest to his father, who bought him a heifer for two pounds. He went back to work after a few months. This time he sent money home for his own and his father's tax. He then returned, bringing with him dress material for his mother and sister, and £4 10s. in cash. He gave his sister ten shillings, and spent the rest on his bride's wedding outfit. Later he again went to work, but returned after a few months owing to illness. He brought with him four pounds, two pounds of which he gave to his father, while the balance he spent with his wife. He returned to Johannesburg for the fourth time early in 1934 (six months after he had come home), and was still there in September, when this information was obtained. While away, he sent home two pounds to pay for medical treatment for his sister, and ten shillings and a blanket for his wife. He also sent a plough for himself, and a door for the hut his wife was building in the new compound to which they were going to move from his father's home, where they had hitherto been staying.

It is not only the men who go abroad. For the past twenty years or so, and particularly during and since the depression of 1929–32, unmarried women also have done so. The chiefs are strongly opposed to migration of this sort, and discourage it as far as they possibly can. Nevertheless, it is maintained by the people that a growing number of women and girls find their way into the Transvaal every year. Figures are unobtainable, but in 1932 I was given the names of twenty-three girls from Makgophana ward alone who were away at the time working for the whites. For the most part they go to the Rustenburg District to pick cotton on the farms, but a fair number enter domestic service in the towns. Many go simply owing to dissatisfaction with the unmarried life they have to lead at home, others because it affords a ready escape from an irksome parental control, and a few because they have no one to provide them with clothes, now that the local income of the tribe has been so greatly diminished by the shrinking value of their produce.

Although it is impossible to obtain accurate information regarding the total difference made to income by the sale of labour, it is certain that most households now rely upon it as an indispensable means of making ends meet. A rough survey I made of Makgophana and Rampedi wards showed that of 126 men no fewer than 106 had at one time or another worked abroad, while five others were locally employed as shop-assistants and herdsmen by traders. The number who can afford to do without wage-labour of some sort is therefore relatively small. As they grow older, of course, men usually stay at home and rely upon the earnings of their unmarried sons, but almost all the younger married men go out several times in order to obtain the means of paying tax and procuring the various household goods they require.

At the same time, not all those going out to work do actually contribute while away to the support of their households. Complaints are sometimes heard that, after a while, they cease to send home money or goods, and also stay away so long that their families begin to be hard pressed to maintain themselves. It is not so much the married men about whom this is said, although occasionally wives do have to appeal to the chief to bring back husbands who have apparently deserted and neglected them. The main culprits are usually unmarried men whose parents are relying upon them. Nkoko's parents, for instance, said of him:

'The first time he went to Johannesburg he did not send us anything; he stayed away for a long time, and did not want to return. Chief Isang then found him loafing in Rustenburg, and brought him back. He had with him a suitcase containing a few clothes. He said that he had no money, because he had been taken away from his work in the middle of the month, and we believed him. Later on we found that he was going about the village buying and drinking beer, and then he began to buy beer for us as well. This showed that he must have had money with him. We say of such a child that he is not fit to have been born. Now he has gone away again; he has been away for over a year, and has not sent us anything or even written, he is just hiding himself.'

Similarly, Boikhutso's mother told me:

'When he first went abroad, he stayed away four years without writing. Some Makgophana people used to see him, he was working on farms, and they came to tell me. At last he went to Rustenburg District and worked there, until I took the train and went to look for him, because he was the only son in our compound. I found him and brought him home; he had no money at all, and I had to pay his train fare with money I had taken when I went there; he had spent all his money on gambling and dancing and buying guitars. Now he has gone back again, and is working at Benoni. Before he went he became engaged, and since then he has written to me and to his fiancée. He sent some dress material for the girl by another man who was coming home, and recently he also sent me one pound, telling me to buy myself dress material for ten shillings and to give the other ten shillings to the girl.'

Summing up, then, we may say that the average Kgatla household produces its own food, builds its own compound, and makes a few of the other goods it requires. The rest of its wants it satisfies partly by the sale of surplus produce, either to fellow-tribesmen or, more often, to the traders. But the main source of additional income is to engage in some form of paid labour, generally for Europeans. A few people have cattle enough, or grow enough corn, not to be dependent upon earnings from wages. Others prefer to eke out a living by looking after cattle and doing other work for more wealthy fellow-tribesmen. But no household today relies as extensively as before upon small-scale subsistence farming.

All Kgatla residents in the Reserve still farm for themselves, but almost all have acquired new wants which can be satisfied only if they also work for others and produce surplus goods for exchange, and of these two possibilities they have resorted increasingly to the former. With it more responsibility has been thrust upon the men, whose earnings frequently make all the difference to a household between extreme poverty and a tolerable existence. This was particularly evident during the famine of 1933, when many of the men working abroad had to send home corn to support their relatives in the Reserve. Two letters written at this time to a young man in Johannesburg, one from his widowed mother, the other from his young sister, may serve finally as an illustration of the straits to which even what is by Kgatla standards a moderately wealthy family was then reduced, and of the reliance it placed upon its menfolk in the towns.

(1) I greet you and ask how you are living. I am sick, my child, I have nothing to say except starvation. You have left me in loneliness. The starvation that is here is very, very serious. I beg you to send me just one bag of corn, so that I can help my child who is at the cattle-post. You must remember that Modise [her eldest son, a loafer] refuses to let me use the cattle, as you well know. The whole day, my child, we sit at the store hoping to get a little corn [as relief rations], but we come back empty. I don't know what to do, but you must know

that I depend upon you, and put all my hopes in you. You must 'carry' us, as you usually do. Other men are striving for themselves, but Modise does not care for anything; he looks to me, but I have nothing to give him. Do not let the eyes of the people look at me [with scorn]. You complain that I do not write to you, but you know that I have nothing with which to buy stamps. That is all I can tell you. Many greetings, my child.

(2) . . . The thing that troubles me very much over here is the starvation. I get up in the morning and go to bed at night without having eaten anything. When I wrote last time I had not eaten anything for about four days, not only myself, but we are all staying without eating anything. When I walk my breath gives out. I tie myself with a belt to hold in my stomach. I am wondering if we are going to live through this starvation. It is the first time I have ever slept without eating since I was borne by my mother. If you could see us you would cry. We seldom speak because we are tired out by hunger. I always feel very sorry for the child [her married sister's infant], who keeps crying and crying. Could you not send us just a little meal, just to keep ourselves going, or a little bit of corn? We always rest our heads wearily when the sun sets. But did you not get the letter I wrote last week in which I stated Modise's fault, when he took away the oxen from us during ploughing? I just want to say that even now he has not brought them back, but at any rate we had finished the first part of the work. My mother does not know what to do with Modise. Many people come to her and say she should report him to the men [of their ward], but she does not want to make cases. I am always in tears. Are we going to die of this starvation? And I always say that if I could have gone to you straight from school it would have been much better, and I feel like coming to you so that I can tell you all by mouth. This is mother's message: 'Look after the orphans of your father and your mother;' and myself I say, 'To whom are you throwing us?' Even as I write I feel very sad, and my tears keep coming down.

6. The Household Routine

In the last chapter we surveyed the various methods by which Kgatla endeavour to secure a livelihood. Let us now see how those who are not working abroad space out their activities at home, and what pattern this gives to the domestic routine. Except at the cattle-posts, where herding is a perennial occupation, there is a well-defined seasonal variation in industry. The preparation of food, and other domestic chores, must be carried on daily, no matter where the people are. But hut-building, pot-making and similar arts and crafts are most generally pursued during the months after harvest, when no work need be done in the fields. They do not demand the same constant attention as the food-producing activities, and are carried on only when occasion arises, or, sometimes, when the inclination exists. With the beginning of the rainy season, agriculture becomes dominant. The periods of most intense activity are during ploughing, weeding, scaring away the birds, and reaping and threshing. There is then little time for anything else but the ordinary household chores, and even these may be skimped if the family is short-handed. During the less strenuous phases of the work basket-work and similar crafts may be carried on, but seldom are to any conspicuous extent.

The months after harvest, when most people are home in the villages, are a time of relative leisure, especially for the men. There is plenty of new Kafir corn, and therefore of beer, that great stimulus to convivial idleness; entertainments are frequent, for it is now that wedding, confirmation and other feasts are mostly held; while tribal meetings and court cases provide constant diversion. The women, tidying up their homes after the long absence in the fields, performing the routine household

tasks, or preparing for a feast, have much more to do, but neighbours are always at hand to relieve the monotony of working
alone, and to lighten the task with gossip and chatter. Towards
the end of this time, in October and November, the increasing
discomfort of climatic conditions and the anxious wait for the
rain are reflected in growing slackness and irritability, but from
July to September, if a good harvest has lifted the ever-present
shadow of want, there is a cheerful atmosphere of liveliness and
variety.

The village day begins early, sometimes before dawn. The
women usually rise first, dress, and go into the backyard to wash
their hands and faces; a full bath, either in the river or by washing the whole body at home, is generally taken in the evening, at
intervals varying from a week to a month according to the season
and personal inclination. If they wish to relieve themselves, they
go out of the compound to any convenient place not too far
away. They squat anywhere to urinate, even on a public road,
and show no concern for people passing by (just as men will
urinate against the first handy tree or fence, no matter who is
about), but for defecation they all seek the privacy of the bushes
or rocks where they cannot be spied upon. On their return, the
women set about their daily tasks. They clear the ashes from the
hearth and sweep the courtyard floor, gathering up the rubbish
in potsherds and dumping it just outside the compounds; they
light the fire and cook porridge, or start stamping corn; they
wake the children, see that they wash, and give them what food is
available; or they go off, their pots on their heads, to fetch water
from the river or bore-hole.

The men with any special work to do or a meeting to attend
may also be up and about by this time. (Public meetings and
court cases almost all start soon after dawn, and are generally
over before the morning is far advanced.) The rest sleep a little
longer, and then, after dressing, washing and perhaps shaving
themselves roughly with a sharp iron blade, they sit about waiting for food, or go straight to the local council-place to gossip
round its fire with any others who may be there. A little later
their food is brought to them by a wife or child, and they share it

with their companions, or they may go home to eat if they feel so inclined, or they may wander off to see where they can beg or buy beer.

There is no regular morning meal. In most cases people eat thick, fermented porridge left over from the night before; some take it cold, others first warm it a little, and many wash it down with tea. If no such food is available, they must wait while the women hurriedly prepare one of the simpler varieties of porridge, or if the corn has first to be stamped they may remain hungry for hours. Children often enough go to school, or take the small stock out to graze, without having eaten anything at all, while men at work or attending a meeting may perhaps also not break their fast until the morning is well advanced. The women usually cook early in the day, but perhaps at any time between say seven and eleven o'clock, depending upon what other work they have to do and how insistent their husbands are. The porridge when ready is ladled into the food-bowls, of which every person, except the small children, has his own. If he is about, he may then eat at once, and when he has had enough he puts away his bowl, to which he returns later whenever he is hungry again. If some one is absent when the food is dished out, his bowl is set aside to await his arrival. People will thus eat at any time of the day, and breakfast is seldom a collective family meal.

By the time the sun has been up for two or three hours, the day's activities are well advanced. The women and girls are almost all busy stamping corn, cooking, fetching water or working at something else. So prominent indeed are the stamping of corn and the carrying of water that at first glimpse they appear to be the sole feminine occupations. The needs of the household generally entail several visits daily to the water-hole, particularly in the morning and afternoon just before cooking. If the source of supply is some distance away, as is often the case, or if it is the height of the dry season, when people must patiently wait their turn at the common village bore-holes, two or three hours may easily be spent on this task alone. Women prefer to make the girls fetch the water whenever possible, but if they have none to help them they must of course go themselves. Then also they must see that the huts and courtyards are swept, the cooking-pots and eating-vessels washed before and after each meal, the sleeping-blankets shaken out and aired, the fowls and pigs given something to eat and firewood fetched if necessary.

Apart from these chores, done mainly in the morning and in the late afternoon, there is no well-defined daily routine, and the women fill in their time with one or other of the many periodical tasks that village life may entail. The care of the compound involves smoothing over the floors of the huts and courtyard at fairly frequent intervals with a mixture of cow-dung and earth. This may take several days at a time, especially if done by only one woman. A new coating of plaster may be needed on the walls, or there are cracks in them to be mended, and for these purposes too loads of earth must first be dug, carried home in baskets and worked into suitable mud. A new hut or granary may be required, and weeks will be spent on building the wall. Supplies of the lime used for cleaning the food-bowls must now and then be excavated and carried home, and as it occurs only in certain localities a day's trip may be necessary. A self-respecting housewife will occupy herself for days painstakingly smearing decorative designs on the walls of her courtyard or huts. The corn in the granaries is periodically taken out and spread in the sun to free it from weevils, after which it is winnowed again and ashed before being replaced. The family clothes are washed once a week or fortnight, in some cases less frequently, and incidental repairs are effected when necessary. Beer must be made, not only for a feast or a work-party, but also for ordinary domestic consumption or for sale, and its preparation is normally spread over four or five days. Specialists, again, may add to their other activities by making pots, baskets, or dresses, ordered by some customer. There is plenty to do, and it depends upon circumstances and personal inclination to which of these various tasks a woman will choose to devote the bulk of the day.

Men, on the other hand, have no regular daily work in the villages, unless they are employed as teachers, shop-assistants, domestic servants in European households, etc. The herding of such livestock as may be at home is done by the boys, who take

the animals out in the morning to graze, and bring them back
again in the afternoon to be watered and kraaled. During the
height of the dry season the men help to water the cattle at the
wells in the river-bed, and at the beginning of this season, soon
after their return from the fields, many will also be kept busy for
a week or two cleaning out and repairing their wells from the
damage caused by the summer floods. The rest of their time they
spend in various ways. They may have to attend tribal meetings
or court cases, or be put on to some regimental work like repairing a road or looking for stray cattle. They may remain at
home twisting hide thongs, making wooden implements, soften-
ing a skin or slaughtering and cutting up an animal; they may go
out into the veld to cut thatching-grass, timber, or bark, or to
fetch an occasional wagon-load of earth or firewood for their
wives; they may engage in some business transaction with others;
or they may take several days or weeks off to visit their cattle-
posts. Specialists like the doctors and thatchers will generally
have something to do almost every day, but the rest seem to work
spasmodically, and frequently spend days on end merely lounging about.

There is no bustle, but the work of the day progresses steadily.
Almost all the women and girls are engaged in some form of
activity; only now and then do we encounter one or two sitting
about in apparent idleness. The men seem on the whole to have
much less to do, judging from the number wandering about, or
gossiping at a council-place or over the beer-pots. Village life
obviously does not impose many burdens upon them, and those
actually at work are in a minority. As the middle of the day
passes into afternoon, even they stop for a while, and slowly drift
homewards to sleep in the shade of a hut or under a tree, or to sit
chatting idly with a neighbour. The women, however, continue
to work, although if possible they too will take a rest in the
afternoon before again starting to stamp corn and to cook.

Towards dusk the village becomes lively once more. Men
return from the veld with wagons or sledges amid a cloud of
dust, cracking their whips or cursing vociferously at their cattle.
The small boys drive in the animals that have been grazing, water

them at a well or at the village dam, pen them in the kraals, to the accompaniment of much shouting and excitement, and then milk the goats. The number of women and girls carrying water suddenly increases. Others loudly call their fowls or pigs to be fed. Blue smoke rises from the hearths where the evening meal is being cooked. The men sit about waiting for their food, or go to the council-places again, or visit friends to drink beer and gossip. By the time the sun has set and it is almost dark, the day's work has ended.

The evening meal is now eaten, either round the courtyard fire or, if the weather is bad, inside a hut. It consists basically of thick, sour porridge, frequently supplemented with tea and with meat, if obtainable, or with some sort of vegetable dish like beans, pumpkins, or wild spinach. Most of the family are home for it, and they eat together in a group. Guests, if any, are served first, then the father and mother, then the sons in descending order, and lastly the daughters. If anybody is not yet there, his food-bowl is as usual set aside to await his return. A small pot may also be filled for the next morning's needs. The meal is leisurely and conversational, and as some of the people may have been hungry most of the day they eat a large quantity. Afterwards the women or girls clean the cooking-pots and food-bowls, feeding the scraps to the dogs, and go into the huts to spread out the blankets for the night. The people then settle down to chat for a while. The younger children, as they begin to doze round the fire, are carried into their hut and put to sleep. It is not long before the adults follow, unless they have visitors or themselves pay a call. The boys and girls, if the evening is fine, may stay up till the early hours of the morning playing and dancing, but otherwise they too go to sleep soon after eating, unless they are courting.

Few people use the raised beds of European make nowadays fairly often seen in the huts. The great majority sleep on ox-hides or woven grass mats laid on the floor, with woollen or cotton blankets serving as sheets, and a soft bundle of some kind as a pillow. They remove all their clothing, but wrap themselves closely in their blankets, and if the night is cold also cover in their heads. The husband, when home, sleeps nearest the wall behind the door, then comes his wife, and then, in ascending order of age, the young children who may be sharing their hut. The older children, as we have already noted, have huts of their own.

And so the days pass, the women carrying on their chores and such other work as they have to do, the men occupying themselves occasionally with some special task or just idling about. Now and then a wedding-feast or some similar celebration breaks the routine, but in the main there is little diversion. In October or November, however, as the rains become due, the people get ready to go to their fields, which are usually anywhere from five to twenty-five miles away. The men overhaul their trek-gear, ploughs, wagons or sledges, replace broken or missing parts, and bring in from the cattle-posts the oxen required for transport and ploughing. Some may go out ahead to make new fields or perhaps clear additional land. The women meantime select the seed they are going to plant, frequently mixing it with medicines bought from the doctors to ensure a good crop. Then, as soon as the rains have begun to fall, there is a general exodus: one can see wagon after wagon, and sledge after sledge, going out laden with ploughs, provisions, water drums, pots and other utensils, fowls and pigs, and whatever else is required for a stay of seven or eight months at the fields. Village life from now on is at a standstill, except for the schools and an occasional tribal meeting, while at the fields there is continuous activity. Each family has a hut or two immediately beside its own field, its nearest neighbours usually being a few hundred yards away.

Formerly, as soon as the first rains had fallen, the chief would summon all the people to hoe and sow his 'tribal' fields. Until they had done so, they might not start cultivating their own. Later they also weeded his fields, and reaped and threshed his crops, before being free to do so for themselves. These restrictions were abolished many years ago by Lentswe, who saw that they prevented people from taking advantage of early local rains and other favourable conditions. Nowadays, therefore, a man may start work on his own fields as soon as he likes, although whenever summoned to the tribal fields with the rest he must answer the call, under penalty of punishment. In other ways, however, the chief still regulates agricultural activity. Together with the missionary, he fixes the day of the 'prayer for rain', which officially opens the new season. This ceremony, instituted by Lentswe after he became a Christian, is generally held in October, when the first rains are imminent. In times of drought it may be repeated in later months. It takes the form of a public meeting in church or in the central council-place, where prayers are addressed to God for rain and good crops. Later in the season the chief tells the people when to stop ploughing, and, once the new crops appear above the ground, he also reminds them of the various seasonal taboos they must now observe until the rains have ended. They may not, for instance, cut certain trees, clear new land for cultivation or castrate young bulls. Violation of these taboos, it is held, will 'spoil the year' by turning the rain into hail that will destroy the crops; and so much importance is attached to them that they have recently become part of tribal law, any offender being punished by a fine. Finally, after the harvest has been reaped, the chief announces when cattle may be allowed into the fields to graze on the standing stalks.

A household ploughs its own fields first, one after the other, usually spending from four to eight days on each, unless interrupted by rain. The work is done in the morning and afternoon, not in the heat of the midday sun. Then, if necessary, poor relatives or friends lacking oxen or ploughs are helped in return for the assistance they have given. Where the ploughing is done by a single family, the husband drives the oxen, the wife holds the plough, and a child leads the span. If a boy is not available, a girl helps instead. The other girls meanwhile fetch firewood and water, stamp corn and prepare the food, and do whatever else is necessary at the family huts. Failing such help, the wife must herself attend to these tasks during the midday rest, so that by the end of the day she is often exhausted.

The next few weeks, from about the middle of January, may be spent in clearing new land for future cultivation and repairing the boundary fences of the planted fields. Most men, however, accompanied by the children, go back to the cattle-posts with the oxen used in the ploughing. They stay there for some time, while the women remain behind, sometimes alone, to inspect the fields and put in fresh seed wherever necessary. When the corn is a foot or two high, weeding begins. It is generally a collective task, done by women and girls working in small groups of relatives supplemented by neighbours. They go through the fields in close formation, rooting out the weeds with the hoe, and at the same time thinning the corn where necessary. When they have finished one field, which may take from a week to a fortnight, according to its size and the number of workers, they go to another, and after their own fields are done they help others still weeding. Regular activity then ceases for a while, during which the women return to the village for additional supplies, or go to the cattle-posts to rest and to feed on fresh milk and game, a welcome change from the monotonous staple diet of porridge.

With the seeding of the Kafir corn, in April or May, another period of strenuous activity begins. The women and children spend all day in the fields, shouting and banging tins to drive away the birds that come in vast numbers to feed on the corn. In May and June, while the crop is ripening, preparations are also made for the harvest. The men build or repair the conical wooden stacks in which the corn is put immediately after the reaping, while the women smear the threshing-floors to give them a clean hard surface. Reaping is generally postponed until after the first frost, which hardens the corn. The whole family takes part, except for the boys at the cattle-posts. The ears, after being gathered in by hand or cut with knives, are carried off to be stacked at the threshing-floors; the stalks are left standing for the cattle. Threshing is done by the women and girls, generally in groups; they stand over the corn heaped up before them, and beat it out with heavy wooden flails to the rhythm of various traditional songs associated with this particular activity. Afterwards they winnow the grain to get rid of the chaff, and mix it with wood-ash to prevent loss from weevils. It is then poured into bags, loaded on to the wagons or sledges and transported to the village by the men. Here it is stored in the granaries attached to every compound. With this the agricultural year comes to an end, and the people move back to their homes in the village, where they remain until the beginning of the next season.

Once the harvest is reaped, few people trouble to do any more work in their fields until it is again time to plough. Cattle-herding, on the other hand, demands daily attention all the year round. At the cattle-posts, twenty to forty and even more miles away from the villages, the easiest time of all is in the late summer and autumn, from about February to April, when there is plenty of new grass and water. In the morning, after the cows have been milked, the main herd is driven out to graze. It is usually sent in different directions on successive days, so that it may graze evenly over the pastures in the vicinity. The calves are driven out separately a little later. Both herds are allowed to roam about unattended, the only problem being to see that the calves do not get to their mothers. In the afternoon first the calves and then the main herd are rounded up, the cows are milked again, and the animals are shut up for the night in their respective kraals, large circular enclosures made from the branches of thorn-trees.

The boys during this season spend much of their time visiting one another or hunting, or stay at the post making bark thongs, wooden spoons and similar objects. In the early morning they generally indulge in their favourite pastime of breaking in young oxen for riding and then racing in competition from one cattle-post to another. They also fetch water and wood, and prepare their own food, unless there are women or girls present to attend to these tasks, as is common at this time of the year. There is sometimes a crude hut at the cattle-post to provide shelter from rain and to accommodate adult visitors, but the boys themselves normally sleep under a tree round a fire kept burning all night to frighten off beasts of prey.

As the days grow shorter and there is less time for grazing, the cattle tend to stay out longer and even sleep in the veld. The boys must therefore be with them continuously to prevent them from straying too far and to see that they come in at night. With the contraction of surface-water supplies, the cattle-post is moved down to a river or bore-hole. Here the daily programme differs in several respects from that of the rainy season. The cattle are let out earlier in the morning, and driven back later in the evening, to give them as much time as possible for grazing. They are first taken to be watered. While there is enough surface-water, the grown cattle and the calves are both driven every day to the source of supply. But as it dries up, and the wells or bore-holes must be used, the two herds are watered on alternate days. At the bore-holes the animals drink from large stone troughs fed from the reservoirs into which the water is pumped. At the wells the boys must bale the water into long wooden troughs, or into shallow depressions made in the ground. This is a tedious and unwelcome task, which often leads to squabbles with neighbours awaiting their turn. After drinking the animals are taken to graze. Their herd-boy accompanies them with his dogs and watches them carefully to prevent them from straying. In the evening he drives them back to the kraal, on the way gathering firewood or water for the camp.

This is the time of year that herd-boys most hate. They have few visitors from the villages, for there is little or no milk, and they themselves have to live on supplies of corn fetched from home; there is no time for riding oxen or similar relaxations; cattle frequently go astray, and days must be spent in tracing them; and disputes with neighbouring cattle-posts over grazing and water rights are a frequent source of trouble. The men who may be with them are worried about the condition of the cattle, and their anxiety is reflected in uncertain tempers and an unwelcome readiness to administer thrashings. It is a great relief to all when the drought at last breaks and the season of plenty starts again.

THE EMPLOYMENT OF LEISURE

From the review just given of Kgatla household activities, it is evident that the incidence of work is unevenly distributed. The women and girls have their daily chores, and are usually also engaged in some special task connected with agriculture, the care of the compound or the making of useful objects. The men work fairly hard during the early and final phases of agriculture, and do odd jobs at home now and then, sometimes of a strenuous nature; they have much to attend to when they go to the cattle-posts; or they may be given tribal labour of some kind by the chief, participate in meetings or court cases or engage in business transactions of various kinds. But these activities do not keep them as continuously occupied as the women, and often enough they may be idle for days or even weeks at a time. It must be remembered, however, that most of the younger men are normally away at European centres of employment, where they have to work steadily if not strenuously for five and a half days in the week. It is only those remaining in the Reserve whose labour activities are spasmodic. This is due more to the nature of the tasks conventionally assigned to them than to any inherent indolence or dislike of work. It is true that men may be found who prefer not to work unless it is absolutely necessary, but the deliberate loafer is an exception, and, as we saw when discussing the qualities of the ideal husband, industry and diligence are highly valued.

Even the women, however, do not have to work hard all day long, except during the more strenuous phases of agriculture. Most of their tasks are more gradual than pressing, and there is no harm in taking an occasional break from smearing a floor or plastering a wall, thatching a roof or moulding a pot. The unfortunate woman who at the moment has no one to help her, and who must therefore see to everything herself, has less time than the others for relaxation, but even she is seldom tied down except by her chores. After weeding, moreover, or whenever else a suitable opportunity occurs, women often go to the cattle-posts, or visit a distant relative or friend, so that they too have periods of comparative rest during the year.

Men with nothing special to do in the village frequent the council-places in the early morning and late afternoon, when others are almost certain to join them and they can while away the time together; or if there is a case on in the vicinity or at the chief's court they may go to listen and perhaps take part in the proceedings. During the rest of the day they may sit about at home talking to their wives or playing with their younger children, and perhaps sleep for a while, but generally they go visiting, or wander about looking for beer. Many pleasant hours can be spent over the beer-pots chatting with congenial companions, and from early morning till late at night one usually sees small groups of men enjoying themselves in this way. Women seldom take part in such informal beer-drinks unless they have plenty of time to spare. They normally rest by sitting idly at home or perhaps dropping in on a close neighbour to chat. The Kgatla are sociable folk, and although if necessary they can remain completely alone even for days, they prefer to have people around them. Women of neighbouring compounds frequently join together to stamp corn or fetch water, just for the sake of company, or if working alone interrupt their task to look in next door for a while. The water-holes and trading-stores are favourite social centres, where people often linger to exchange gossip with others before proceeding on their way.

It is in idle lounging and visiting of this kind that most people spend the free hours of the daytime. There is little else they can do, for, except when someone is giving a feast, or there is an important public meeting or ceremony, village life has few entertainments to offer, and life at the fields none at all, apart from the occasional bustle of a work-party and the ensuing beer-drink or collective meal. The children, of course, have games of many kinds to keep them pleasantly occupied by day and night. But adults have very few pastimes. Now and then a couple of men may spend some hours playing *morabaraba* (a game similar to draughts), or, if they get jolly enough at a beer-drink, they may start singing or dancing, or indulge in their main form of humour by teasing one another vulgarly. A very few of the more literate people may entertain themselves by reading newspapers or books, but this is a habit still foreign to the Kgatla in general. Even at night many adults have nothing better to do than watch the young people dancing, and their vociferous enthusiasm as spectators then contributes greatly to the gaiety of the occasion.

The others are probably drinking beer, visiting or entertaining friends, chatting at home, indulging in amorous adventure or already in bed.

Visiting is actually the main relaxation that most people have. Apart from being pleased to see their relatives or friends, they appreciate the break in the monotony of the day, and the prospect of entertainment with both food and gossip. Neighbours drop in casually on one another, but if someone intends to visit people farther away he usually informs them beforehand, so that they may know when to expect him and can prepare accordingly. Visits are generally paid in the evening, or during the slack hours of the early afternoon. An intimate friend or relative, however, may come in the morning and stay the whole day. Husband and wife frequently go visiting together as well as separately, but it is seldom that they are accompanied by their children. The latter do their own visiting, unless it is an occasion when they must be formally escorted to a relative's home to take part in some celebration.

There is little ceremony about an ordinary social visit. When a woman calls on a friend, the latter, if at work in the compound, may continue with what she is doing; the visitor meantime sits nearby chatting to her, or may even help her if the task permits it. But a mere acquaintance or an important relative should be taken at once into a hut, given a mat to sit on and receive polite and constant attention. Male visitors should similarly be provided with chairs or stools, and shown every other courtesy. If married, they chat at first with the host, while their wives chat with the hostess, but after a while the conversation tends to become general. But if any one has come for some special purpose, say on a business transaction or to convey an official message, he discusses this privately with the person concerned, and may then either leave at once or stay on as an ordinary visitor. Unmarried youths, again, are waited upon by the girls whom they have probably come to see, and it is considered good form for the parents to leave them alone after a while. At some time during the visit food is usually prepared and produced. The visitors are always served first, and given the choicer portions. Finally, when they depart, their hosts accompany them part of the way to see them safely on the road.

It is the rule that all visitors should if possible be given some food, or at least offered an apology if there is none at the moment. Ordinary friends and acquaintances are usually entertained with porridge, beer or tea, but for a person of some importance, like a son-in-law or accepted suitor, a fowl may be killed. Hospitality of this kind is a virtue highly stressed. 'Stranger, arrive,' say the Kgatla, 'so that food may appear.' A generous and willing host soon becomes popular, and is usually a welcome guest when he in turn visits others. A niggardly or grudging host, on the other hand, is secretly or even openly despised, and people will refrain from visiting his home or inviting him to theirs. And since most Kgatla want to be liked and respected by their neighbours, avoidance of this kind may be the cause of much unhappiness. It is here that a wife's quality is often put to the test. She may, according to her behaviour, attract or keep away visitors, and so be either an asset or a liability to her husband. Since she is responsible for the provision of food, the popularity of her home depends mainly upon the extent of her hospitality. Again, if she is discourteous or openly rude, she readily offends visitors, whereas if she is polite and considerate to all, no matter how unwelcome they actually are or how ill-timed their visit, she comes to be regarded with liking and admiration. 'The village is centred in the home,' the Kgatla say, and by this they mean that a man's social standing and influence are often determined by his reputation as a host.

Apart from paying such visits within the village itself, or calling on neighbours at the fields or cattle-posts, people with sufficient time to spare may go to stay with relatives or friends in other parts of the country. Their hosts put a hut at their disposal, and they stay as long as is convenient to both. Now and then they may help in such work as is going on around them, but in the main they lead an idle life. They are taken round to their hosts' local relatives and friends, so that they need never lack company, and if men they should also be introduced to the chief or village headman, so that he may know where they come from and why. If possible their hosts slaughter a goat or sheep to provide meat for them during their stay, and it is customary that before they depart they should be given small gifts like baskets, pots or food-bowls. Children also are often sent to live with relatives either for a holiday or in some cases more permanently. I shall discuss in a later chapter the various reciprocal obligations that the latter entails.

So far we have been dealing with the routine of ordinary working days. Since Lentswe's acceptance of Christianity, however, Sunday has come to be regarded as a day of rest. This applies to the tribe as a whole, and not merely to members of the Church. There is a tribal law that wagons should not be driven in or out of the village on Sundays, and most people refrain then from other major activities as well. At the height of the ploughing season, it is true, they frequently violate the Sabbath by working in the fields, a fact to which missionaries have sometimes publicly attributed the occurrence of droughts. Normally, however, little work is done apart from the essential household chores. The women, especially, welcome this opportunity for greater relaxation. People who do not belong to the Church spend the day in comparative idleness. Communicants, if at the fields, come together to pray and sing hymns. If in the village, they make a more elaborate toilet than usual in the morning, put on their best clothes (if they have more than one set), and go to church. After the service they visit their friends, or themselves act as hosts. Sunday has become the favourite day for visiting, and a more substantial meal than usual is generally prepared for the occasion. In the afternoon there is another church service, which however is not so well attended as in the morning, many people preferring to enjoy themselves sociably at home. At night, after the evening meal, local prayer-meetings are held here and there by the orthodox, but for the rest there is the usual routine already described.

Sunday is not the only break in the ordinary household routine. Every now and then, as we saw in the last chapter, people may be called upon to work for the chief, or to help relatives or friends engaged in some major enterprise. Interruptions of this sort, while they do not mean any respite from labour, are nevertheless a diversion from one's own household occupations, and the cooperation of so many people provides an opportunity for much talk and laughter, sometimes enlivened by the prospect of a beer-drink or minor feast at the end. Often enough, again, there is a birth, a wedding, a confirmation or some similar domestic celebration, in the vicinity. A feast may then be expected, and for days, occasionally weeks, beforehand there is considerable excitement. Even the people not directly involved bustle about with offers of help and take a lively interest in all that is happening, and the event is of course also a welcome source of gossip and comment. The feast itself, especially at a wedding, attracts almost all the neighbours, whether invited or not, and with eating and drinking, singing and dancing, flirting and squabbling, they enjoy themselves noisily and happily. The death of a relative or neighbour is again a diversion, sorrowful though it is. All who can do so abandon work for the day in order to attend the funeral and ensuing cleansing-feast, and subsequently pay formal visits of condolence to the stricken family.

It is in this manner that most people spend the time when they are not actually working for themselves. The schools provide more entertainment for the children in the form of organized games and drill, and now and then a concert or football match is arranged that attracts many adults as well. A high Government official may visit the tribe, and for days beforehand preparations are made to receive him in state. An agricultural show may be held, and again the daily routine must be varied immediately before and during its progress. Once in a while a political crisis occurs in the tribe, and the men are too occupied with meetings, both public and secret, to be able to spend much time on their work; or a new regiment is created, to the accompaniment of much feasting and rejoicing. Events of this kind all disturb the normal course of household affairs, and help to relieve the monotony of what at best is hardly a colourful existence, even to the people themselves. Those old enough to remember the days when the chief used to organize dances for the adults in his council-place, or publicly celebrate some ceremony connected with rain-making, agriculture or the renovation of the town charms, complain sadly that the times have become dull, and ancient warriors regret still more the passing of the inter-tribal raids that contributed so greatly to the excitements of life.

FAMILY GATHERINGS

The routine described above tends to scatter the members of the Kgatla family. To start with, one or more of them may be resident in European labour centres for considerable periods of time. Inside the Reserve, the older boys are generally at the cattle-posts, where they remain all the year round except for an occasional brief visit home. Wives, daughters and the younger sons are normally together, although during the greater part of the agricultural season, from the end of January onwards, some of the children may be at school in the village while their mothers are at the fields. Husbands are usually at hand to help in the ploughing and reaping, when the whole family, except those working abroad or at the cattle-posts, is busy in the fields, to which even the school-children go every week-end. But during the intervening months, or when the people are back in the villages, the men are as often as not away from home, sometimes only for a day or two, sometimes for weeks on end, according to the nature of the activity on which they are at the moment engaged. Again, as we have seen, people may go visiting in other parts of the country, or children may be sent to live for a while with some relative.

This fluctuating dispersion is due in the main to the organization of Kgatla economic life. The well-defined separation of villages, fields and cattle-posts leads inevitably to a scattering of the population, which labour migration has greatly intensified. So far as the family is concerned, the result generally is that husbands and wives do not live together all the year round, and that older boys are seldom with their parents, except when the latter visit the cattle-posts. It is in fact very unusual to find all the members of a family under the same roof for more than say a fortnight or so at a time, unless the children are still fairly small; and the momentary composition of the average household changes frequently. It is therefore not surprising that real intimacy and sympathetic understanding are often lacking in family relationships. This, of course, cannot be attributed solely to the looseness of the residential tie, but, as we shall see in later chapters, the latter has certainly contributed to the widespread prevalence of infidelity among wives and of indiscipline among children. Home life, in the ordinary European sense of the term, does not really exist among the Kgatla; the compound is not a place where all the members of the family habitually spend at least part of the day together, but is a centre from which the men and older boys are frequently absent and where they seldom remain continuously for long.

There are certain occasions, however, when parents and children are expected to come together. In the old days the most conspicuous of these occasions was the annual eating of the first-fruits. This ceremony was held as soon as the earliest crops of the new season began to ripen. It started in the chief's council-place, where the people of his own ward assembled on a specified day, bringing with them pumpkins from their fields. The heir to the chieftainship was given a slice of raw pumpkin; he bit off a piece and spat it out, then bit off another piece, which he chewed and swallowed. The slice was passed to the senior son of the chief's next brother, who tasted it in the same way, and the rite was repeated, in descending order of precedence, by the senior sons of every other man in the ward. The remaining wards of the tribe were then free 'to bite the pumpkin' as well. They assembled in their council-places, where they carried out the rite along the same lines as in the chief's ward. Each family then went home for the domestic part of the ceremony. Some pumpkins were cooked, and tasted first by the children, in descending order of age, then by the father and lastly by the mother. In a polygamous household the ranking of the wives was strictly observed at this time, the children of the first preceding all those of the second, and so on. Considerable importance was attached to this, for it demonstrated clearly the exact standing of each person in the family.

Today the public eating of the first-fruits has long been abandoned, and the succeeding domestic rite is also no longer
observed, except by a few magicians and other conservative
people. Most families, on the other hand, still try to come
together when a new compound or hut is being doctored. Part of
the ceremony consists in the people themselves being ritually
'protected' against sorcery and other evils, and for this purpose it
is necessary, or at least desirable, that everybody should be there.
The officiating magician treats the father first, then the mother
and then the children in descending order of age; each is inocu-
lated on various parts of the body with medicines, or may be
given them to swallow instead. Even Christians usually have this
ceremony performed after building a new home, for they feel,
like the rest, that without it they may not be able to live there in
peace and security.

Domestic gatherings are also held whenever a birth takes place
in the family, or a confirmation, initiation, betrothal, wedding or
death. All the children actually in the Reserve, even if already
married, are expected to join their parents on such occasions,
while for particularly important celebrations, like those connected with marriage or death, the children working abroad will
also come home if possible. Again, when someone is seriously ill,
or involved in a court case or in trouble of any other kind, the
adult members of his family usually rally round to cheer him up
or to support him.

On such occasions, however, the other relatives also participate, so that the gathering is never restricted to the family
itself. If the occasion calls for a feast, these relatives help too in
the necessary preparations, and, if they can afford it, contribute
gifts of food. The maternal uncle is particularly expected to do
so, but the other brothers and sisters of the husband and wife
likewise help as much as possible. For this reason domestic celebrations are most frequently arranged for the months after the
harvest, when people generally have more leisure from
work and so are easily able to attend. Again, if a person has to go
to court, his relatives generally discuss the case with him first and
decide what line to take at the hearing, where they support him

with all the arguments at their command. It is indeed one of the main obligations of kinsmen to stand by and help one another whenever necessary, and failure to do so is bitterly resented and usually gives rise to considerable ill-feeling, followed sometimes by accusations of sorcery if anything disastrous afterwards occurs. On the other hand, the family itself is obliged on all occasions of domestic importance to inform its relatives of what is happening, and to invite them formally to attend the associated discussions and ceremonies. Thus, as we have seen, when parents are arranging the marriage of a son, or have been approached for the hand of a daughter, they should consult the child's uncles and aunts, particularly the maternal uncle, before making a final decision. These relatives must similarly be referred to before an estate is divided, the fate of a widow settled, or any other matter dealt with that affects not only the family itself but the wider kinship group. Even those who live in some other part of the Reserve must be sent for specially on the more important occasions, and nothing should be done until they arrive.

A few actual episodes may serve to illustrate concretely some of the circumstances under which kinship gatherings are held, and who are the people that attend. Modise became engaged to Dikeledi in 1933. He visited her frequently at night, and after a while she became pregnant. When questioned by her widowed mother, she said that Modise was to blame. He also admitted this. Her mother reported the matter to MmaDintwe (Modise's paternal aunt, who had been the female intermediary when the betrothal was negotiated). MmaDintwe told him what she had heard, but for some reason he now denied having impregnated Dikeledi. MmaDintwe thereupon related the whole story to his mother. The latter, who was also a widow, consulted her husband's younger brother Mongale, the male intermediary in the betrothal negotiations. Mongale summoned all the other close relatives at hand. A meeting was held in Modise's home, at which there were present his mother, his two paternal uncles (Mongale and another), his father's paternal aunt (the oldest female member of the group), his maternal uncle, his paternal aunt

(MmaDintwe), and a paternal grandfather's son. His mother told them what had been reported to her. They sent for him, and after a while got him to admit that it was really he who had impregnated Dikeledi. Then they dismissed him, and settled down to discuss the question of 'fetching her home' as his wife. They finally decided that the ceremony should be held just before the child was due to be born.

Shortly afterwards Dikeledi became ill, and complained of pains in her stomach. Her mother at once sent for Modise's mother, and for some of her own relatives. Apart from the two mothers, Modise himself, one of Dikeledi's paternal uncles, her maternal uncle, and the latter's wife, attended the discussion. They decided between them that a doctor should be called to divine the cause of the illness, and also which doctor it should be. It is usual in all the more serious cases of illness to have a conference of this sort, so that a doctor may be chosen whom everybody trusts. Any close relative not specially notified and summoned may feel that he is no longer regarded as friendly, or even that the people suspect him of having caused the illness by sorcery or some similar means.

In 1932, again, a girl named Bitsang was being confirmed. As is usual, her family gave a feast to celebrate the occasion. According to custom, they should have notified their relatives formally that she was going to be confirmed, and afterwards should have invited them individually to help in preparing the feast. Bitsang's mother omitted, however, to convey the necessary invitations to her husband's maternal uncle and paternal aunt's son. She said afterwards that she had thought they would come in any case, since they were so closely related to the girl. The result, however, was that both men felt slighted and stayed away with their families. Their absence robbed the feast of almost all its gaiety, and it soon fizzled out. The matter aroused a good deal of discussion, and almost everybody blamed the mother for having acted so improperly. The relatives concerned, in particular, felt very bitter against her, and complained that she apparently did not want them to take any interest in her daughter's well-being.

These instances show that although the family is normally somewhat scattered, any event out of the ordinary will bring it and its immediate relatives together again. The routine of everyday activity may favour dispersion, but reunions are held sufficiently often to counteract in some degree the disintegrating tendencies of frequent separation. On such occasions, moreover, the presence of the relatives shows that family affairs are not considered a purely private concern. The Kgatla family is not an isolated, self-contained unit; it is part of a wider kinship group within which mutual aid and responsibility are strongly developed. The way in which relatives insist upon being notified of all family events, and their readiness to take affront if they feel that they are being ignored, indicate clearly enough the importance attached to the ideal of kinship solidarity.

The subordination of the family to the kindred is revealed in still another context. Whenever any fairly serious dispute arises between husband and wife, or parent and child, or between two people otherwise closely related, it is always dealt with in the first instance by their own family-group. 'Outsiders should not interfere between children of one womb,' it is said, and it is expected that if possible the matter should be settled privately without recourse to the official tribal courts. The senior male member of the group in line of descent takes charge of the proceedings. He is assisted by the maternal uncles of the people concerned, by the other men of the group, and sometimes also by the married women. They try by all means possible to reconcile the contending parties, but may also thrash or fine the one who is clearly to blame. There is a right of appeal from their decision to the court of the local ward-head, but it is not very often exercised. The authority of the group as a whole is usually sufficient to restore friendly relations and to prevent the matter from going any further. We shall see more fully how this informal court works when we come to discuss the personal relationships between the members of the family. For the moment it is sufficient to note that we have here one more type of the occasions when domestic life departs from its normal daily routine.

7. The Sexual Aspect of Marriage

SEXUAL RELATIONS BETWEEN HUSBAND AND WIFE

When discussing with Kgatla the relations between husband and wife, I was continually struck by the open importance they attached to the sexual aspect. They have very little prudery in matters of this kind. Certain standards of decency must be observed in speech and in dress, but sexual behaviour in itself is not a topic that must be veiled in deliberate obscurity or if possible ignored altogether in society. The physical relations between men and women are spoken about freely and with relatively little embarrassment, even in mixed company, for sex is considered a normal factor in human life, which not even Mission teaching has succeeded in tarnishing with the concepts of shame and sin. Nor is any attempt made to keep it a sacred mystery where young people are concerned. The ignorance until recently held to be so desirable in European women before marriage is never looked for in Kgatla girls. From an early age children are familiar with the nature of copulation, and much of their play consists of games with a definitely sexual character. As they grow older, they are given special instruction in matters of sex, girls especially being told by their mothers of the connection between menstruation and fertility. Once past the age of puberty, boys and girls indulge freely enough in full sexual relations, and it is taken for granted that by the time they are married they will have acquired personal experience of intercourse.

The result, as we have seen, is that very few Kgatla enter marriage with no sexual experience at all. But sex now assumes a new importance in their lives. Coitus is no longer merely the closest form of intimacy in which two lovers can indulge, and the highest favour a girl can bestow upon a boy. With marriage it becomes also a duty that husband and wife owe to each other. The Kgatla are well aware that conception is due to sexual intercourse, and, since marriage is regarded primarily as a union for the production of children, husband and wife are expected to sleep together so that she may fulfil her destiny of becoming a mother. Failure on the part of either to consummate the union is readily accepted as a ground for divorce, while if a husband stays away too long from his wife public opinion will not condemn her for taking a lover by whom she can bear.

But the Kgatla do not regard sexual intercourse as an act indulged in merely to procreate children. They acknowledge candidly that it gives them very great pleasure. That is why a woman is explicitly instructed at marriage to submit to her husband's attentions whenever he wants her. It is her duty to afford him carnal satisfaction, and no attempt is made to disguise it. There is much less emphasis, in everyday talk, on the desirability of his likewise gratifying her sexual desires, but that she also can find pleasure in coitus is well recognized.

'When I sleep with my husband,' a young wife confided, 'I like to lie on my back, I don't like to lie on my side or in any other way. And while he is busy, I feel very, very nice, I shiver with pleasure, and as he keeps pushing I feel it nicer than anything I have ever had under the sun, and I like him more and more. I feel my inside itching, and my stomach comes together, I don't know what happens, my whole body gets hot, but I think it's my veins that make the body hot, because they are so taut. I shut my eyes with pleasure, and at that moment I find that I have given all my life to him. And when he discharges into me, it is nicer than ever, but I wish that he would not then pull out, but remain lying flat upon me.'

Women frequently complain of the manner in which a husband makes use of his rights. Many told me bitterly that however tired they were they received little consideration, and that if they refused or resisted they were usually beaten into submission. One, only recently married, said that if she had known what was before her she would rather have remained single, for then she could at least have chosen her own times for sexual intercourse, instead of having to yield to her husband every night. In a divorce case heard in the chief's court in 1929, the junior wife of a polygamist complained that her husband had been so excessive in his demands, forcing her even when she was completely exhausted by work, and thrashing her with a leather strap when she refused, that at last she had no alternative but to run away. The husband was found the innocent party because his wife had deserted him. It is seldom that such extreme forms of protest are adopted, but quarrels owing to a husband's failure to consider his wife's wishes are a commonplace feature of Kgatla married life. The men, however, take up the attitude that intercourse is a duty every woman owes to her husband, and that she must carry it out faithfully (hence the verdict in the case just mentioned). 'These women can't stop us,' I was told; 'we have given *bogadi* for them, and so we are entitled to make use of their bodies.' Occasionally, however, a woman is strong enough to resist her husband with success, and then, as one informant put it, 'They fight about it, and later on the husband complains to his friends, and says that while he is himself forced to empty out the chamber-pot he yet does not get his fair share of the blankets' (i.e. of sexual intercourse).

Many women, on the other hand, complain that they do not receive as much sexual attention as they desire. Adultery is so commonly practised by men after a few years of marriage, when the novelty of perpetual access to the wife's body has faded, that women frequently find themselves neglected, and in sheer desperation may take lovers of their own, or resort to masturbation. Most humiliating of all is when a husband comes home late at night from some other woman, and is so 'worn out' that, to quote one angry wife, 'he is no use at all to me, his penis dangles like that of a baby, and nothing can arouse it'. Even if a husband is reasonably faithful and attentive, he is so often away, either at the cattle-post or for a long spell in town, that his wife is forced to seek some other form of sexual relief.

Women who do not take lovers almost invariably practise masturbation. This generally takes the form of rubbing the finger about in the vagina, or of playing with the *labia minora*. Some women have small sticks covered with rags, which they keep carefully hidden when the husband is at home, and use as a substitute penis whenever he is away. Occasionally two very close friends sleep together and indulge in homosexual play by fondling each other's *labia*, or, more usually, one slips her fingers into the other's vagina and rubs them about, while the latter, 'feeling very nice', responds by moving her body about as if copulating. But there do not seem to be any instances of genuine homosexual affairs among women, involving the total exclusion of men. All those with whom I discussed the matter said that the practices just described were employed merely to obtain gratification in the absence of their lovers or husbands. The vast majority of women, if not all, prefer normal coitus to all other forms of sexual activity. Nevertheless, the prevalence of such practices among them, as contrasted with the men, among whom masturbation is seldom found after adolescence and especially after marriage, indicates clearly enough that wives often fail to receive adequate satisfaction from their husbands.

There are, of course, married couples who lead a fairly well-adjusted sexual life. The husband need not necessarily be faithful to his wife, but he tries to satisfy her and does not force her when she is unwilling. But the general impression I obtained was certainly that the women suffered either from excessive demands or from inadequate attention in matters of sex. The readiness with which wives could always be induced to discuss their grievances suggests that Kgatla husbands have much to learn about the art of married love.

In fairness, however, it must be added that men in turn sometimes accuse the women of being insatiable, and point to some who are notorious for promiscuity. 'She is everybody's meat,' the local gossips say of such a woman; 'her sexual parts are always on fire, and cannot be quenched.' It is mainly widows or unmarried girls against whom these accusations are made, and not women whose husbands are still living. Nevertheless, one middle-aged husband complained to me about his wife:

'A woman does not like a man who sleeps a lot at night; she wants him to be awake and talkative, and shakes him to talk to her. This is one of the troublesome things in the house. You are fast asleep, and she shakes you to wake up and talk, but this is just an excuse; what she really wants is "the hyena that eats people" (i.e. the penis), because when you married her you married her for sexual intercourse, and now she wants you to keep on fulfilling the promise you made to her through marriage. And if you want to "use" her at night, and she refuses, then leave her; and after a while you'll find that she begins to push up against you; you move away, and she coughs and says: "Did you not say that you want to do something with me?" Then don't sulk, but do it, or you will never have peace in your home.'

As we shall see later, there are certain occasions when sexual relations between husband and wife are forbidden, and almost all husbands also visit their cattle-posts frequently, or, if still comparatively young, go off to work in the towns. It is, in fact, hardly ever that husband and wife stay together continuously for more than say two months at the most. Every married couple, therefore, observes periods of mutual abstinence, extending over a fairly long time in some instances. But when they are together, and still newly married, intercourse between them is said by informants to occur daily, 'because their love is still very strong'. Later it is stabilized at from three to five times a week. Women said that they prefer coitus three or four times a week, but not more often, as they are sometimes so tired, after a heavy day's work, that they long only for sleep. Some men also hold that daily intercourse is injurious to bodily health, and warn young husbands of the dangers of excess. 'You laugh and laugh,' goes the relevant proverb, 'but the slippery places are still ahead,' i.e. copulation at first is enjoyable, but in time becomes troublesome and fatiguing.

Normally two or at the most three acts of coitus take place during the night; once before sleep, and once on awaking at dawn, seems to be the common practice. Occasionally men are much more vigorous, especially when they have returned after a long absence, or a period of ritual abstinence has expired, and then they sometimes have coitus as much as six or seven times in succession. But excesses of this kind are generally condemned, for they are said to make a person lean and feeble. In the old days, at the initiation ceremonies, boys were deliberately warned to be temperate in their sexual life, and similar advice is still freely circulated among the younger people. Two obscure sayings, both part of the ancient teaching, are frequently quoted in this connection: 'It bites, although it has no teeth,' and, 'The blunt knife cuts without your noticing it.' The reference in both cases is to the vulva, which is said to 'bite' or 'cut' a penis entering it too often in one session. This is the explanation usually given for the fact that after a riotous night the tip of the penis may be badly bruised and urination difficult.

It is widely held by both men and women that coitus can be very painful if the vagina is too 'tight' to permit of easy penetration. Men express a decided preference for a woman with a fairly wide vagina, and, as old Maswe said, 'Her husband uses her excessively because the enjoyment is so great, and then he hurts himself because he tries to have too many orgasms'. On the other hand, they generally look askance at a woman with so little experience that she has not yet been 'worked loose', and, in some cases at least, a virgin is regarded with marked disfavour. For this reason many girls, from the age of about sixteen or so, practise systematic dilation of the vagina. They begin by pushing in the tip of the finger, and keep on doing so night after night, until the whole finger enters easily. At first only the bare finger is used, but in time it may be reinforced by a covering of rags or the soft leaves of the *modubu* tree, or sometimes two or three fingers are used simultaneously. This practice is so common that it can well be regarded as a standard custom. Its avowed object is to facilitate sexual intercourse, 'so that when a girl sleeps with a boy, he must not find it difficult to locate the vagina, or feel sore when he puts in his penis, and she also must not feel sore while he is pushing'. Sometimes a woman, if expecting her husband back from the cattle-post, or awaiting the visit of a lover, will in the late afternoon wash her body with warm water, lie back, put one or more fingers into the vagina, and work them about to 'loosen' or 'stretch' it. 'Then when the man sleeps with her, it is not as sore as it would otherwise have been.'

Judging from this practice, and from the various comments noted in connection with it, it seems that coitus is at times accompanied with greater pain, especially for the women, than need be the case. One old woman went so far as to say that 'drunk people, when they quarrel in the night, often shout that they want to leave their husbands, because the latter hurt them, they have got terrible "things" '. And a common saying among the women is that 'the men carry a stabbing-spear, they pierce you with it, and then go on their way'. Nevertheless, since most women are already accustomed to sexual intercourse by the time they get married, they seldom experience the painful shock of the wedding night which is said to be so common elsewhere. But the bungling and difficulties that often accompany defloration are shown by the fact that of fourteen girls whom I questioned on this point, all said that they felt very sore and bled, while several added that when the penis entered they felt as if a stick had suddenly been thrust into them. The account I quoted in Chapter 2 of a girl's first seduction illustrates this. And Manyama, who when she was married at the age of twenty-two still happened to be a virgin, said that on her wedding-night one of her aunts said to her: 'When your husband tries to sleep with you tonight, he will hurt you; but don't shout or scream or resist, because people will laugh at you, and we shall be disgraced, everybody will hear that you refused your husband.' 'I had it very hard that night,' she went on, 'the blood kept coming out, but I stuck it out, having been told to bear it and be patient.'

Almost invariably coitus is preceded by some form of love play. Girls attach considerable importance to this, and readily distinguish between 'good' and 'bad' lovers by the skill displayed in arousing excitement. Kissing is a fairly recent innovation, brought in by the children who have been to school abroad. It is on the whole confined to the more 'sophisticated' classes. The girls sometimes like it, but mostly regard it with repulsion. As one of them said, 'It is a waste of time, and eating dirt, because you swallow each other's saliva.' The usual approach among the younger people, whether married or not, is for the man to fondle the woman's breasts and suck her nipples; he then caresses her buttocks and hips, and gradually brings his hand round to the mons pubis; finally he tries to handle the vulva itself, but most women are very sensitive about this part of the body, and it is only in the heat of the moment that they will allow him to touch them there. Occasionally the woman herself makes the first advances, seizing the man's penis and rubbing it up against her body, especially if he is not particularly keen on sleeping with her just then. But it is very unusual for women to play an active part at this stage; several said that however 'excited' they felt they would just lie still, lest the man think they were over-keen on coitus.

The more mature married people seem to dispense with most preliminaries other than fondling the genitals. In this connexion the woman's *labia* are of outstanding importance. As we have seen, the stretching of these parts is admittedly practised for the direct sexual gratification of both men and women. As Manyama's mother said:

'The *labia* adorn a woman. If a woman hasn't got long *labia*, we don't call her a woman at all, but a child. When you hear husband and wife quarrel at home, this is the main cause of their quarrel, because this is the place where the husband plays every day, and if his wife has not got them, there is no peace at home, for then he has nowhere to play, while other men boast to him about how they play with their wives. The man plays with the *labia*, and even if he is not intending to copulate with his wife, and just puts his hand there, he gets an erection, then he has intercourse with her, and afterwards plays there again.'

And a married man commented, similarly: 'If you marry a woman with long *labia*, you love her more than one who has not got them, because you play with them and they help to give you an erection, and so we call them "the exciter of the bull".' These statements indicate clearly enough the high erotic value attached by the Kgatla to the *labia*. Women say also that it adds greatly to their own enjoyment when the penis rubs up against the *labia* during coitus.

Several positions of coitus are known. In the most common, the woman lies on her back, and the man on top of her with his legs between hers. Sometimes she lies on her left side instead, with the man facing her, and puts her right leg over his body.

Both forms are described to women at marriage by their older female relatives, and they are also told to try the second if they find the man's body lying too heavily upon them. But the first is generally preferred, because, as one woman said, 'When I am lying on my back, the penis goes right in.' Sometimes, especially if the couple are out in the open and must hurry to lessen the risk of discovery, they have coitus standing, the woman supporting her back against a wall or tree. For variety some people experiment with *coitus a posteriori*, the woman either lying on her side or crouching on her arms and legs, 'like an animal'. Apparently no other forms are generally known or practised, and such perversions as *coitus in anum* are very seldom if ever indulged in.

Men prefer it greatly if the woman is an active partner during intercourse, if, as they put it, 'she shakes her body, and knows how to hold one'. This, too, is one of the things about which a young bride is told on her wedding-day, and which was formerly included in the teaching given at the initiation ceremonies. On the other hand, men apparently pay little attention to the desirability of bringing the woman to an orgasm. Some are even unaware of its true nature. 'Women deny that they ever have ejaculations like those of the men,' a young man told me, 'but they say this because of shame. Because sometimes, before you even have coitus with a woman, you find that she is already wet, her "blood" has come out, and so we say that women "finish" first.' There is obvious confusion here between orgasm and the vaginal secretion. 'We never know whether a woman is satisfied or not,' another man said, 'because she never tells us.' Others recognize that she is experiencing an orgasm 'when she suddenly clutches you tightly, or folds her legs round your back'. But some men, since they hold that a child will look like its father if he has the orgasm first, try deliberately to reach the point of ejaculation as soon as possible. It is no wonder therefore that women complain that the men do not stay on them long enough, but quickly ejaculate, 'and then want to rest and sleep, while you are still feeling excited'.

The outline just given, since it is based mainly upon the confidences of only a few informants, is of course far from complete. On some points I could receive no information at all, but there were also many about which I failed to make the necessary inquiries while I had the opportunity. A few additional details are provided in a description of sexual intercourse written for me, in the vernacular, by a young teacher. Although it refers to unmarried lovers, it is sufficiently interesting and comprehensive to be worth quoting in full as an illustration of procedure and technique probably employed also in the early stages of married life.

The boy and the girl sit together outside her hut talking, until her parents go to bed. Then he pleads with her to sleep with him, and because she is shy she will at first refuse, but when he says that if she refuses it is because she does not love him, she will consent. She goes into the hut to spread her blankets on the floor, and then calls the boy to come in. He sits on a chair, and she sits beside her blankets, and they talk. Then he puts out the light in the hut, takes off his clothes, and gets into the blankets; he calls to the girl to come to him, and she also gets into the blankets, and then takes off her clothes.

As they lie together like this, the girl turns her back on the boy, while he faces towards her. Then he begins to trouble her by feeling her body, he fondles her buttocks and breasts, and all over, stroking her. He keeps stirring her body uneasily, and she will keep on saying: 'What are you doing? Leave me alone, why do you feel me all over?' The boy will keep reassuring her, saying, 'What are you afraid of? I am just admiring your body.' Sometimes he kisses her, but many girls will not allow him to do so, for they regard the kiss as an awful thing. Then he tries to touch her vulva, and she will jump, because she does not like him to do that, and she will tell him not to insult her, because she does not want her private parts to be seen. But the boy will say to her, 'I am not insulting you, I am just caressing your body to make you feel well;' but she will refuse to let him do so at first, but when she gets hot, then perhaps she will not mind so much.

Sometimes it happens that the girl takes the initiative. She begins to feel the boy's body in the same manner; she is hot, but afraid to ask him to start doing it now, so she tries to arouse him, and may catch at his penis to make it stand, and may even put it at the mouth of the vulva. But some girls have much shame, so that even although they are hot they simply lie still and pretend not to be troubled, so that the boy must be the one to begin.

When they are both hot, the boy gets on top of the girl. She lies on her back and opens her legs, and he will begin to feel for the vagina with his hand and put his penis in. If he does not find the vagina, he will ask the girl to show him; and sometimes she catches the penis and puts it in, but sometimes she refuses and says, 'You can find it for yourself,' and this is due to shame. Then they begin to copulate. The boy presses hard on her, he breathes deeply and perspires freely. And while the boy is working, the girl sometimes folds her legs over his back and clasps him firmly, but sometimes she is nervous and simply lies still. If she is still young, she feels sore, and she will begin to cry softly, saying, 'You are hurting me, be gentle, be slow, it is enough;' but the boy will just continue, and then she keeps quiet, she is feeling the sweetness of it. Some girls, if already much used to this thing, keep quiet altogether, and say nothing, but others, because they like it very much, keep saying, 'Push harder, man.' The boy, as he keeps pushing, talks softly of the pleasure he is getting: 'Oh, you are treating me well tonight, my wife, my love; when I used to say you must love me, I meant that you must treat me like this; oh, how nice it is! One can die of it.' And just when he ejaculates, he says, 'Man, it is so nice that I could cut off my neck; oh, what a wonderful sweetness, it is coming out of my ears!' He gives a deep breath, and becomes weak and loose all over. Sometimes he ejaculates into the girl, sometimes outside. And sometimes the girl, after he has ejaculated, will hold him firmly with her hands and not allow him to get off, telling him to continue, because she still feels the sweetness; but he will refuse, and tell her that he cannot do so because his semen is all out. And when she is absolutely convinced that he will not continue, she will let him get off.

Now they lie down again next to each other. If she is a good-mannered girl, she will always have a towel near her pillow, and as soon as they lie down she quickly takes it and cleans his genitals and her own, and wipes the sweat from their bodies, so that the blankets should not be stained. They keep quiet for a while, then the girl embraces the boy, and says: 'You boys have it hard, you keep on breathing hard and working at this.' And the boy will say, 'Yes, it is hard work, but it is also very nice, so much so that one could cut off one's neck.' And the girl says, 'Oh, is that so? But you boys are naughty, and you have terrible wishes, you can't even lie quietly for a short time before you must be at it. You boys are thieves, why can't you just stay without it?' And the boy will reply, 'We cannot stay without it, we are not doing it blindly, we have it hard unless we can do so.'

Sometimes he copulates with her three or four times that night, and then he leaves early in the morning so that he may not be seen by the people. And once they have slept together like this, they begin to love each other very much almost as if they were man and wife.

The way in which a polygamist may regulate his sexual life is indicated in the following statement by Natale, which represents the only actual evidence I have on this point:

'I live with my wives very cleverly, I have handled them properly, so that they get on with each other. At first I had only one wife, and then I married a second named Mogatsa. And when I found that Mogatsa did not wish to live harmoniously with my senior wife, I slept only with the latter for many days in succession, without going to see Mogatsa at all except in the afternoons. Then she said to me: "Why is it that you don't come into my blankets, did you marry me just in order to laugh at me?" And I replied, "Well, when I married you I did not say I was going to divorce my other wife." And she said, "If your senior wife does not want you to come to me, tell me, and I shall know where to take the matter." Then I saw that this was likely to lead to a serious quarrel, and so I said to her, "No, I am staying with that wife just to finish the month, then I shall come to you." Thereupon she was satisfied, and when the month was over I came to her, and began to sleep with her. And it was also then that I took the medicine about which I told you, and secretly gave it to them both to drink, without their knowing what its purpose was. Since then there has been no trouble, they help each other at work, and they even eat together. I have laid down the rule that I shall sleep with each one for four days in succession, and then go to the other. I find them both equally desirable, but when I have slept with one for three days, by the fourth day she has wearied me, and when I go to the other I find that I have greater passion, she seems more attractive than the first, but it is not really so, for when I return to the latter again there is the same renewed passion. A woman does not weary one out except when you come home after drinking beer, it is then that she wearies you tremendously, you find when you sleep with her that you have no strength, because your heart is longing for sleep, and even although she urges you to mount her you are already tired before you even begin to have intercourse with her, and you just fall asleep upon her. Long ago Chief Lentswe said that after a plentiful harvest the Kgatla did not procreate, and this was the fault of the men, because they drank so much beer, and he wanted to stop beer-drinking altogether, so that the people could make children again.'

SEXUAL TABOOS AND THEIR SANCTIONS

So far we have been concerned mainly with the personal aspect of sex relations in marriage. The sexual life of married people is, however, affected not merely by individual desires and varying proficiency in the art of making love, but by social regulations of several kinds concerning the occasions when coitus is specially desirable, or, on the other hand, should be carefully avoided. These regulations for the most part reflect the prevailing belief that sexual intercourse at certain times, or with people of certain classes, will result in sickness or some other misfortune. So strong is this belief that children past the age of puberty are repeatedly warned by their parents or companions of the dangers attaching to careless promiscuity, while in the old days they were explicitly taught at the initiation ceremonies when and with whom to avoid sexual relations. Among both married and un-married people, the consequences of neglecting these regulations form a frequent and always absorbing topic of conversation, both generally and with reference to specific individual instances, and little difficulty is experienced in getting them to talk on the subject.

The restrictions on sexual intercourse are associated with the idea that at certain times a person's blood becomes 'hot', and until he has 'cooled down' he is in a condition harmful to others with whom he comes into very close contact. Both men and women still capable of bearing children are 'hot' immediately after intercourse, and, since they presumably lead active sexual lives, they are accordingly debarred from taking part in certain forms of ritual. Thus, in some of the rain-making ceremonies, and on similar occasions, only children who have not yet attained puberty, or women who have passed the menopause, can be employed, for they are not yet or no longer able to be 'hot'. Widows and widowers are also 'hot' for about a year after their bereavement. A woman is 'hot' during her menstrual periods, during pregnancy (especially in the early stages), and immediately after childbirth. If she has aborted, she is 'hot' until she menstruates again. Her condition in all these instances is shared by her husband or the man responsible for her pregnancy. A few other states of 'hotness' are not so directly the product of sexual activity, but may in turn affect it. People are said to be 'hot' when they have just returned from a long journey, from a funeral or from visiting a newly-confined mother; a doctor is 'hot' for two or three days after one of his patients has died; and a woman is 'hot' if she has during the course of the day been mixing earth or smearing the walls and floors of her compound.

In most cases of 'hotness', especially those resulting from sexual behaviour itself, it is believed that if the person affected indulges in coitus before 'cooling down', his partner in the act will be stricken with disease and may even die. This belief rests upon the idea that during intercourse the woman's vaginal secretion, which is identified with her 'blood', enters the man's body through his urethra and 'summons' his semen (also termed 'blood'), with which it is then ejaculated. But if her 'blood' is 'hot', it is too 'strong' or 'heavy' for the man; it thickens inside his body, and cannot all be ejaculated, but settles in his hips and loins. The result is that his body starts to ache, 'his stomach swells and his intestines burn', and, above all, his urethra becomes blocked, so that he cannot urinate at all, or only with very great pain. As the Kgatla put it, 'The woman closes him up,' and unless he is successfully doctored he will remain crippled or may die. He may also become impotent, for the 'bad blood' he has absorbed weakens his own, and deprives it of the 'strength' needed to form a child.

Similarly, if a man with 'hot blood' sleeps with a woman, his 'blood', instead of mixing with hers in the womb to make her conceive, flows over into her hips, where it remains to trouble her. It is said that a woman suffering from this affliction of 'bad hips' does not at first feel any pain, but after a while her body begins to ache, especially round the hips, and unless doctored she will have irregularities of menstruation and may ultimately become sterile. It is believed that a woman promiscuous in her sexual favours will likewise acquire 'bad hips', through the accumulation in her body of the 'bloods' of many different men. 'These bloods fight one another, they do not agree and they poison the woman's body.' The condition is held to be contagious. Girls are therefore warned by their mothers not to wear someone else's clothing, for if the latter has 'bad hips' they will become similarly afflicted. Furthermore, any man sleeping with such a woman will not only himself become affected, as already described, but will infect any other woman with whom he afterwards has intercourse.

The symptoms in both men and women, as described by informants, are almost certainly those of gonorrhoea. This disease, although according to medical reports it is fairly common, is not specifically identified by the Kgatla, a fact that can only be due to its being regarded as one of the complaints arising from infection by 'hot blood'. Syphilis, on the other hand, which is also widespread, is recognized as a distinctive disease. But, although its connection with sexual life is well known, it is not held to result from 'hot blood'. In fact, according to some informants, many people do not regard it as contagious, and have little hesitation in sleeping with persons infected with it. The Native doctors seldom treat it, saying that it is a European disease, and can therefore be left to the Mission doctor. On the other hand, they have a large variety of remedies for 'bad hips' and kindred ailments. These remedies are designed in most cases to purify the blood and so remove the infection.

Because of the dangers of 'hot blood', all people with it are expected to refrain from sexual relations until they have 'cooled down'. It is difficult to say how faithfully the rule is observed in practice. In everyday speech, as well as in the teaching given to children, it is certainly stressed very strongly. Thus, to quote a girl of about twenty:

'When I began to understand things, my mother said to me: "Look, Tsholo, my child, this world is standing on its feet, this world does not want you to act carelessly. Don't mix too much with boys. If you love one boy, let it be that boy alone. And be careful of the boys with whom you sleep, for sometimes boys sleep with wrong girls, with girls who have syphilis or bad hips, and then the boy will come to you and put these sicknesses into you, and when you have grown up you will not be able to bear children. I strongly advise you to keep only one boy, so that even if he has these sicknesses, when you are sick everyone will know that it could have come only from him." And she said to me: "My child, you see many girls hurt boys by sleeping with them when menstruating. If a boy sleeps with such a girl, it is a dangerous thing, because the boy will die, and you will remain alive, so you must be careful never to sleep with a boy when you are menstruating." '

The frank assumption that the girl will in any case have lovers is worth noting as an index of the modern attitude towards premarital chastity, but the advice itself is very much to the point in view of the beliefs regarding sexual diseases. These beliefs are reinforced by the instances quoted to show the effects of violating the taboo. In 1933, for instance, a man named Setimela died two days before his marriage. The story at once went about that his death had been caused by his sleeping with his fiancée during her menses. Another man, Moeketse, whose legs are completely paralysed, is pointed out as an example of what can happen to a person sleeping with a widow newly bereaved. Natale, the doctor with two wives, told me that the second, formerly a widow, had become sterile from a similar cause. Her first husband was also a polygamist. His other wife died, and according to rule he could not sleep with anyone else until he had been purified. His mother-in-law specially warned him about this, but he pestered her daughter (his remaining wife, now married to Natale) until at last she gave in to him, 'and then her womb closed up for good'.

The general impression I received was that most people certainly do try to avoid intercourse with those suffering from one or other of the 'blood' complaints; and girls told me that they can almost always escape the attentions of an ardent but unwelcome lover by falsely pretending that they are menstruating. Occasionally, however, even this does not help. The young teacher whose description of coitus I quoted above told me that he once wished to sleep with a girl, who pleaded menstruation as a genuine excuse for refusing. He was all 'heated up' and very persistent, however, and said that if he did become sick he would get a doctor to cure him. Thereupon she reluctantly agreed, warning him not to blame her if anything happened to him. He had intercourse with her, and as he did not want to make her conceive he practised *coitus interruptus*. When he withdrew his penis he found it covered with blood; but he suffered no ill effects. This, instead of shaking his faith in the taboo, merely provided him with a new variation of the standard belief: he now holds that it is only if you ejaculate into the vagina that the woman's 'blood' can enter your body to affect you! Apparently few other Kgatla, however, would have ventured to take the risk. And a further incentive to conformity is provided by the proverb often quoted in this connexion: 'A suicide is not mourned,' i.e. if you deliberately sleep with an unclean woman, and become affected, no one will sympathize with you, for it was your own fault.

Between husband and wife the taboo on sexual intercourse during periods of 'hotness' is subject to certain modifications that do not apply to their relations with others. They are, for instance, not prohibited from sleeping together when the wife is pregnant. Her condition, as we shall see more fully in the next chapter, is attributed to the mixture of her menstrual blood with her husband's semen, and consequently he himself will not be injured if he sleeps with her. He is in fact expected to do so, so that his semen may continue to add to the flesh of the child growing in her womb. It is only some one not responsible for her pregnancy and sleeping with her who will be affected, for the 'blood' in her womb does not come from him, and will therefore react disastrously upon him when it enters his body during inter-course. For this reason, a wife pregnant by a lover sometimes refuses to cohabit with her husband, a fact that will readily make him suspect her of infidelity.

The following instance will illustrate the hold this belief has upon the people. Mmadikhukhu had been betrothed as a child to Ramfatshe. When she grew older, she objected to marrying him, but was forced to do so. She refused to consummate the mar-riage, and as a result quarrelled so much with her husband that she ultimately left him and went home to her parents.

Ramfatshe's people thereupon claimed the return of their betrothal gifts and *bogadi*. The case came before the chief, who ordered the couple to be put into a hut, where their parents were to see that the marriage was consummated. Mmadikhukhu thereupon protested that she could not sleep with her husband now, as she had become pregnant by some one else, and would therefore hurt him and even kill him if he had coitus with her. This was accepted as a valid ground for refusal, and the marriage was dissolved.

While on this point, we may note that, unlike many other primitive peoples, the Kgatla do not prohibit sexual relations between husband and wife while she is suckling a child. Intercourse between them is forbidden for the first two or three weeks after childbirth, when she is still secluded in the hut, but the husband is then allowed 'to cross the poles' (laid outside the hut as a sign that it contains a 'sick' person) and to have coitus with her. After this they may sleep together when and as often as they like, subject to other taboos. It is their duty, however, to see that she does not become pregnant again until the child has been weaned. They must therefore practise either *coitus interruptus* or one of the other contraceptive methods described in the next chapter.

On the other hand, sexual relations between the couple are forbidden if either has just come back from a long journey and is not yet 'cool'. Nowadays this restriction lasts only until the morning after the return, but formerly it is said to have continued for a week. Similarly, if a man is about to depart on a long journey, he should not sleep with his wife the night before he goes. 'Coitus,' say the old people, 'may not be taken as provision for the road,' lest the man, owing to his 'hot blood', falls sick on the way. If a woman has miscarried, she and her husband may not sleep together until she menstruates again, and they have both been ritually purified. A doctor, again, may not sleep with his wife immediately after the death of a patient. Similarly, during the rainy season the chief and his official rain-maker are both expected to remain continent until the new crops have sprouted. It is held that if they indulge in coitus during this time, and so become 'hot', their efforts to produce rain will be nullified, and the crops will fail.

The main prohibition for all married people, however, is during the wife's menstrual periods. In addition to fearing the consequences to which I have already referred, women say that they themselves feel no sexual desire at all during this time, and therefore object strongly to having intercourse with their husbands. Formerly they not only slept apart, but the wife could not even touch her husband or hand him his food directly. These usages are no longer observed, and today married people share the same blankets even during the wife's periods. Most men have been so firmly impressed since boyhood with the dangers of indulging in sexual relations with menstruating women that they apparently make no attempt to do so now with their wives. But some women complain that 'a husband can never last these three or four days without actually doing something, even if it is only letting his penis play about on your body', and they sometimes have great difficulty in preventing him from actually forcing them. As usual, it seems as if the wife has to take all the precautions, and that the husband fails to act with sufficient consideration.

Many squabbles also arise from the fact that married people may not be careful enough in their affairs with outsiders, with the result that, should they become infected, their spouses will likewise suffer. It is therefore held to be an important duty of every wife to inform her husband which of the neighbouring women has 'bad hips', so that, even if he is unfaithful, he will at least know whom to avoid! It is because they fear the infection he might bring them, thereby possibly rendering them sterile, that many women object to their husband's love-affairs.

The story of Ramasilo and his wife Dorika bears on this point. Ramasilo was attracted by another woman, and wished to take her as a second wife, but Dorika objected. He nevertheless slept with the woman, who bore him a child, and according to custom he performed the rite of 'crossing the poles', i.e. he had ritual coitus with her while she was still confined to her hut. He then returned to his own home, and slept with Dorika. Soon afterwards she became so ill that she almost died. While she was recovering, one of her friends told her that Ramasilo had 'crossed the poles' of her rival. She asked him if it was so, and when he admitted it, she became furious and left him. The matter came to court, where she complained that her husband was trying to kill her, because he had come to her straight from a woman with 'hot blood'. She insisted on a divorce, saying that she could not stay with a man acting like this, and after a good deal of trouble, she was granted it by the chief.

On certain occasions, it is particularly incumbent upon a husband to remain faithful to his wife. Thus, when she has just given birth to a child, he must stay away from all other women, even her co-wives, until he has resumed sexual relations with her by 'crossing the poles'. It is said that if he violates this taboo, his next visit to his wife will cause the new-born child to die owing to the bursting of its navel, or it will grow up weak, stupid and deformed. Some informants maintain that the husband should remain faithful to his wife during her pregnancy as well, lest he weaken the child in her womb or cause it to be aborted. Others say that it does not matter whether he is faithful or not, provided that he still cohabits with her frequently. Since, however, his own 'blood' is 'hot' owing to her condition, any other woman with whom he sleeps at this time will acquire 'bad hips'. Similarly, a woman, after giving birth to a child, should not sleep with any one else until she has resumed sexual relations with her husband, or the child will suffer in health and physique. She must also be faithful to her husband while he is out hunting, or at war, or engaged in some other enterprise of a dangerous nature. It is held that if she commits adultery at this time he will meet with some serious misfortune or accident. Formerly this taboo applied also to women whose husbands were away working in the towns, but it is certainly not observed today, as we shall see in the following section.

Apart from the sexual prohibitions, people with 'hot blood' must refrain from certain other activities. So far as a married couple are concerned, these additional restrictions do not affect their behaviour towards each other so much as their behaviour towards other people, but since they are derived partly from the incidents of sexual life we may refer to them briefly to round off our picture. In the first place, men and women with 'hot blood' should not visit sick people or women confined after childbirth. It is believed that breach of this injunction will cause them to 'trample' upon the patient or mother, and greatly retard recovery. Women during their periods are further prohibited from entering a cattle-kraal, or walking through a flock of sheep or goats, lest the animals abort or die. Some also will not work in the fields at this time, lest the crops become spoiled, nor will they drink fresh milk, lest the cows be disastrously affected; but these two forms of abstinence are not very common. All the restrictions just mentioned apply also to newly-pregnant women and to women who have recently miscarried, to the husbands or lovers of these women and to newly-bereaved widows and widowers. Such people have various other special observances to keep, which will be described in due course when I discuss pregnancy and widowhood respectively.

MARITAL INFIDELITY

It is already evident that the sexual relations of Kgatla husband and wife do not involve merely the universal problem of satisfactory adjustment to each other's desires. The customary restrictions we have just discussed, based as they are upon locally-accepted ideas of disease or other misfortune caused by wrongful indulgence in sex, enter very prominently into the life of every married couple, and the conflicts that may arise from their neglect are obvious even from the few actual episodes I have cited. There remains still another powerful source of domestic discord founded upon the sexual relationship, and that is infidelity.

From what has already been said, it will have been gathered that adultery is fairly common, among both men and women. In theory, husband and wife should remain faithful to each other. It is a breach of marital rights if either has sexual relations with any other person. This does not apply, of course, to men who are polygamists, or who cohabit with the widow of a close relative to raise up seed to the deceased. But any man sleeping with a woman other than his wife or wives, except for the reason just given, is held to be violating his matrimonial obligations, and so is a woman sleeping with anybody but her husband.

Like so many other peoples, however, the Kgatla do not take a husband's infidelity as seriously as a wife's. They hold that a man is naturally inclined to be promiscuous. 'A man, like a bull, cannot be confined to a kraal,' says their proverb. The institutions of polygamy, the levirate and the sororate, gave explicit recognition to this principle by allowing a man access to a number of women, even if he was not married to them all. Today, when owing to the influence of Western civilization these institutions have suffered decay, there is less justification for promiscuity, but an erring husband is nevertheless regarded with general tolerance. In Kgatla law his wife has no direct remedy against him. She cannot desert or divorce him merely because he is unfaithful, although she may do so if his behaviour is accompanied by other forms of neglect or ill-treatment. In marriages contracted under the European civil law, however, a husband's infidelity is accepted as a ground for divorce. But I know of only one instance where it was used for this purpose, and here the issue was aggravated by the fact that he had driven away his wife and put another woman into her hut.

The reasons men commonly give for their infidelity include some interesting examples of rationalization. Occasionally a man will admit frankly that he is tired of his wife, or is attracted by some one else, or is unable to be satisfied by one woman alone. He will say that at certain times, as we have already noted, he is expected to refrain from sleeping with his wife, and, since he cannot curb his sexual desires, he must seek relief somewhere else. More often than not, however, he will seek to justify himself by pleading that the decay of polygamy, and the prolonged absence of many men in the towns, have led to a preponderance of dissatisfied women at home, and that he is doing them and the tribe a service by consorting with them. There is a widespread impression that fewer children are being born nowadays than before, so that men distributing their favours among several women are actually regarded with approval by some. 'They are the bulls of the tribe,' said an enthusiastic informant. Even respectable members of the Church, who unknown to their missionary have one or more concubines as well as a wife, have advanced this argument to me as an excuse for their 'immoral' conduct. 'There are these women,' they say, 'young and ripe for bearing children, but the laws of the white people will not allow us to have more than one wife. Why should their fertility go to waste, when they can be used to increase the numbers of the tribe?'

'As for adultery,' said Natale, 'I have many concubines. There is Refeng, and there is Moagi, and several others as well. I live with the first two as if I were married to them, but the others I sleep with for only one night, and then abandon. And when I go to these other women, my junior wife gets jealous and complains, but the older one does not. And when the junior wife gets angry with me, I buy beer and bring it to her, and we drink together, and when she has drunk it she becomes reconciled to me again. And in any case I once found her also sleeping with a lover, I caught him in her blankets, but I forgave him; this was at the time when the Prince of Wales visited us.' (1925.)

Sometimes a man's mistress is a woman whose husband is still living. The affair is then generally kept as secret as possible, meetings being confined mainly to the occasions when the husband is away. Many men, however, 'use' the older unmarried girls, or widows who have not married again. Often enough, when this is so, the man openly and regularly visits the woman at her home, and her people acquiesce in the relationship, so long as he feeds and clothes her and the children he has by her, ploughs for her, and helps her in other ways. She is, in effect, a true concubine. If she is unmarried, it seldom happens that he is called upon to pay the usual damages if he makes her pregnant. But, so long as nothing has been done to convert the relationship into marriage, neither party is under any legally enforceable obligation to the other. The man is not bound to support the woman, nor she to remain with him, and no right of action lies if

one abandons the other. Occasionally he may afterwards take her
as an additional wife, but he is generally reluctant to do so. His
own wife may also object, and threaten to leave him if he marries
her rival.

One important motive for concubinage is the barrenness of a
wife. In the old days this was usually circumvented by the sororate, whereby she would get her parents to provide her husband
with her younger sister, or some other close relative, to bear children in her place. If the parents refused or were unable to provide such a substitute, the husband could send his wife back if he
wished, and demand the return of his *bogadi*. Today the sororate, in this form, seems to have died out almost completely, and
it is in any case forbidden to Church members. Informants maintained that it is still sometimes practised, but could give no recent
instances in proof. What usually happens instead is that the husband either takes an additional wife, or, more frequently, resorts
to a concubine. Legally the children he begets by the latter belong
to her own people, and not to him. But by contributing to their
support while they are still young, he can sometimes gain custody of them without actually marrying their mother. Should his
wife object to his taking a concubine, and this sometimes
happens, he will threaten her with divorce, and may thus succeed
in stifling her opposition.

Wives vary greatly in their attitude towards an unfaithful husband. Often enough a woman is fairly complaisant, or at least
resigned, so long as her husband continues to look after her decently, sleeps with her regularly, and does not obviously favour
his concubine. One of my informants said that at his wedding-
feast he was greatly attracted by two of the girls present, and
asked his wife if he might take them as mistresses. Her reply was
in his eyes eminently reasonable. 'Well,' she said, 'you are still a
young man, so I suppose that you need more than one woman,
but don't make your affairs too public, and remember that we
also must have a baby of our own.' This attitude is by no means
unusual. Accustomed to a tradition of polygamy, women regard
it as natural for a man to distribute his attentions, and many a
wife, provided that her husband does not talk of marrying again,

and does not humiliate her by openly flaunting his infidelity, judiciously refrains from making it a bone of contention, except when she is thoroughly angry with him over something else as well.

But the wife is not always so accommodating. She may object to being neglected for some one else, she may fear the possibility of her husband's infection by one of the 'blood' diseases, she may resent the indignity of not being regarded as sufficiently attractive in herself, and she may simply and furiously be jealous. As one embittered woman said, whose husband had recently been carrying on with a younger and more prepossessing rival: 'If a husband would only listen to his wife when she tells him to stop going out, there would be peace in the home. When our men keep going out at night, we feel very jealous, because they make these other women know the insides of our homes and all the secrets of our lives. We wonder what it is that a husband really wants, for his wife's body is there every day for him to use.'

Where the wife is, from the husband's point of view, so unreasonable, he tries to conceal his intrigue as much as possible. But women are soon able to discover that they are being deceived. It may be that the husband frequently comes home late at night, and is then either unwilling or unable to copulate with his wife, a fact that always makes her suspect he has just come from a rival. Sometimes, again, she finds one of her female neighbours suddenly trying to become very friendly, a move that instead of diverting suspicion usually arouses it. Or, as is almost inevitable, the village gossips will soon enough enlighten her. Then there is a violent quarrel, often ending up with an open fight. If the husband stays out night after night, the wife will at last complain to his parents. They take him to task, telling him that they did not get her merely to come and live in his house, while he goes about giving children to other women. Sometimes their reprimand achieves its object for the time being, but usually it is not long before the husband resumes his former ways. If really jealous and angry, the wife may then deliberately seek out and fight with her rival. Village life is often enough enlivened by squabbles of this kind, in which obscene abuse is freely bandied about, and actual scratching and biting may occur, with possibly an ultimate sequel in court. A less violent woman will resort instead to magic, getting medicines from a doctor either to bewitch her rival or to keep her husband by her side. To counteract this, the doctors also have medicines by means of which an erring husband can not only pacify his wife but even make her friendly with and reconciled to his concubine. Polygamists with relatively peaceful homes are almost invariably credited with possessing medicines of this kind, and Natale, the doctor with two wives, told me that his own medicines were so effective that whenever he scolded one wife the other always took her part.

Sometimes the wife leaves her husband and goes back to her parents. When he comes to fetch her, the whole matter is discussed by the family council, usually with the result that he is severely blamed for his conduct, and told that he can get his wife back only if he promises to reform. It is seldom that she then refuses to return to him, although this may happen if she has been sufficiently annoyed. I shall discuss more fully in a later chapter the procedure on such occasions.

A wife's principal defence, however, and one to which many resort, is to get a lover of her own if her husband persists in associating with his concubine. Opportunities for such intrigues are common enough, for the husband is often away at his cattle-post or may be working in town, so that there is comparatively little risk of discovery. A husband's infidelity, however, is not the only reason for his wife's following his example, although it is the one most frequently advanced by women. Sometimes the wife may have been forced into an unwelcome marriage, and to spite her husband she will deliberately continue her affairs with the man or men she previously favoured. This, as we have seen, is one of the principal reasons why men dislike marrying women who have already borne children to some one else. And, of course, it happens often enough that after marriage a woman may meet some one more attractive than her husband, and yield to his welcome advances. Then, also, it is by no means uncommon for a woman coming home drunk from a feast to allow herself to be seduced by the man escorting her. For this reason a husband usually insists that his wife should always go to bed before him, so that she may have less opportunity of deceiving him.

Many a husband, although fully aware of his wife's infidelity, prefers to ignore it, especially if he too is unfaithful, or if the marriage is barren. In the old days it was indeed a recognized custom for an impotent man to allow some trusted companion secret access to his wife, in the hope of procuring a child in this way. Any children born of such a union were always considered the legitimate offspring of the husband, because of the rights he obtained by giving *bogadi* for the wife. This custom is still practised at times, although, as the matter is kept as secret as possible, it is difficult to say to what extent. Usually the wife herself takes the initiative in finding a lover who will enable her to bear. The husband does not as a rule interfere or protest very strongly, unless he dislikes the man she has chosen. Even if he does object, the tribal courts may refuse to give him satisfaction. It is considered the duty of every husband to see that his wife should become a mother, and if he is himself not able to impregnate her, or neglects her for some one else, she will not be blamed for resorting to other men.

Within relatively recent times, too, adultery on the part of women seems to have increased considerably as a result of labour migration. Often enough a husband stays away so long from the Reserve that his wife can no longer control her sexual desires, and begins to look round for a lover. If one may judge by village gossip, the number of women unfaithful to their absentee husbands is very great indeed. Many a man has come back to find that his wife has during his absence given birth to one or more children of whom he is not the father. Legally, the children are his, and usually he takes no action in the matter, recognizing that he is to blame for having been away for so long. In the few cases where he has brought a charge of adultery against the wife's lover, the court has generally found him in the wrong for having stayed away until she could no longer resist temptation. It is maintained that her procreative power should not be allowed to lie dormant, and that she is acting rightly in cohabiting with men by whom she can bear. All this, nevertheless, tends to make family life very unpleasant after the return of the husband, especially if he is inclined to be jealous.

Where a husband objects to his wife's infidelity, he usually punishes her with a sound thrashing. If she is persistently unfaithful, he may send her away and so divorce her, but he is apparently not entitled to do so for a casual affair. He prefers instead to annoy and humiliate her in other ways, like neglecting her for a concubine, although if he is fond of her he will soon forgive her if she mends her ways. On the other hand, he is also entitled to take legal action against her lover, a right that she cannot exercise against his concubine. Normally he claims damages in cattle, but if he catches the couple red-handed he may take the law into his own hands and thrash the adulterer severely. 'A bug must be squashed against the wall,' goes the relevant proverb. Formerly, it is said, he could even kill his betrayer, but no instance was quoted where this had actually occurred.

Most cases of adultery are in fact settled out of court, for the wife's lover knows that he is in the wrong, and will pay what the husband demands. The number of cattle claimed usually varies from four to eight, and it is only if the lover considers it excessive, and refuses to pay, that the matter will be tried before the ward-head or chief. Frequently a smaller amount is accepted, especially if the two men belong to the same ward. The husband may even overlook the offence altogether for the first time if the adulterer is a close friend or relative, but if it is repeated he will take action, and can then claim comparatively heavy damages.

The husband has no case unless he catches the couple red-handed, or can produce other reliable evidence. Mere hearsay or suspicion is not enough. What usually happens, when he is not absolutely certain of his wife's infidelity, is that he lays a trap for her and her lover. He tells her that he is going to his cattle-post, and asks her to give him food for the road. But instead of making the trip, he spends the day out in the veld, and then returns home late at night to see if he can surprise the guilty couple. In one instance, in 1934, which because it involved a prominent ward-head caused a good deal of mirth and joyful gossip, the lover, caught by the unexpected return of the husband, escaped through the window of the hut and ran home completely naked. The next day he sent his own wife with four pounds to pacify the injured husband and secure the return of his clothes.

It is also good evidence if the wife becomes pregnant in circumstances ruling out the possibility that her husband is responsible. He will then force her to reveal the name of her lover, and takes whatever action he thinks suitable. A pregnant or newly-confined woman will sometimes voluntarily confess to adultery, for fear of the 'sickness' she may inflict upon her husband if he cohabits with her, since the 'blood' in her body is not his. The husband must then stay away from her until the rite of 'joining their bloods' has been performed. The doctor called for the purpose cuts them both on the pubis. He wets his finger with the blood flowing from the husband, dips it into his magical paste, and rubs it into the cuts made on the wife. He then repeats the rite by transferring the wife's blood in the same way to the husband. After this, the couple may sleep together in safety. Many women, however, fail to confess in time for the rite to be performed, with the result, according to local opinion, that husbands often suffer sickness as well as other unhappiness through being deceived.

If we now review generally the sexual relationship between husband and wife, it is, I think, evident that there is a good deal of maladjustment, to which labour migration has obviously contributed greatly. If I appear to have stressed the unhappy marriages too much, and to have paid little attention to the happy ones that do also exist, it is because the latter, so far as I could judge, are comparatively rare. Few of the women I got to know well enough to talk to on this topic pretended to be living harmoniously with their husbands. Almost always there were complaints of sexual ill-treatment or of infidelity, and the characteristic female attitude was one of resignation rather than of happiness. Newly-married couples are often very much in love with each other, and the wives will speak most affectionately of their husbands, but after a few years little of this remains except in isolated instances. Many women grow reconciled and manage to lead a tolerable existence with husbands who are not unduly inconsiderate, others find some sort of relief by being unfaithful themselves and some are acutely miserable. The men are not always to blame, for the wanton wife is common enough, and the jealous shrew is by no means unknown. Many men, too, are by Kgatla standards fairly considerate, and live peacefully enough with their wives. But the polygamous ideal still prevails and the virtually enforced monogamy of today has not been accompanied by the true companionship upon which a successful union should rest. To this point I shall return when discussing the stability of marriage.

8. Procreation and Childbirth

KGATLA THEORIES OF PROCREATION

The Kgatla would readily agree with the Anglican Prayer Book that marriage is 'ordained for the procreation of children'. To them it is inconceivable that a married couple should for economic or personal reasons deliberately seek to restrict the number of its offspring, or even refrain from having any at all. They insist rather that a wife should bear her husband as many children as she can, provided only that she does not become pregnant until she has weaned the child already at her breast. A woman with a large family is honoured as highly as she would be in any modern Fascist state, while a childless wife is an object of pity, often tempered with scorn.

With the birth of their first child, married people acquire a new dignity. The husband has proved his manhood and become the founder of a line that will perpetuate his name and memory; the wife has fulfilled her supreme destiny, and freed herself from the most humiliating reproach that can be made against a married woman. To their respective relatives, too, the birth is a matter for rejoicing and congratulation. The husband's people are pleased that the woman they 'sought' for him, and for whom they gave or will give *bogadi*, has rewarded their choice by helping 'to build up their village'; her own people are happy that she has saved them from shame, and that her married life will henceforth be more securely founded. The enhanced status of the couple is reflected in change of name. They now become generally known by the child's name, preceded by the affix *rra* (father) or *mma* (mother), as the case may be. Thus, if the child is named Molefi, its father will be called Rra-Molefi (father of Molefi), and its mother Mma-Molefi (mother of Molefi). As more children are born, the parents gain in prestige. Children mean additional help in labour, and increased self-sufficiency in production; they ensure that their parents will have security in old age; when they marry they extend the range of people with whom their family is allied, and so consolidate its standing in the tribe. 'The cunning of the *phala* antelope comes from its young,' says the proverb, i.e. a person with children cannot be lightly molested, for he is always sure of protection and support.

The desire for children is reflected in the various customs already described, whose avowed purpose it is to overcome the barrenness of a marriage. An impotent husband, for instance, may place his wife at the disposal of some intimate friend or relative, while if the fault lies with her she may procure another woman from her family to bear him children instead. Both customs are considered immoral by the Church, and are forbidden to its members. But that even Christians still approve of them was shown by the reaction to the code of Church laws published in 1933 in *Lesedi la Sechaba,* the local Mission journal. It was laid down there, *inter alia,* that no wife, even if barren, might get another woman to bear children in her place. This drew a protest from two of the leading young men of the tribe, both members of the royal family. Writing in a later issue of the same journal, they say of a newly-married couple:

> How cruel it will be to them if God, after bringing them together, denies them children, and yet, because of this Church law, they cannot plan to comfort themselves. The custom of the wife's introducing a substitute for herself is our custom, and there can be no objection to it if carried out properly. She does it owing to the great love she bears her husband, because a child is so greatly desired that otherwise he would roam about to beget one somewhere else.

The Church attitude, nevertheless, accompanied by the general spread of other 'civilizing' influences, has led to the decay of these particular usages. Their place has been taken by increasing indulgence in adultery and concubinage, and, as we have seen, public opinion tends to be tolerant of childless people breaking their marriage vows, and actually approves of the men who consort with young widows and neglected wives. A wife's failure to bear is almost always a source of conflict with her husband, it is one of the few inducements men still have for practising polygamy, and it is among the principal reasons for the adoption of children. Moreover, as we shall see more fully below, there exist various magico-medical rites by means of which the local doctors try to cure barrenness, and to which childless couples, whether heathen or Christian, almost invariably resort. It is not merely in speech, therefore, but also in custom, that the desirability of having children is stressed.

Procreation itself is surrounded by various theories and beliefs that in turn are reflected in custom. Young children, on inquiring where a baby comes from, are usually told that its mother fetches it from a pool in the river. But, as I have already mentioned, all adults, and most of the older children, are well aware that conception is due to sexual intercourse. It is for this reason, quite apart from the question of sexual desire, that they consider it a husband's duty to cohabit regularly with his wife. Any theory denying the existence of physiological paternity seems to them utterly fantastic. They themselves hold that a child is formed in the womb by a mixture of the man's semen and the menstrual blood of the woman. Some assert that only one act of coitus can make a woman conceive, 'if her blood agrees with that of the man'. The majority, however, maintain that at least three or four successive nights of intercourse are required, so that enough semen may accumulate to blend with her 'blood'. I know of several young people who actually based their contraceptive practices on this belief, taking precautions only on the third or fourth night, with occasionally unexpected and undesired results.

The Kgatla hold that no woman can conceive unless she menstruates regularly. Her blood, they say, is needed to form the child. It accumulates steadily in the womb to form a large clot, which, unless she is pregnant, must break every month and flow out, but which, once she has conceived, is absorbed into the body of the foetus. Their association of menstruation and fertility explains the tolerance shown towards the sexual play of the younger children, which they know cannot result in pregnancy.

But once a girl begins to menstruate, her mother warns her that she is now capable of bearing a child, and must therefore be careful in her relations with boys. It is vaguely believed that menstruation is due to the growth of the breasts, but just how or why nobody was able to say. Menstruation is also linked with the changes of the moon, and is in fact euphemistically termed 'the sickness of the moon', but here again I failed to get any specific explanation.

A woman dates her pregnancy from the cessation of her menses. In the words of Manyama:

'She knows that she is pregnant when she misses her periods. If she ordinarily misses her period, it may be just because she is sick, her blood is no good; but then she will get well again. But if she has recently met a man, then she knows that she is pregnant, because she is used to having her periods regularly. As soon as she is pregnant, she tells her husband that she has failed to menstruate, and he is very pleased. But she tells nobody else, for they might bewitch her, and then she will have difficulties in labour. Her pregnancy is noticed by the other women in the third month, when her complexion becomes light in appearance, her breasts begin to swell, and her hips expand; and in the fourth month it is obvious to everybody, because her belly is becoming large. And when eight new moons have passed since she last menstruated, she knows that her time is at hand.'

Few Kgatla have any clear idea of what happens in the womb after intercourse. The men generally say that knowledge of this kind is confined to the women, or they may hazard wild theories of embryology based partly upon what they have gleaned from their wives, and partly upon guesses of their own. Some of the older women, however, whose experience in dealing with cases of miscarriage had given them opportunities of inspecting the foetus at various stages of its development, were able to give me information showing that on the whole they were fairly accurate observers. During the first two or three months of pregnancy, they said, 'the womb shakes about; it mixes up the bloods of the man and the woman, so that they become thick, like cheese, and form the seed'. 'If two months pass without your menstruating after you have slept with your husband,' Mmampotele told me, 'you know that his blood is fighting with yours in your intestines to make the child; you feel your stomach not sore but palpitating, and when the third month comes you feel, near your navel, pulse-beats just like a heart.' It is during this early period of gestation, 'when the bloods are fighting each other', that, as we have seen, the woman's blood is particularly 'hot'. By the fourth month the 'bloods' have coalesced completely, and the foetus has taken form. At this stage it is said to look like a lizard, with nothing to indicate that it is human. In the fifth month it acquires human characteristics, and is complete with head, body, arms and legs, but lacks hands, feet and eyes and other facial features. These appear in the sixth month, when it is fully formed. Thereafter it grows steadily in size. 'In the seventh month you feel the child moving from one side to the other; in the eighth month he begins to stand on his legs and stretch himself, and then sleeps again; and in the ninth month he plays about in your stomach, waiting to be born.'

Both parents contribute to the build of the child. Its blood, say the people, comes from its mother, 'because before a woman conceives she menstruates regularly, and this is nothing but blood, while after she is pregnant her menses stop, and the child starts to be moulded, so it is obvious that she gives her blood to the child'. The father, on the other hand, contributes the flesh, 'because of the heavy lumps [of semen] that he puts into the mother'. As a result, children are usually expected to resemble their father, 'unless the blood of the woman has been stronger than that of the man, then the child will look like its mother'. Should a man deny paternity, say in a seduction case, the people sometimes wait until the child is several months old, and then compare its appearance with his. They believe that if he is really its father it will have his eyes, ears and nose, and the same markings on the palms of the hand, as well as any special physical peculiarities he may possess.

All married people wish to have sons to whom they can leave their property, but they prefer both sons and daughters in roughly equal numbers. There is no well-defined theory of sex determination. Some doctors profess to have medicines enabling them to influence the sex of an unborn child. These medicines generally consist of powdered roots, to be mixed with the food the woman eats before she conceives again after the birth of a child. They are said 'to change her womb', so that if all her children have hitherto been sons, she will in future bear daughters only, and vice versa. Many people are sceptical of this treatment, and even some doctors deny that medicines can help, 'for', as Rapedi said, 'it is God who decides whether a child shall be a boy or girl, and how can we alter his decision?' The fact remains, nevertheless, that parents anxious to have children of a particular sex do resort to the doctors for aid, and sometimes claim to have received it. Chief Isang himself, for instance, told me that in the case of his own family he had found the services of a doctor named Rantshwarang invaluable and unfailing in ensuring the birth of sons. The art of the doctors, however, is more generally employed to cure barrenness and to prevent the recurrence of a miscarriage; and here, as we shall see, the treatments pursued by them are on the whole consistent with the theory of procreation outlined above.

THE SIZE OF THE FAMILY

No official records are kept of births, marriages and deaths. Nor does the Administration make any other attempt to collect vital statistics, except when the decennial census is held. The information then obtained, however, not only is unreliable, owing to the crude methods employed to secure it, but also throws no light at all upon the marital condition of people and the number of children per family. It is therefore impossible to discuss these particular topics for the tribe as a whole. The only data I have bearing upon them was obtained by collecting genealogies and by questioning a number of people personally. Information of this sort, while useful enough as a rough guide, cannot on the other hand be regarded as thoroughly reliable, owing to the strong probability that, in some cases at least, it was not always accurate or complete. For this reason I shall not try here to analyse it in detail, but propose merely to direct attention to what appear to be its outstanding indications.

In all I obtained information about 439 families (out of an estimated total of 3,500 in the tribe). Four hundred and seventeen were monogamous, in twenty-one the husband was a bigamist, and in one he had three wives. The monogamous families included thirty-six in which there were widows or widowers, either remarried or not; but owing to the smallness of the numbers involved I have not here separated these special cases from the rest, especially since widows, if they do not marry again, frequently take lovers and so continue to reproduce. In the group as a whole, the average number of children born alive per family was 3.9; in the monogamous families alone, it was 3.6; in the bigamous families, it was 8.7; while the man with three wives was the father of twenty-two children. The group, however, is made up partly of women who have reached the menopause, and partly of women potentially capable of still bearing children. If we confine ourselves to the former class, we find that the average number of children born to each of the 184 women in it was 5.4. The following table shows the distribution of live births per 100 women for the monogamous group as a whole (the others are too small to be of much service), and for the old women of this group. (For convenience I have adopted the following rough classification: 'small' family, one to three children; 'medium' family, four to six children; 'large' family, seven children or more.)

VARIATIONS IN SIZE OF FAMILY

(a) *Live Births per 100 Families*

Kind of Family	Whole Group	Old Women
Childless	10	4
Small	44	19
Medium	31	36
Large	15	41

Of the 1,699 children (860 male, 839 female) collectively produced by the 439 families, 1,229 (592 male, 637 female), i.e. 72 per cent, were still alive at the time of my inquiries. This gives an average of 2.8 per family for the group as a whole, 2.9 for the monogamous families alone, and 6.4 for the bigamous families, while the number surviving to the man with three wives was 11. The average number of children surviving per woman in the group past child-bearing age was 3.7. The percentage distribution of living children per family was as follows:

VARIATIONS IN SIZE OF FAMILY
(b) *Children surviving per 100 Families*

Kind of Family	Whole Group	Old Women
Childless	14	7
Small	55	47
Medium	27	39
Large	4	7

The following table, finally, shows the number of children dying per family:

DISTRIBUTION OF DEATHS PER 100 FAMILIES

Number of Children dead	0	1	2	3	4	5	6
Whole Group	42	29	16	9	3	1	1
Old Women	32	28	22	12	5	1	1

For our immediate purpose, we may conclude from these figures that the average monogamous family will produce four children, of whom three will survive to maturity. Roughly three families out of five will lose one or more children, and roughly fourteen families out of every hundred will lose three children or more. By the time a wife has grown too old to bear any more, she will on the average have produced between five and six children, of whom perhaps three or four may still be living. Roughly two women out of three will have lost one or more children each, and roughly nineteen out of every hundred will have lost three children or more.

In considering these figures, it must be noted firstly that the interval between one birth and another is normally longer than it need actually be. This is due to the rule that a woman should not become pregnant again until she has weaned the child she is suckling, which seldom happens until it is already able to walk about steadily. Since few of the Kgatla yet reckon their ages in terms of calendar years, I was unable to get much accurate information on the spacing of births. I found, however, that in 22 families, each of three children or more whose ages were definitely known, 7 of the 125 children were born the year after their predecessors, 40 two years afterwards, 36 three years afterwards, 14 four years afterwards, 3 five years afterwards and 1 seven years afterwards.

The lengthy absence of a husband in European labour centres does of course now contribute to the spacing of births, assuming that his wife remains chaste while he is away. The original and more general explanation, however, is to be found in the practice of contraception. A husband may resume sexual relations with his wife once she emerges from her confinement a month or so after the birth of her child, but as soon as she starts menstruating again they must take precautions to prevent her from conceiving. It is believed that if she does become pregnant the child she is suckling will suffer because it must now be weaned before its time. 'It cannot suck the milk of the child in the womb, so it will be given lots of porridge, and its stomach will swell, but it will remain very lean, and sometimes it becomes deaf, or stupid, or does not grow properly.' A woman who normally starts menstruating again soon after parturition may therefore actually try to delay the reappearance of her menses. She goes to another, who does not menstruate until long after giving birth, and is smeared by her with fresh cowdung, in the form of a cross, on the back and on the abdomen. This, it is thought, will communicate to her the same fortunate immunity as is possessed by her friend, and will therefore prevent her from conceiving too soon.

The commonest method of contraception locally practised is *coitus interruptus*, spoken of as 'spilling the blood outside'. It is widely employed not only by married people, but also by unmarried lovers. A very few educated men have in their experience outside the Reserve learned the use of condoms, which they obtain in the towns or through a local trader. They regard this method as more reliable than *coitus interruptus,* but one youth remarked that girls are not always keen on its use, fearing that the condom might break in the vagina and be carried with the semen into the womb.

Apart from these two methods, where the responsibility rests with the man, there are measures that a woman herself may take to prevent conception, and about which she is told when getting married. When, for instance, she feels her husband or lover 'pushing more rapidly', and so realizes that he is about to ejaculate, she may move her hips slightly so that the penis slips out of the vagina and the semen is ejected on to her thighs, or she may turn over quickly on to her side and push the man off. 'But if you do this,' a young wife remarked, 'your husband usually quarrels with you, and says, "Why do you stop me just when I am enjoying it?" ' Some women turn over on to their bellies immediately after coitus, or go outside to urinate, hoping to get rid of the semen in this way. Others drink medicines instead, the commonest of which is prepared from the *phukutsa* shrub, a well-known purgative. Married women, however, almost all rely upon *coitus interruptus,* or, if their husband fails to practise it, upon their own methods of preventing ejaculation inside the vagina.

If in spite of such measures, or in their absence, a woman becomes pregnant, and does not wish to bear the child, she tries to induce an abortion. As far as I could learn, married women seldom resort to this, except when particularly anxious to conceal an adulterous intrigue. Unmarried girls, however, practise it fairly extensively: in a group of forty-four I found no fewer than eight who had done so. The reason sometimes is that the girl is engaged, and fears that her fiancé may break with her if he discovers her infidelity; or she may be urged on by her lover, who does not want to get into trouble for seducing her; or she may be anxious to continue passing as 'unspoiled', and so still have the opportunity of making a good marriage. Among the commonest abortifacients are ordinary writing ink, sometimes mixed with the pulverized heads of matches, and strong solutions of washing blue or of potassium permanganate. These can all be obtained from the traders. Various Native medicines, mostly purgatives, may also be employed, but they are apparently not very efficient, judging from the marked preference for European substances. One unfortunate girl, mentioned in Chapter 2, successively tried croton oil, washing blue, epsom salts, castor oil, and some local herbs and bleeding the veins of her foot, but failed to achieve her purpose.

Induced abortions are always kept as secret as possible, so that very few cases ever come to light. It is only if the girl's condition was previously obvious to all, and she suddenly recovers her normal physical appearance, that inquiry may be made into the matter. Even then the people of her ward will try to hush it up, partly through pity for her, partly for fear of the trouble that would ensue. Her action is generally condemned, however, for, as a local song says:

> To force out the womb is grievous,
> the knot of the cradle-skin is a flower

i.e. a woman always derives great happiness from carrying a child slung on her back, so that one should rather let it live, even if it is illegitimate. But when publicity cannot be avoided, and this very seldom happens, for in matters of this sort women generally stick together, the girl is reported to the chief. She is then thrashed severely, and so is her lover, if he is known. Her body is also smeared with the irritating juice of the *mogaga* bulb, a plant widely used in ritual cleansings. This is done because her 'blood' is hot, so that wherever she goes she will 'scorch' the land and keep away the rain. Similarly, if an aborted foetus is discovered lying about, all the older girls in the vicinity are summoned and their breasts are tested for milk, to see who is responsible. The culprit is then treated as already described. The tribal rain-maker is also sent to doctor the place where the foetus was found, so that the land may become 'cool' again. The foetus itself is put into a small pot and buried inside the girl's hut or in some other shady place where it will always be 'cool'.

Unwanted children may also be disposed of by infanticide.

This was formerly practised as a standard custom in regard to a child born feet first: it was smothered with manure immediately after birth, and buried in the hut, while the news would be spread abroad that it had been stillborn. It was regarded as an evil omen, which had to be done away with as soon as possible lest it bring disaster upon its parents. In such cases, of course, no action was or could be taken by the tribal authorities. Today, however, a child of this kind is usually allowed to live, much to the disgust of some old people, who attribute to its presence the evils that are now besetting the tribe.

The only other form of infanticide, practised very occasionally, is when an unmarried girl kills a child she has not been able to abort. Here again the matter is hushed up if possible. Failing this, the girl was formerly punished in the chief's court, in the same way as if she had been guilty of procuring an abortion. In one instance, which occurred not so many years ago, the girl immediately after bearing her child exposed it to the pigs. They ate its whole body except for a leg. This was found by another woman, who reported it to the ward-head and through him to the chief. The chief ordered all the young women of the locality to be gathered, and their breasts were tested for milk. The culprit was in this way discovered, but nothing more was done to her than to wash her body with *mogaga*. In another instance, however, the girl's own mother reported her to the chief, who ordered several men to thrash her with sticks until she was very badly hurt. Today, in theory, a case of infanticide should be handed over to the Administrative authorities for trial and punishment, but I do not know of any instance where this has actually been done.

The various practices described above all serve to limit the size of the family. Another factor of considerable importance in this connexion is the high rate of mortality among children. Here again we have no statistics for the tribe as a whole, and even in the genealogies I collected it was not always possible to get exact information about the age of death; in many cases, too, I failed at the time to make the necessary inquiries. The number of women for whom I can regard my data on this point as thoroughly reliable was only 80. None of them, I may add, had yet reached the menopause, so that the figures for women who had completed their child-bearing career would probably have been higher. The collective reproductive history of these 80 women may be summarized as follows: Total pregnancies, 227; natural abortions (including 2 stillbirths), 21 (i.e. 9 per cent); children born alive, 206; since dead, 57. Of the children born alive, therefore, 28 per cent failed to survive to maturity. Three out of every 100 born alive died while the mother was still confined to her hut, i.e. within a month or at the most two after birth; 8 died after emerging from the hut, but while they were still being suckled, making a total of 11 per cent who died before weaning; and 16 died in later childhood, making a total of 27 per cent who died before reaching adolescence.

According to the local medical officers, the principal causes of infantile and child mortality, excluding accidents, are dysentery, gastro-enteritis, bronchitis, broncho-pneumonia and especially syphilis, which is apparently very widespread. After heavy rainy seasons malaria may also be responsible for many deaths, but normally it is not an important factor. The high mortality after weaning is, however, said to be due mainly to malnutrition. The diet of the people, for many months on end, consists of little more than Kafir-corn porridge. The fields and cattle-posts are on the whole too far away from the villages to enable the inhabitants to obtain adequate supplies of green food and milk all the year round. While at the fields they can supplement their staple diet with melons, pumpkins, peas, beans and other vegetables, but after returning home they have little of these auxiliary foodstuffs. Thick milk is often sent during the late summer and autumn to the people in the villages or at the fields, but fresh milk can as a rule be obtained only by actual residence at the cattle-posts. Meat, again, is eaten so rarely as to be considered a luxury, people often going for weeks without ever tasting it. The result is a diet so deficient in protein and vitamin content that many Kgatla are of conspicuously poor physique, and easily susceptible to disease. This is particularly marked in the children, who are almost all very thin, with hollow backs and protuberant bellies, and compare unfavourably in weight with European children of corresponding age.

The frequency of miscarriages and natural abortions is perhaps another indication of the extent to which syphilis is affecting the people. The Kgatla themselves, however, maintain that these phenomena are due to sorcery, or to the breach of some taboo incumbent upon a pregnant woman. A woman who has miscarried and her husband are both held to have 'hot blood', and must observe many special restrictions. The aborted foetus must first be carefully buried in some shady spot, e.g. beneath the floor of a hut. A doctor is then called, who gives the woman medicine 'to clean her stomach, and to restore her blood to its former purity'. From now on, until she menstruates again, both she and her husband must refrain from sexual relations, even with each other. They may not visit any sick person or confined woman; they may not enter any hut but their own unless they first smear cow-dung on its wall, failing which they will bring sickness upon its inmates; they may not handle babies, whom they might infect with a dangerous form of rash; and they may not drink milk, lest the animals from whom it comes also abort. Moreover, they must carry a *mogaga* bulb with them wherever they go, and when they come to any crossroad or cattle-kraal for the first time since the miscarriage they must peel the bulb and throw its flesh about on the ground. Should they neglect to do so, they will 'dry up' the land, and so keep away the rain, and cause any livestock crossing their tracks to abort. When at last the woman menstruates again, she and her husband are given medicines in which to wash themselves. They are then free to resume sexual life and go about as usual. Manyama, whom I quoted in the first section of this chapter, observed all these usages when she had a miscarriage in 1931, and she was only doing what the great majority of women in a similar position are equally careful to do to prevent a recurrence.

So far I have been dealing with marriages that are fruitful. But of the 462 women (including the wives of polygamists) in our original group, forty-seven (10 per cent) had produced no chil-

dren at all.* They include some, however, who, judging from
their age, are still potential mothers. A more accurate picture of
the final result can therefore be obtained if we again confine
ourselves to the women who have reached the menopause. Of the
184 women in this particular group, only seven (4 per cent) were
childless. This shows that although the people employ contraceptive methods, they do not do so to the extent of refraining
from having any children at all. As I have already emphasized,
all married couples desire to have offspring, and if they are not
themselves fertile they resort to various devices to overcome their
misfortune.

These devices include special treatment by the doctors. If,
after a year or two of marriage, a woman shows no signs of
bearing a child, her husband usually calls in a doctor known to
specialize in such cases. The doctor first consults his divining-
bones to ascertain the cause of her barrenness. It may be that she
was bewitched by some one able to get hold of her menstrual
blood, and use it 'to reverse her womb'. The doctor treats her
accordingly, and then, 'if God wills', she will be able to bear
children like any normal woman. More generally, barrenness is
attributed to some deficiency in the 'blood' of either the woman
or her husband. Conception, it is held, can take place only if 'the
man's blood agrees with the woman's'. If it does not, her womb
will fail to hold the semen, which flows out again. Most cases of
sterility are ascribed to this rejection (*pusa*) of the semen. *Pusa*, it
is said, is most frequently due to the fact that the woman, before
marriage, led a very promiscuous life, and consequently absorbed
so many different kinds of male 'blood' that they 'spoiled' one
another and flowed out of the womb, which thus became accustomed to rejecting the semen. It may also be due to her having at
some time induced an abortion, and so 'spoiled her blood' permanently, or she may have been infected with 'hot blood'. Sometimes, again, it is due to some anatomical abnormality: the womb

* The rate among the Mpondo of South Africa is 12 per cent. M.
Hunter, *Reaction to Conquest*, Oxford, 1936, p. 146ff.

may have too small a 'mouth' to allow the semen to enter; it may be twisted, so that the passage of the semen into its interior is blocked; or it may be dotted with pimples or sores, making it unable to retain the semen.

Where the woman's sterility is due to the defective quality of her 'blood', the doctor gives her certain roots to boil every morning and evening in water, which she then drinks. 'These medicines work inside the stomach, they go into the womb and dry it up, so that the blood should not run out.' As long as she is taking the medicine, her husband should not sleep with any one else, or the treatment will fail. Sometimes the doctor 'joins the bloods' of the couple by cutting them both on the pubis, and transferring the blood from the husband's body to the wife's, and vice versa, in the manner already described. Where her sterility is due to an abnormality of the womb, he makes a more detailed diagnosis in the following manner. He asks the husband to provide a she-goat, and gives it medicines to drink. It is then made to lie down next to the woman for a short while, after which it is killed. It is skinned, and carefully cut open, and the doctor will tell from inspecting its womb what is wrong with that of the woman. He chooses accordingly the medicines he then gives her. The treatment is kept up in each case until the woman ceases to menstruate and knows thereby that she is pregnant. Most people believe that, by methods such as these, the doctors are capable of curing barrenness, but it is also said that children born as a result of their treatment are generally delicate.

The barrenness of a marriage is occasionally held to be due to a husband's impotence. The old people say that they can tell in a man's early boyhood if he will be impotent: they notice that when he urinates his penis does not stiffen, but dangles loosely, and they regard this as a sign that he will never be capable of having an erection. 'He has been formed like this by God, he has not been given strength and he can never be cured.' His only remedy is to get some one else to sleep with his wife. But impotence may also be due to the man's having become infected through intercourse with a woman suffering from 'hot blood'. In such cases the doctors generally give him medicines to drink, made as a rule from the roots of certain plants which, because of the red juice they contain, are considered particularly useful for treatments of this kind.

All these practices, as well as the others to which I have already referred, show how very anxious people are to have children. It should be mentioned in this connection that a widespread impression prevails locally that women are less fertile than formerly. This is variously ascribed to promiscuity before marriage, and to the effects of labour migration. The information I have does not enable me to judge how well founded the first alleged reason is. Many unmarried girls, of course, do become pregnant, and each of the genealogies I collected contains several instances. Of forty-four single women, old enough to be married, who figured in them, fifteen had one or more living children each, and eight others had procured abortions. But I cannot say how many lovers each of these woman had had, although, according to village gossip as well as the various instances I know of myself, few unmarried girls content themselves with only one. On the other hand, as we have seen, the continued absence at work of many young men has resulted in raising the general age of marriage. There are now many young women at home with few prospects of soon becoming wives. Even when allowance is made for those having children out of wedlock, it seems evident that most women will begin their child-bearing life at a somewhat later age than formerly. In the case of a married woman, again, the long intervals sometimes occurring between the home-comings of her husband suggest that, if she remains faithful to him, she will be less prolific than she might otherwise be, despite the practice of spacing out births. The complete absence of reliable statistics for past as well as present generations, however, makes it impossible for us to regard these deductions as more than hypothetical.

PREGNANCY AND CONFINEMENT

Now that we know what the Kgatla believe and how they behave in regard to the act of reproduction, let us follow briefly the career of a pregnant woman who intends to bear her child. As among so many other primitive peoples, she and her husband enter upon a new series of special observances. We have already noticed that while she is pregnant he should sleep with her regularly, so that his semen may continue to build up and strengthen the child in her womb. We have also seen that it is considered fatal for any one to cohabit with her at this time unless he is actually the begetter of the child she is carrying, and what effect this belief may have upon the relations between a husband and his unfaithful wife. The only other important usages associated with pregnancy are the taboos, previously described, on the woman's visiting sick people, entering a kraal containing cattle or walking through a flock of sheep and goats. All pregnant women, as far as I could learn, scrupulously observe these taboos, the first of which also applies to their husbands. The woman may as a rule eat what she likes, apart from the flesh of a cow that has died in calf; this must be avoided by all young and middle-aged women, whether pregnant or not, lest the same fate overtake them during labour. It is recognized that individual women may have peculiar likes and dislikes during pregnancy, especially in matters of food, but these are not customarily defined. Sometimes, however, a doctor will advise a woman to avoid taking strong medicines, especially purgatives, which might disturb her 'blood' and bring on a miscarriage, nor should she bind anything about her waist, lest she force the child higher into the womb and so have difficulty in labour.

The woman carries on with her usual domestic tasks as long as possible, but generally avoids the heavier forms of work during the later months of her pregnancy. If she is in the fields when her time approaches, she goes into the adjoining family hut. If she is in the village, her first confinement should always take place at her mother's home, where, it is held, she will receive better care and be more protected from sorcery. On subsequent occasions she usually remains in her own compound. Formerly her husband was expected to stay at home at this time, lest she have a difficult or protracted labour, but today he is often away working in the towns, and is therefore unable to play his part in the associated ceremonies. I could not discover that his absence is still believed to have the evil results formerly attached to it.

Birth-giving is considered so essentially a feminine process that few men know anything at all about the usages observed, and the women themselves keep the details as secret as possible. I was therefore unable to obtain as much information about them as I would have liked, but some of my female acquaintances were willing to confide in me to a certain extent. According to them, the parturient woman is usually alone in her hut during labour, but her mother, or some other elderly woman of her family, waits outside to give help if required, and keeps coming in to see that all is going well. The woman sits or reclines against the wall, with some old skirts under her hips to support her, and holds her legs apart with her hands. There is some dry cow-dung on the ground beneath her to absorb the blood and amniotic fluids. As soon as the child has been born, she calls her attendant, who, when the afterbirth has also been expelled, and not till then, ties the umbilical cord with string and cuts it with an iron blade. The baby is then washed in cold water, and laid on some blankets or skins beside its mother. The afterbirth, and the cow-dung on which the blood and fluids have fallen, are put into a small pot and buried in a hole made in the floor of the hut. This will prevent an enemy from getting hold of them and mixing them with medicines to bewitch the woman so that she cannot bear again.

If labour is difficult or protracted, as is apparently often the case, the woman is given drugs to relieve her pains and hasten the birth. A purely magical rite is generally added: after she has drunk the medicine, the cup containing it is immediately dashed to the ground, so that the child will also rush out! Sometimes the attendant lubricates the woman's vulva with fat, 'to loosen the skin and prevent it from splitting', or gently massages her abdomen, or rocks the trunk of her body to and fro. If this does not help, the aid of a doctor is sought. The more enlightened people nowadays send for the European doctor attached to the Mission, but the majority still prefer their Native practitioners. Male doctors, who are not allowed inside the hut, usually give medicines to the attendant to administer to the woman. There are some female doctors, however, specialists in this work, who are said to be experts at massaging and other forms of manipulation. 'Sometimes she puts her hand into the vagina, and keeps feeling for the place where the child is stuck, and if she finds its hands or shoulders caught presses them down, and then keeps shaking the child until it drops.' A similar treatment may be followed if the placenta delays unduly in coming away.

After the birth, if all has gone well, the mother and baby remain secluded in the hut for one or two months. The period varies according to the rank and wealth of the family, poorer people generally staying in for a shorter time than others, occasionally for as little as three weeks. This post-natal seclusion is regarded as necessary because of the weakness caused in the woman by labour and its after-effects, and is also held to give the baby time to grow stronger. During the whole period of seclusion, from the moment the birth has taken place, some long sticks, known as 'cross-poles', are laid flat in the courtyard just outside the hut. This is the conventional sign that there is a 'sick' person inside. As long as the poles lie where they are, all men, and all women with 'hot blood', are forbidden to enter the hut, lest they 'trample' on the woman or her child, and injuriously or even fatally retard their progress. Her husband, if at home, must likewise stay away from her, and during this time sleeps somewhere else.

The original attendant, or some other woman, shares the same hut at night as the mother and child, and also looks after them by day. While doing so she must refrain from sexual relations, and may not go to a funeral or any home that has recently been bereaved. The news of the birth is meanwhile conveyed to all the relatives on both sides of the family. Those living nearby come to inquire after the mother and child; the men sit outside in the courtyard, while the women, if not debarred owing to 'hot blood', enter the hut to chat with her. The women bring with them corn to feed her during her seclusion, and also either send their daughters or come themselves to help prepare the food, fetch water and wood, and do the other routine tasks to which she herself cannot now attend.

The woman while secluded lives mainly on thin porridge, tea and milk. Her husband or father, if he can afford it, kills an ox or goat to provide meat for her and her attendant. The chief or local ward-head may also send an occasional gift of meat if the family is very poor. The woman may not take any of her food with her hands, which are said to be 'dirty' from touching the baby, but must use a special spoon. So much importance is attached to this that the phrase, 'A confined woman eats with her hands,' is used to describe a time of such scarcity that when she sees food coming she grabs at it with her hands because she is so hungry from starvation! The baby is fed from the beginning on its mother's milk. It is sometimes given weak tea before the milk is available, but this is not usual. If it does not take kindly to the breast, some roots are cooked in cow's milk, which after cooling is given to it to drink. Some of the doctored milk is also smeared over the mother's breasts, to which the baby is then put. Similarly, if the woman has previously had a miscarriage, her breasts must be washed with medicine before the baby is allowed to suck. If the mother dies shortly after giving birth, the people sometimes try to raise the child on cow's milk, or if possible give it to some other relative to suckle, but more often than not their efforts are unavailing and it also dies.

The baby is generally doctored soon after birth, as a means of warding off the convulsions with which it may become afflicted 'because of sorcery'. Many people nowadays use patent medicines for this purpose, buying them specially at the store. Others rely upon the traditional procedure. This normally consists in burning certain roots, in whose smoke the baby and its mother are both made to bathe. The ashes are then ground, and some of the powder is given to the baby to eat. The rest is mixed with fat, and used as an ointment with which its ears, nostrils and fontanelles are regularly smeared. Moreover, when the new moon appears for the first time after the birth, the attendant takes the baby out into the courtyard, and, holding it in the palms of her hands, raises it towards the moon, and says: 'There is your moon.' She then takes the child back into the hut. This particular rite has no standard explanation. 'It is just our custom,' most people say, but some interpret it as a form of invocation to give the child a long life.

Soon after the presentation to the moon, occasionally even before it, but in any case invariably after the navel cord has fallen away from the child, its father is for the first time allowed to enter the hut to see it. As already mentioned, it is held that if he has been unfaithful to his wife between this moment and the time when she went into confinement, his entrance will cause the child's navel to burst, or affect the child disastrously in some other way. Even the educated Kgatla believe in this. If, however, nothing so unpleasant happens, the father should on this occasion have sexual intercourse with his wife, to mark his 'crossing the poles' and consequent release from his taboo. He is required to practise *coitus interruptus,* and must afterwards smear his semen on the child's back, in the form of a cross, in order 'to strengthen its spine'. Some informants say however that this is not necessary unless he associates with other women as well. After this he may come into the hut whenever he wishes by day, but he may not sleep there until the period of seclusion has come to an end. If he is not at home when the child is born, this rite cannot of course be performed. But his wife must then remain faithful to him until his return, for if any one else cohabits with her first the child's health or intelligence will suffer. Many women nowadays, whose husbands are away working in the towns, practise another method of 'strengthening the spine' of the child. As soon as they emerge from their seclusion, their first act is to go to the river early in the morning to fetch some mud and water, which on their return they smear on the child's back and chest in the form of a cross. I failed to inquire if this would relieve them of their obligation of fidelity.

While the woman is still secluded, her husband or some other male relative, preferably her brother or maternal uncle, slaughters a sheep or a calf, out of which he makes a cradle-skin for the child. The skin must never be made before the birth of the child, lest misfortune results. In fact, the proverb, 'A cradle-skin is not cut for a child still in the womb,' is the Kgatla equivalent for, 'Don't count your chickens before they are hatched.' The cradle-skin is used for the first time after the baby leaves the hut and begins to be carried about on its mother's back. There is no ceremony to mark the occasion.

As long as the baby remains in the hut, it has no name, but is spoken of simply as 'the child'. Just before it is due to come out, the attendant goes to its father to ask for a name, by which it will henceforth be known among his people. He in turn appeals to some older relative, usually the head of his line. The name given is often that of some senior relative of the same sex, whether living or dead, or it may commemorate some conspicuous event occurring about the time of the birth. The mother's people are similarly asked to select a name, by which the child will generally be known at their home. The children of Christian parents receive still another name when they are baptized, a month or so after the end of the seclusion period. The name in such cases is almost invariably European in form, and often enough Biblical. All these names are kept unchanged throughout the child's lifetime, and he is generally known and addressed by them until he has himself married and become a parent. He is then, as we have seen, more frequently known by the name of his first child, to which the appropriate prefix is added.

Soon after it has been named, the child is taken out of the hut. Its mother generally leaves her seclusion and resumes her normal household occupations about a week earlier. When the child at last emerges, a small feast is made, to which all the close relatives and friends are invited, especially those who have been helping the mother. This feast is termed 'manure', because it symbolizes the cleansing of the child from its baby-dirt. Wealthy people may slaughter an animal for the occasion, but the majority simply brew beer. If the birth took place at the mother's parental home, she and the child now go back to her husband's compound, where another small feast may be held. The hut in which the baby was born is next cleansed, its floor being smeared afresh, and it can then be entered freely by those hitherto excluded. The husband, if the hut is in his compound, may also start sleeping in it again and resume ordinary sexual relations with his wife.

THE NURSING PERIOD

From the time it is taken out of the hut until it is weaned, some two or three years later, a child is continuously in the care of some older female relative. At first it is looked after by its mother and grandmother, but after a few months it is also entrusted to a special nurse, generally a sister, or, failing one, some other young girl lent for the purpose by an uncle or an aunt. Most of its daily life is spent on the back of its mother or nurse, where it is fastened securely in a blanket or the cradle-skin. One commonly sees a woman fetching water, visiting the trading-store or a friend, or even threshing or working in the fields, with her baby slumbering peacefully on her back, or a group of young girls similarly encumbered playing about in the streets. At home the baby, if still tiny, may be left sleeping alone in a hut, but as it grows older it is always kept under direct observation in the courtyard, if the mother or nurse is working there. At night it sleeps in the same blankets as its mother until it has begun to walk, when it is generally given a bed of its own.

An infant is almost always treated with constant indulgence. It is never left to cry; at the first whimper its mother or nurse or some other woman will hurry to pick it up if it is lying alone, and try to comfort it by playing with it or letting it suck. People seem genuinely fond of very young children, caressing them frequently and lavishing upon them other demonstrations of affection, and taking a keen interest in their development. Whenever women come together, inquiries about the welfare of one another's babies and the usual little anecdotes of their cleverness figure prominently in the talk, and if the infants themselves are present they are openly admired and petted. Even the men, who generally take little notice of older children, unbend for the babies, and the proud father playing with his latest child is a by no means unusual sight. It is very seldom, however, that a man will carry his enthusiasm so far as to give a baby food, hush it to sleep or clean it when it is soiled.

Little attempt is made to regulate the feeding of the child. It is put to the breast whenever it cries, or when it wakes after sleeping, or when its mother feels her milk troubling her. From about the age of four or five months, it is also accustomed to other forms of food. Two or three times daily it is given liquid porridge specially prepared for it. It sits in the lap of its mother or nurse; she takes some of the porridge in her left hand, holds it close to the baby's mouth, and pushes it down with the middle finger of her right hand, until the child's stomach bulges to capacity. By the time it has cut its first teeth and begun to crawl, it is fed on ordinary porridge, and as it grows older it is given other soft food, such as wild spinach and the more tender pieces of meat, cut small so that they can easily be swallowed. Weaning therefore introduces not so much a pronounced change of diet as the child's deprivation of the comfort and pleasure it has come to associate with the breast. So marked is its dependence upon sucking as a means of gratification and refuge from trouble that one sometimes sees an old grandmother try to soothe a crying child by putting it to her long-wizened bosom.

As soon as the child begins to crawl, efforts are made to induce it to stand and walk. Its mother or nurse, or sometimes its father, holds it under the armpits or by its hands and walks backwards facing it and encouraging it to try using its legs. It is thought that without practice of this kind the child will become lazy and be unable to walk even when fairly big! Similarly, most parents try to teach their children to speak. Lesaane described the process as follows:

'Some parents teach their children by making corrupt abbreviations of real words, e.g. *tatê* for *ntatê* (father), *lobala* for *robala* (to sleep), *lôgô* for *morôgô* (wild spinach), and *nnatê* for *monate* (pleasant, nice); these are repeated over and over again by the mother or nurse, until after some time the child begins saying them to itself, and the mother will continue repeating them until they have been learned. The child sometimes learns to speak by making all sorts of sounds that may occasionally form words, like *a, a, ala, lala*; the mother or nurse will keep repeating these sounds after it, and then make a word from them. Or the mother, whenever she sees the father coming, will point to him and say, *tatê, tatê* (for *ntatê*), until the child associates the two, and will itself say *tatê* on seeing him; it will know that *tatê* means "father", that particular man, and not any one else. And if the mother sees the grandmother coming, she will point to her and say, *koko, koko* (for *nkoko*), and the child will look there; then the mother will say *koko ka o mo kee* (for *nkoko tla o mo tseye*, "grandmother, come and take it"), and when the grandmother comes, the baby will lean over from its mother's arms to be taken by her. But most mothers say that God is the one who teaches children to speak!'

Care is also taken to teach the child habits of bodily cleanliness. Infants carried on the back frequently soil the blanket or cradle-skin wrapped around them. At first the mother or nurse contents herself with cleaning the child and its covering, but as time goes on she will try to make it learn to pass water or defecate before being taken on the back. She holds it and says, *sss, sss, sss*, until it has relieved itself, and will from time to time take it down from her back and repeat the performance, until the child has learned to cry whenever the need arises. She tries in the same way to teach it not to soil its blankets when sleeping at night. Once it begins to walk, it is taught not to make a mess in the hut or courtyard, but to go outside whenever necessary, and it is shown also how to hold its little fringe-skirt or skin-flap horizontally so as not to soil its clothing. As it grows still older, if it is seen relieving itself in the courtyard, its mother will hit it with a little stick, and say, 'Go outside.' She keeps doing so until it has learned its lesson.

By the time the child is between two and three years old, it is associating more and more with its nurse and her companions, returning to its mother only when it has to be fed. Once it is able to walk fairly steadily and go on little errands in the compound, it is considered ready for weaning. The process is ably described in a text written by Sofonia, which embodies most of the essential points:

'Weaning generally takes place when the mother's milk begins to fail, or when she is pregnant again. They start by keeping the infant away from her for a longer time than formerly; for instance, she tells the children to take it and go to play far away. When they come back, she does not simply give the infant her breast, but waits for it to say "I want it." Then when it cries and wants to suck, she lets it do so; but the nurse says to it, "What are you sucking?" and spits, *nthwa*! She points to the nipple, saying, "You are sucking a worm," and snatches it away from the infant's mouth, squeezes out a little milk, and says, "A worm! Don't you see? Don't you see?" to draw the infant's attention to it. Then the infant looks at the nipple. Perhaps it continues to suck. This keeps on for some time, perhaps two weeks or so. Whenever the baby sucks, the nurse will say something like this, or she snatches it away from its mother and runs away with it. Then when it cries they give it porridge. Then the mother, after squeezing out a little milk from her breast, sprinkles snuff over her nipple; the child sucks, and finds it bitter, and its little nurse laughs at it, and says, "I told you so." She takes it up and runs away with it, and as it cries says, "Hush, my child, you must not suck any more." Next time the baby wants to suck, they tell it, "The nipple is a worm;" then it fears to suck, and just sits by its mother and cries. Or, if it still wants the mother's breast, she puts some other bitter substance there, and when it cries, after tasting that, they give it porridge and say, "Eat this." Then the baby will always fear to suck. Once the mother says, "I don't want the baby to suck any more," the little nurse tries to stop it from doing so, especially as it always interferes with her play, since whenever it cries she has to take it home to suck. So she is anxious to get it past sucking. Now the baby may still wish to suck at its mother's breast, but whenever it sees the nipple it will cry and not suck it, fearing the bitter stuff.'

Weaning, as here described, and as I have seen myself, is obviously a difficult process. To the child it means a change from the loving attention of its mother to the rougher society of its playmates, from the warm shelter of the breast to the harsh realities of a more detached existence. Many children do not take kindly to the process, and it is not uncommon to find them showing resentment of the babies who have supplanted them. To get over the immediate difficulty, such children are sometimes sent to the cattle-post for a while with an older sister, or they may be put in the home of some relation, where it is believed that they will soon forget their former attachment to their mother.

9. Parents and Children

With parenthood, men and women acquire the new responsibilities of rearing and educating the children they have produced. Their duties in this connection are specifically defined in law and custom, and public opinion is usually quick to condemn any marked dereliction, and if necessary to intervene on behalf of the children. To start with, parents must feed and clothe their offspring, preserve them from difficulties and hardships, have them doctored when sick and in general do whatever else is required to ensure their wellbeing. 'My parent is my shield and my shelter,' says the Kgatla proverb, in almost Biblical language. Parents should prepare a child for participation in tribal life, by teaching it the moral code to which it must conform, and the various occupations it will have to pursue in making a living. They pair off the children according to sex and age, make them known to their other relatives and instruct them in the corresponding kinship obligations. They teach them their proper standing in family, ward and tribe, and how to behave towards their seniors and juniors respectively. They should, if possible, send them to school, and must see that they are duly initiated into membership of the age-regiments. They must afterwards ensure that daughters find husbands reasonably soon, and must carry out the customary betrothal negotiations and collect *bogadi* to provide wives for their sons. Christian parents should have their children baptized and confirmed, see that they receive religious instruction and bring them up according to the tenets of the Church.

These duties are common to both parents, but each also has specific responsibilities of his own. The burden of looking after the children while they are young rests mainly upon the mother.

She prepares and gives them their food, sees that they are properly dressed, washes their bodies and clothes and nurses them when they are sick. Her other obligations are ideally expressed in two proverbs: 'The mother of a child is the one who seizes the knife by the blade,' i.e. if necessary she will sacrifice herself to save it from harm, and again: 'A woman's child cannot get lean or die' (from starvation), because she will always stint herself rather than see it want. Daughters in time learn to cook, mend and wash clothes, and clean out the huts, but sons until married remain dependent upon their mother or sister for these and similar domestic attentions. A mother also instructs her daughters in women's work and 'the facts of life', especially in regard to menstruation and other 'blood' diseases, and should restrain them from having illicit love-affairs. When they get married, she provides them with utensils and seed-corn to take to their new home, and afterwards visits them frequently, aids them in their major household tasks, and advises them on the problems they encounter. She attends them when they are sick or confined, and subsequently helps to bring up their babies. She tests and trains her daughters-in-law while they live in her compound, and when they and their husbands have moved out helps them in the same way as she does her own daughters. Her interest in the welfare of her children does not cease till the day of her death, for even as an old woman she continues to serve them as well as she can.

The father has comparatively little to do for his children during their early youth. In any case his personal dealings with them never involve such intimate services as are required of the mother. His duties lie rather in the spheres of household management and public life. When the children are born, he formally recognizes them as his own, by giving them a name and providing for their mother during her confinement. He sees to it that she is subsequently able to rear and feed them, by assigning to her cattle, fields and other property. If possible, he also gives his sons one or more heifers each to form the nucleus of a personal herd, and when they marry helps them to obtain the land they need for residence and cultivation. As founder and legal head of the family, he must answer for the conduct of his children, and can be held liable for their debts and misdemeanours. He is their guardian and public representative, and if they are involved in a lawsuit appears for them. He should consult with his older sons, especially in matters of property, and inform them of everything he does in connection with household affairs. His livestock and other possessions are held to be destined for them, and should not be squandered recklessly.

In the old days, the father was also expected to sacrifice periodically and pray to his dead ancestors on behalf of his whole household, especially in times of trouble or festivity. No one but the head of a family could carry out these rites, upon which the well-being of every person was held to depend; he was consequently able to control his children effectively, owing to their dependence upon him for supernatural aid and protection. Nowadays, ancestor-worship is virtually extinct, and Christianity has provided no comparable form of ritual in which the father is also household priest. Nevertheless, he is still obliged to procure supernatural aid to safeguard the fortunes of himself and his dependants. Whenever necessary, he hires a magician to doctor his whole family, his compound, his cattle or his fields, for protection against sorcery and similar evils, and for ensuring prosperity and good health. Moreover, as already mentioned, he and his wife observe various taboos in connection with pregnancy and childbirth, for the sake of their offspring as well as themselves.

A person must carry out these duties not only to his own offspring, but to any children he may have adopted. It sometimes happens that a child is sent to live with some relative, especially a maternal uncle or aunt. This is occasionally done if it is sickly or unhappy at its own home, and its parents feel that a change of scene will do it good. Usually, however, the relative concerned may have no children of his own, or children of only one sex, in which case he will be given a girl to help in the home, or a boy to look after the cattle, according to his need. Sometimes he may himself ask for the loan of such a child, but often enough parents agree beforehand that their next child will be 'born for' some particular relative, to whom it is accordingly given soon after weaning or perhaps somewhat later. In Sikwane village (1929) there were adopted children in five of the 130 households, and in Rampedi ward (1932) there was an adopted child in one household of the sixteen.

An adopted child may return to its parents after several years, but if its foster-parents have no children of their own it sometimes remains with them until married. They look after it and provide for its needs, and it is subject to their authority. Its own parents, however, must visit it from time to time, and contribute occasional gifts of food, clothes or money, towards its support. Failing this, they may have to pay one or two head of cattle as 'maintenance fees' when they ultimately reclaim it. If the child remains with its foster-parents until it is an adult, they may give it some property of its own and even arrange its marriage. An adopted son may also inherit the property, but not the official status, of his childless foster-father.

Even if relatives do not adopt a child, they are bound to take an active interest in its welfare, and to see that its parents treat it properly. As we have already noted, their homes are always open to it for food and shelter, and they have not only the right but the duty to intervene in case of conflict between it and its parents. These obligations apply to all close relatives, but especially to the maternal uncle. They provide one of the most powerful controls existing in Kgatla society over domestic relations. To a much greater extent than is common amongst Europeans, a child's kinsmen share with its parents the responsibility of bringing it up. Many of them live immediately around its home, and so are intimately aware of all that happens to it. Unless it is obviously in the wrong, they generally support it in case of ill-treatment or neglect, and if necessary take its parents severely to task. Kgatla parents differ just as much as any others in the devotion and care they give to their children, but the influence of the other relatives helps greatly to check any marked evasions of duty.

The Kgatla child is thus assured from birth of certain rights and privileges, not only from his own parents but also from his other kin, and in the last resort, as we shall see, he has the protection of the law if he is treated very unjustly at home. On the other hand, he himself has many obligations towards his parents, these obligations increasing in scope and importance as he grows older. Here again there is general agreement regarding the ways in which a child should behave, and failure to comply with them meets with immediate correction or punishment.

For the first few years after weaning children lead a fairly independent life. They seem to be remarkably unspoiled, despite the constant indulgence of their parents during infancy, and seldom pester their elders for attention. They may occasionally be sent on an errand, but are otherwise free to amuse themselves as they wish. They spend most of their time playing about in the streets and open spaces near home, usually in small groups drawn from the same neighbourhood, and with one or more nurse-girls in charge of those still too young to go about alone. Boys and girls have their distinctive games, but as often as not can be seen playing together. In the early evening they join up with the older children who have been working, and the village then becomes lively with the noise of their merriment as they romp about or play the many singing games that figure so prominently in their repertoire. At this stage of their lives they are particularly attractive. Solemn and often bashful in the presence of adults, they are delightfully cheerful and happy when by themselves; a whining or petulant child is the exception, and parents are on the whole still easy-going and tolerant.

As the child grows older, however, it comes to participate more and more in the routine work of the household. Girls, from the age of about six or seven, are made to help in fetching water, firewood, earth and ornamental clay, stamping corn, and cleaning the huts and courtyards. They start by imitating these activities in their play, and are gradually drawn into actual service under the instruction of their mothers and elder sisters. Somewhat later they begin to cook, serve the food, clean the eating utensils and help to smear the walls and floors of the compounds. But their most constant occupation is that of nurse, and one frequently sees them, at work or at play, carrying a baby strapped to the back. Soon they begin to help also in agriculture, at first by scaring away the birds that come to feed on the growing crops, and later by weeding and reaping alongside of their mothers. By the time they are adolescent they are performing most of the tasks normally done by women, and are expected more and more to lighten the burdens resting on their mother. Unless they are attending school, their daily life is one long round of work, even if carried on somewhat leisurely, and it is only in the evenings that they can relax completely.

Young boys, again, are early put to herding the small stock kept in the village, and as they grow older look after such oxen as may be at home. In the mornings they drive the animals out to graze on the surrounding veld, and remain there with them all day, bringing them back in the late afternoon to be watered and kraaled. This appears to be the only duty regularly assigned to them, apart from going on errands. Then, at the age of about ten or so, they are taken to the cattle-posts. Here, at first, they herd the small stock and calves, under the supervision of their elders. Later they are sent out with the grown cattle, do the milking, and help build the kraals, dig for water, look for stray animals and do all the other work associated with cattle management. From time to time they are also called to help their father plough, inspan and drive the wagons or sledges, cut wood for building purposes, etc. In due course they will themselves take charge of the cattle-post, their father visiting them periodically to see that all is well. Formerly they remained at the cattle-posts until called home to go through the initiation ceremonies, after which they went back again until it was time for them to marry. Today, however, they seldom stay as long as this, preferring instead to seek work abroad, and those with younger brothers to relieve them may also be withdrawn after a few years and sent to school.

Children are therefore required from early youth to help in maintaining the household, until by the time that they are adults they are themselves doing most of the work, while their parents mainly supervise. As people grow older and less active, their children become directly responsible for supporting them. In the old days, anything sons acquired by hunting or serving other people belonged to their father, who could do with it as he pleased. A father had the right to hire out his son to herd cattle for someone else, and poor people still do this sometimes as a means of procuring livestock. Nowadays, however, unmarried youths are as a rule expected to go abroad to work for the money with which to pay tax and buy clothes and other wants for themselves and their parents, and any savings they bring back should be handed to their father for disposal. Married sons should likewise help their parents plough, give them occasional presents of money, food or clothes and assist them in various other ways. Married daughters, too, must help as far as they can, particularly with labour and gifts of food or clothes.

Children should also obey and honour their parents. This is a duty on which the Kgatla lay very great stress. 'A child's parent is its god,' they say, and so children must without hesitation or question do as they are told, especially by the father. 'The child who does not hearken to the law of his father will hear that of the vultures,' says another relevant proverb, and tribal courts will usually punish an insubordinate son or daughter severely. Children should consult their parents about most private and all business affairs, and do nothing important without their approval. A son still living at home may not even dispose of his own property or enter into any agreements without his father's consent, which is also necessary before he can marry. Coupled with obedience are the duties of respect and humility. Children should fear and honour their parents, and behave towards them and in their presence with becoming modesty and deference. The most insulting language a person can use towards someone else is to refer abusively to the latter's parents. 'Your father's testicles', or 'Your mother's anus', two of the most common expletives, are considered highly offensive when used as a deliberate taunt. This often leads to a fight, or, if the aggressor is junior in age or rank, to a prosecution at court in which he may be punished by thrashing or a fine. The fourth commandment appeals very greatly to the Kgatla.

Finally, children are expected to conform to the many rules of etiquette and correct social behaviour impressed upon them at home. They are taught to respect and submit to the authority of all their elders and tribal superiors, and to greet them with the conventional terms of politeness; to distinguish between their different classes of relatives and to behave towards each in the suitable manner; to be sympathetic and generous with their companions, and to treat their juniors with consideration; to take a pride in personal appearance and bodily cleanliness; and to refrain from greediness, helping themselves to food without permission or begging it from neighbours, swearing, telling lies, interrupting older people, stealing or being cheeky. A girl is brought up to entertain visitors politely, sit modestly so as to avoid exposing herself indecently, refrain from visiting young men in their homes, strictly observe the taboos relating to menstruation, and be temperate in her love-affairs or preferably have none at all. A boy is brought up to wait respectfully upon the men of his ward and to help them willingly whenever he can, to conduct his love-affairs with discretion and not pester the girls unduly, and above all to know his proper standing in the tribe and to give honour to whom it is due. Children living up to these standards are spoken of with approval as 'well-mannered', while those falling short are said to be 'disobedient', and are continually held up as models of reproach to the rest. Here again the child is duty-bound to his parents. By conforming to the general code of behaviour he gains them esteem, or at least saves them from shame and disgrace, and he should at any rate try to avoid doing whatever might injure their standing in the community. Kgatla gossips find great pleasure in pointing the finger of scorn at respectable parents whose daughters have become pregnant though unmarried, or whose sons have been publicly thrashed for insulting behaviour.

TRAINING THE YOUNG

The conduct demanded from a child is impressed upon it in the household of its parents, in its relations with other people, especially its kinsmen, and in the company of its coevals. But its training is primarily the duty of its parents, and parents are often judged by the conduct of their children. 'What is a habit comes from the beginning,' says the proverb, i.e. a child's behaviour originates from its parents, either from what it sees them doing or from what they teach it. And just as some parents are well-mannered, and others ill-bred, so will the conduct of their children vary. But, recognizing that children may turn out badly however good the parents are, they also console themselves by reflecting that 'A good milch cow does not necessarily reproduce its own kind.'

In their early years children are more directly under the control of their mother. They are always at home with her, and so become more attached to her; she gives them their food, helps them in their little troubles and comforts them in their distress, and in general keeps a close watch over them. On the other hand, most scoldings and whippings inevitably come from her at this stage, with the result that she may inspire more fear than love. The father is often away, so that his authority is less continuously felt. Sometimes he is almost a stranger to them, and they seem to fear and avoid him, because they are not accustomed to him. I have seen little children cry and even swear when their father tried to pick them up and play with them, and when they want food, or are in trouble, it is almost always to their mother that they run. Occasionally, however, a child becomes really fond of its father, who is usually more indulgent at this stage than is its mother, and if, as sometimes happens, she is harsh with it and tends to beat it frequently, it will immediately run to him for consolation. Quarrels between husband and wife over the treatment of children are by no means uncommon, and a child is generally quick to learn who is its champion, and to adapt its behaviour accordingly.

As the children grow older and begin to work, there develops a differentiation of authority, best summarized in the saying: 'A boy takes his law from the council-place' (i.e. from his father), 'a girl takes her law from the compound' (i.e. from her mother). Girls are always at home with their mother until they are married. They work together with her, and most of their domestic education comes from her. They are generally on better terms with her than with their father, and she is often their guide and confidante in matters of love. Boys after they go to the cattle-post are freed to a considerable extent from the control of their mother. Their work now brings them into much closer association with their father, whom they come to know more intimately and to appreciate. They learn from him the behaviour expected of men, and must always be ready to please him. They are apt at this stage to be rather scornful of their mother, and when at home seldom show her due respect or obedience, except when the father is about. On the other hand, they still depend upon her for food, care of their clothing and similar domestic attentions. Moreover, they need not be as formal and restrained with her as with their father. Adolescent boys usually find their mother the more sympathetic and indulgent parent, and she is often enough the medium through whom they convey requests to their father. But she seldom inspires the same fear and respect as he does, especially as she too is obviously in a position of dependence upon him.

The domestic training in conduct and character is not carried out in any set manner, but through exhortation or reprimand, as well as by chastisement, as the occasion arises. Mistakes are corrected, ignorance is dispelled, good behaviour is applauded and insolence or disobedience are immediately followed by punishment. This generally consists of a scolding or whipping. Small children are slapped with the bare hands or lightly beaten on the buttocks with a wooden switch or reed broom. Adolescent girls are generally beaten with switches on the body or shoulders. Adolescent boys are made to lie face downwards at full length, and are whipped on the bare back with a cane. The Kgatla say that thrashing makes a child wise, and helps it to remember what it has been taught. Some people are ruthless in their infliction of punishment, and beat their children mercilessly. I know of cases in which a particularly disobedient child was taken into a hut and thrashed simultaneously by its parents and other relatives until it was badly hurt. But Kgatla do not as a rule believe excessively in the power of the rod. 'A growing child is like a little dog,' they say, and even although its behaviour may be annoying one must exercise patience and forbearance.

The right to punish children formerly extended also to the

community in general. Any man or woman insulted or otherwise annoyed by a child was entitled to beat it on the spot. Nowadays this is still sometimes done, but parents are apt to resent it strongly, and it is more usual for the offended adult to complain to them, so that they may themselves punish the child. But if a boy is caught stealing food from a field, or allowing his cattle to damage standing crops, the owner has the right to thrash him at once, and seldom hesitates to do so.

The authority of parents was in the old days greatly strengthened by the belief in the power of the curse. If a child shamefully and persistently neglected his father, or indeed any senior relative, the latter would deliberately invoke some evil upon him, and it was firmly believed that the curse would take effect. The case is often quoted of Rakanyane, who, when his father became old and feeble, took charge of the family cattle, and refused to feed or clothe his parents decently. The old man became so disgusted by this treatment that at last he said to his son, 'The day I die I shall drag you after me into the grave, so that my cattle will be inherited not by you, but by your children.' And within a month of his father's death Rakanyane also died suddenly!

Even the mere anger of the offended person was thought to be supernaturally potent. If some one fell ill soon after a family quarrel, the diviner would often attribute the illness to the anger of a senior relative. This illness, known as *dikgaba,* was believed to have been sent by the ancestral spirits as a punishment for the breach of respect to one's elders. It could not be cured until the anger of the offended person had been appeased. He would then wash the patient with certain medicines, saying at the same time, 'If it was I who caused the illness, may he recover.' Even at the present time the belief in *dikgaba* is still very strong, and a child refusing to go on an errand is often warned: 'If you refuse to obey when old people send you, they will afflict you with *dikgaba.*' Many instances are cited of disobedient children having been punished in this way. Miscarriages by pregnant women are often attributed to *dikgaba* sent by a disgruntled relative, and indeed any serious misfortune may be so interpreted by the diviners, who know only too well that strained family relationships are sufficiently common to give credibility to their diagnosis.

Formerly the period of adolescence ended in elaborate rites, when the children, each sex by itself, were initiated into the ranks of adults by being organized into an age-regiment. These initiation ceremonies, held at irregular intervals several years apart, were among the most important occasions in Kgatla life. Through them a child was removed from the sole control of his parents, and made to assume responsibilities towards the chief and the tribe that previously did not apply to him. They included a systematic course of instruction, concentrated but given in particularly awe-inspiring circumstances, in the behaviour henceforth expected from the initiates, whom they also subjected to a severe routine considered by old people to have been a very efficient form of training in discipline and self-control. The details of the ceremonies were kept hidden from non-initiates, and although they have long been abandoned full information about them is still very difficult to obtain. 'We shall die with puffed cheeks,' the old people say when questioned, i.e. we would die rather than open our mouths.

As far as I could learn, the essential features of the boys' ceremony were as follows. All the eligible boys round about the age of twenty, led by a son or brother of the chief, were initiated simultaneously in a group. They were secluded out in the veld, for three months or so, in a camp specially built for the occasion. On getting there, they were first circumcised in descending order of precedence by rank. Once their wounds had healed, they were taken out early every morning to the nearest pool to bathe in the cold water. On their return, they were gathered round the central tree of the camp, and taught tribal laws and songs by the old men. Meanwhile the 'shepherds' (the young men of the preceding age-regiment) went to fetch and cook the food that the boys' mothers had to bring every day to a special rendezvous. After eating, the boys were taken by their 'shepherds' out into the veld, where they hunted game or ran long distances at speed as a test of endurance. On their return, they were again given instruction while the food was being prepared. Then they ate, after which they danced and sang until late at night.

The instruction given to the boys took the form of songs that had to be correctly learned and rendered. The most important, known as 'the songs of the law', exhorted them to honour, obey and support the chief; to be ready to endure hardships and even death for the sake of the tribe; to be united as a regiment and to help one another; to value cattle as the principal source of livelihood and herd them carefully; to attend the council-place regularly, as this was the place for men; to honour and ungrudgingly obey their parents and other elders; and to abandon all childish practices. They were also taught the accepted theories of sexual physiology, the duty of procreation and other rules of conduct in married life, and the dangers of intercourse with ritually unclean ('hot-blooded') women. Much of this teaching was in cryptic language that only initiates could understand. The boys were further taught tribal traditions and religious beliefs, and the tribal songs of war and triumph. To harden them they were occasionally subjected to starvation and many other rigorous forms of discomfort, and those notorious for their unruly or insolent behaviour in the past were here singled out for treatment with special severity. Any slip was seized upon as an excuse for a whipping, while more serious faults were punished by various ingenious forms of torture.

As long as the ceremony lasted, many taboos were observed both in the camp and at home. The boys themselves had to practise specially prescribed ways of sleeping, sitting, talking and eating, any deviation being immediately punished with the cane. When they were out in the veld with their 'shepherds', and any woman or stranger was seen in the distance, they sang and shouted loudly as a sign of warning to withdraw, which if not heeded might lead to severe and even fatal assault. None but the initiated could approach the camp, and even they were not allowed to enter unless sexually 'cool'; moreover, before being admitted they had to respond correctly to a series of passwords put to them at the entrance. The women at home who cooked for the boys or brought food to them were also obliged to refrain from sexual intercourse, nor were dancing or other forms of festivity permitted in the villages.

When their seclusion came to an end, the boys smeared their bodies with red clay and dressed themselves in new skin garments specially made for them by their parents. Then, closely surrounded by the men, they set out for home, singing in triumph, while the camp and all its contents were burned behind them by the 'shepherds'. They marched to the chief's council-place, where they were received with great jubilation by all the people. The chief announced the name of the new regiment they now constituted, and gave them some further advice, warning them particularly that they were now men and must discard the practices of boyhood. Several of his advisers spoke in the same strain. The boys were then allowed to go home, where they were enthusiastically welcomed, and given presents of cattle and clothes by their parents and other relatives.

This ceremony, known as 'the white initiation', from the ashes with which the boys smeared their bodies daily while in the camp, was followed after a year or so by 'the black initiation', so termed because they now smeared themselves with ground charcoal mixed with fat. It was held in the great cattle-kraal adjoining the chief's council-place. The boys remained here for a few days only, during which they were made to go over the laws they had previously been taught, and received some additional instruction, accompanied as usual by many painful forms of discipline. After this they were given their first task to perform as a regiment: they might be sent on a cattle raid, or to kill a lion or to hunt for the chief. They were then regarded as men, and were free to marry, after their leader had done so.

The initiation of the Makuka regiment, in 1901, was the last occasion on which these ceremonies were performed. Chief Lentswe had by then become a Christian, and since the missionaries refused to countenance circumcision and its associated rites, which they regarded as most immoral, he decided to discontinue them. When the next regiment (the Machechele) was formed in 1911, he simply called the boys together, told them that they were now men, and gave them their regimental name. But a more elaborate system of initiation has gradually developed again, in response to the general feeling that this was not enough, and that the boys should receive at least some sort of instruction before being organized into a regiment.

Today, when the chief, after consulting his advisers, decides to create a new regiment, he tells the men to bring their sons to a selected spot in the veld. They come in wagons, bringing their provisions and weapons. For the next three or four weeks they live out in the veld, camping according to their wards. The greater part of each day is spent in hunting, and the camps move from one place to another following the game. In the mornings and evenings the men in charge talk to the boys about the behaviour henceforth expected of them. They stress the virtues of loyalty to the chief and tribe, respect for one's seniors, and obedience to the other tribal laws, but there are no references to matters of sex. The boys are also taught the various tribal songs, and shown their proper standing in the tribe. As part of their routine, they fetch water and wood early every morning, keep the camp clean, prepare the food, and perform any other tasks of the same nature that may be imposed upon them. A severe discipline is maintained, the slightest breach of conduct being punished by thrashing. But there is no longer any secrecy about the ceremony, nor are the other taboos still observed. It is even no longer essential that a boy must actually pass through the rites before being accepted into his regiment. Schoolboys are exempted, and those away working consider themselves as a matter of course members of the same regiment as their age-mates.

The creation of a men's regiment is usually followed within a few months by the creation of a women's regiment, which will be given the same name, to show that the two are coevals. In the old days the associated rites were held in the village itself, in selected compounds carefully screened off from the public view. They began with an operation on each girl, which is said to have consisted in cutting her on the inside of the right thigh and twisting the glowing end of a burning stick into the cuts. After their wounds had healed, the girls spent the greater part of each day out in the veld. Here they were instructed by the older women in matters concerning womanhood, domestic and agricultural activities, sex and behaviour towards men. In the evenings they danced and sang at home, semi-public masquerades in honour of various 'deities' forming a conspicuous part of their routine. Like the boys they were subjected to severe punishments and other hardships, and had to observe many taboos; they wore distinctive dresses made of corn-stalks, and painted their bodies white with lime; no man might come near them, under penalty of severe assault with the hooked sticks they habitually carried; and everything that went on in the enclosures was supposed to be kept secret from non-initiates. After a month or so of all this, the girls were formally given their regimental name in the chief's council-place, and were now considered ready for marriage.

The modern ceremonies are far simpler. For a week or so the girls of each ward sing and dance about the village at night, under the guidance of the old women, but by day they carry on their normal occupations. They are then taken together in a single group into the veld for one day. Here they are lined up ward by ward in order of seniority, lectured on the conduct henceforth expected of them, and ceremonially whipped. Afterwards they run down to the river to wash, and are then marched back to the council-place, where the chief gives them their regimental name.

In the old days people who had not yet been initiated could not marry or appear before a court as litigants, nor, if they were men, could they attend tribal meetings or even sit at the council-place with their elders. These discriminations are no longer so rigidly observed. Some women, as I have previously mentioned, are already married and even mothers by the time they are initiated. But membership of a regiment is still considered indispensable to full recognition as an adult. With it, however, a man's education does not cease. He should now, if at home, frequent the council-place regularly, and attend court cases and tribal meetings, in this way acquiring a knowledge of public affairs and procedure; while the work he may be called upon to do for the chief with the other members of his regiment impresses upon him his wider tribal responsibilities. Similarly, as we have also seen, a woman at marriage receives explicit instruction in the behaviour becoming to a wife. Through the regimental organization, moreover, the principle of respect for one's elders receives new and emphatic expression. The regiments are graded in seniority according to their order of enrolment, and people are expected and can be forced to behave respectfully towards those belonging to regiments formed prior to their own. For instance, any man swearing at or insulting someone of an older regiment can be tried and punished by fining or thrashing, while if he does so when the regiments are out together all his age-mates with him at the time suffer the same penalty as he. A similar discipline prevails among the women.

To these traditional forms of training has now been added formal education in the schools erected under European influence. The first schools were established by the Mission very soon after it came to the tribe in 1864. In 1878 the local missionary recorded that 'books and clothes have already become the fashion among the young Kafirs, although unfortunately they then become very conceited. Such people are in general worse than the heathens, who wish to know nothing of books or clothes.'* Early in the twentieth century, under the influence of the Rev. P. Stoffberg, there was a marked development of educational activity. A report written in 1905 by Mr E. B. Sargant shows that there were then over 1,000 children in school, and comments favourably upon the enthusiasm of the people. The teaching given seems, however, to have been most elementary, and confined in the main to religious preparation and the rudiments of literacy. At a meeting held with Chief Lentswe, Mr Sargant noted that 'the discussion in regard to education was unusually free from complaints as to unsatisfactory relations between the tribe and the missionary; it turned chiefly upon the various ways in which the schools could be improved; for instance, by the employment of better teachers, by industrial training, and by the use of more English'.†

* *De Kerkbode*, vol. xxx, 1878, p. 289.
† *Report on Native Education in South Africa: Part III – Education in the Protectorates*, London, 1908, p. 43.

In later years, however, the Mission policy in regard to education became increasingly distasteful to the tribe, which felt that, for reasons mainly personal, far less zeal and interest were being shown than in the past. As a result, the schools began to suffer. In 1915 there were some 500 children at school; in 1918 the number on the registers had dropped to seventy-five. In 1920, finally, it was agreed to transfer the control of the schools from the Mission to a tribal committee on which the Administration, the Mission, and the tribe were all represented. The school attendance for the year immediately rose to 480. About the same time the Administration created a general Native Development Fund, financed by an annual contribution of three shillings (later five shillings) from every taxpayer, which facilitated the revival of education by providing more funds. In 1923 a magnificent school was erected at the tribal expense in Mochudi. In 1930 all education in the Protectorate was taken over directly by the Administration, and a much sounder policy was introduced.

The chiefs have always fostered education zealously, the ex-regent Isang being particularly active in this connection. They have made it more or less obligatory for parents to send to school all the children who can be spared from cattle-herding and other domestic work. There are two large schools in Mochudi, and one in each of the outlying villages, and education is free, except for a small entrance fee and the cost of books. In 1932 there were some 950 pupils at school. In 1937 the number had advanced to some 1,400 (said to be approximately 50 per cent of the children of 'school-going age'). Of these, however, no fewer than 1,170 (83 per cent) were girls.* The main reason for this striking disproportion is that most of the boys are still compelled to spend the greater part of their youth at the cattle-posts, which are far from the villages and so from the schools. To meet this particular situation, the Education Department in 1935 instituted the experiment of sending an itinerant teacher out to the cattle-post areas. The results so far are considered promising, but it will

*Annual Report of the Director of Education ... 1937, App. G and H.

obviously be long before as many boys as girls are receiving instruction.

The people appear on the whole to have realized the advantages of education, especially as a preparation for a life that nowadays involves so much contact with Europeans. Few, however, yet send all their children to school. This often creates jealousies, especially since those going to school require better clothing than the rest, do less work at home, and have various other privileges. Many parents, moreover, soon complain that they cannot do without the help of their children, and so take them out of school after only two or three years. This is officially stated to be the average length of attendance. Very few, in consequence, ever get beyond the lower classes. In 1937 approximately 70 per cent of the children attending school were in the first two sub-standards, and less than 3 per cent in Standard VI, the eighth year of the primary course.

The Education Department, aware of this fact, which is common to all the tribes of the Protectorate, has accordingly adopted the policy of teaching the children to read and write, giving them 'a sound knowledge of elementary numbers', and establishing 'habits of good health and conduct'. Increasing emphasis is being placed on the use of the vernacular as a medium of instruction, a tendency not altogether welcome to the people, who feel that a knowledge of English would be of more economic value. Some training is also given in arts and crafts, and several school gardens have recently been established, where the children are taught to grow green vegetables for their own consumption in order to counteract malnutrition.

There were no facilities for secondary education in the Reserve until 1937, when the National School at Mochudi began taking pupils beyond Standard VI. Previously the few wishing to proceed further had to go to Tiger Kloof or some similar institution in the Union or Southern Rhodesia. They generally either qualified as teachers or specialized in a trade. Most of the teachers afterwards managed to find work in the Reserve, or among the Kgatla in the Transvaal, but not all could do so. On the other hand, only a few of those who acquired trades were afterwards able to practise them at home, owing to the very limited demand for special services of the kind they are able to render. The majority in consequence have had to seek employment elsewhere, and some have never returned to the Reserve. The tribe has thus lost young men who should have been potential leaders to progress.

As we shall shortly see, school education has contributed to the changing relations between parents and children. It has also brought knowledge about things that formerly played no part at all in tribal life, and many of which are still unrelated to the environment in which most of the Kgatla, especially the girls, will always remain. It has led to the spreading use of English as a spoken language, and to the increasing importance of letter-writing as a means of maintaining contact between the men working abroad and their families and friends at home. Finally, it has introduced many new games to the children, such as football and hockey, and given them the advantages of participation in organized youth movements modelled on the Scouts and Girl Guides.

Another new educational agency is represented by the Church, which has come to exercise a considerable influence upon the lives of the younger people under its jurisdiction. Its catechumen classes take up much of their time, and its confirmation ceremonies are eagerly anticipated and made the occasion of feasts, while at Christmas time the girls organize themselves into choirs which go about the village singing, the tunes generally being of a European character, while the words also are often in English. Its forms of discipline, like censure for moral lapses and expulsion for repeated or grave delinquency, constitute new and sometimes powerful sanctions of behaviour. Attendance at church and at local prayer meetings provides a welcome diversion from every-day activities, and the Sunday service is also an opportunity for parading in one's best and making assignations. Some of the children take their religion lightly, but others experience all the thrills and emotions of conversion with which we are familiar in adolescents of European society. They apparently become sincere in their outlook on religion, fill their letters with pious sentiments and Biblical quotations, and may even try to lead their less enthusiastic parents along the paths of righteousness, with results to themselves that are often unwelcome. This fervour seldom lasts for long, however, and by the time they reach adult maturity most Kgatla take their religion as a matter of course, and rarely allow thoughts of their possible fate in the next world to affect their daily life in this to any appreciable extent. The scarcity of male communicants, in particular, is troubling the Mission authorities greatly, and a Church conference in 1932 gloomily visualized a time when the elders, the evangelists and ultimately even the minister would all be women! 'This matter was discussed a long time, and with very sore hearts,' adds the report.

'THE REVOLT OF MODERN YOUTH'

We have just seen how in their own tribal culture Kgatla children were instructed at home in the occupations they would have to follow as adults, and how both here and later at the initiation ceremonies they received a character training which, with all its defects, was apparently an efficient agency in making them conform to the social standards of their people. The Kgatla aimed essentially at bringing up children to be obedient and devoted to their parents, respectful to all their elders, loyal and submissive to their chief, and competent and industrious at work. They did not encourage originality, or consider it the function of education to develop a child's 'personality'; they sought merely to make him a useful member of his family, and a law-abiding citizen of his tribe.

Civilization has destroyed some of this old educational mechanism, and substituted for it the church, the school and the industrial environment of the towns. In none of these new agencies does the Kgatla child receive the same grounding in conduct that was, and to some extent still is, provided at home. Nowadays, in fact, complaints about the behaviour of the children have become very common. It is said that they are cheeky and ill-mannered, showing little respect for their parents and still less for other elderly people; except when compelled, they seldom do as they are told; they take little interest in domestic work, and do not support or help their parents as they should; they have no morals in matters of sex, and their promiscuity is ruining the tribe and filling it with bastards; they have lost all discipline, and think only of their own pleasure.

Exaggerated as this indictment obviously is, it is not merely a case of 'the good old days', when everything was so much better than now. There is a widespread conviction that parental authority and tribal discipline have decayed, and that young people today are more independent and unruly than ever before. Thus, at a meeting of the local Church Council in 1932,

It was stated also [I quote from the vernacular report published in *Lesedi la Sechaba* for October of that year] that boys are nowadays lawless and uncontrolled, they do just as they please, and even the parents at home have abandoned their responsibilities towards the children. The children of Christian parents dance and sing at night, and the boys do not honour grown people. It was discussed how to cure this disease. The Council agreed to put the matter to the chief, and ask him to use his authority to help stop these things. Christian parents should also look after their children, especially the girls, and prevent them from going to the dances at night. But above all, the Church members should pray. Another topic discussed was the impregnation of girls. This had already been dealt with frequently at previous Church meetings, but no remedy has yet been found. It is not that girls are seduced only by boys, but by married men also. A remedy for this is still being sought. It was agreed to ask the Church women for suitable suggestions, and get them to speak to the girls, and also to send delegates to the chief, for this is a thing that is weakening and spoiling the tribe.

And the chief's paternal aunt actually besought me to find her daughter work in Johannesburg or Cape Town, for she feared that the girl's virtue would suffer if she remained any longer in Mochudi.

In trying to account for the present situation, the older Kgatla generally stress the changed character of the initiation ceremonies. Previously, they say, children known to have been disobedient or insolent towards their elders were treated with special severity in the initiation camps, which accordingly served as a powerful disciplinary force. Parents would exercise every possible control over the behaviour of children, who themselves would behave with restraint, for fear of the additional hardships and tortures they would otherwise have to suffer when being initiated. Moreover, the ceremonies themselves included a very thorough training in character and self-discipline, given under conditions that impressed it firmly upon the minds of initiates. The moral training given at the modern initiation camps is not nearly so comprehensive or emphatic. Moreover, since labour migration provides a ready means of escape from participation in the ceremonies, excessive punishment there need no longer be dreaded. As a result, parents have gradually become less vigilant, while among the children there has been a growth of irresponsibility and even licence, manifesting itself more particularly in regard to sex.

School children have been affected as much as the rest. Some of my most detailed information about the sexual activities of young people came from boys and girls still at school, and few of them were without any experience at all, while many were maintaining standing liaisons. The teachers appear to exert no control in this direction, and as a class have indeed set a bad example to their pupils. Barely a year passes without at least one teacher being dismissed for immorality, and village gossip surrounds many others with well-founded scandal. What little training is given in conduct and the formation of character is therefore not very successful. Some parents blame education for further ill effects. The children not at school envy their more fortunate companions, and resent being deprived of the same opportunities, with the result that they become sulky and recalcitrant. The school children, on the other hand, acquire a feeling of superiority through learning to speak English and wearing comparatively good clothes, and so often affect to despise their parents as illiterate and uncouth.

The young people who have been to schools abroad, and the others whom they have influenced directly at home, have certainly tended more readily than any other section of the community to embrace the ways of the white man. They regard it as fashionable to speak and correspond in English even among themselves, they show a preference for European foodstuffs and such relatively novel articles of clothing as pyjamas and bloomers, they have taken up ballroom dancing, to the music of the gramophone, and they have begun to practise kissing as a part of love technique, to employ European contraceptives, and even to read the works of Dr Marie Stopes and kindred authors. All these are recent innovations, many dating back not more than ten years or so, and they are regarded with disgust and dismay by the more conservative members of the tribe. The youths, on the other hand, complain bitterly about the lack of the social amenities to which they became accustomed abroad, and profess an anxiety to break away from the tribe and seek more 'civilized' surroundings. In the meantime they seem to find a fairly congenial outlet for their unrest in sexual intrigues, in which they indulge very freely, and some have latterly begun to dabble in tribal politics as rowdy partisans of their former boon companion, the exiled Chief Molefi.

Religion does present some form of control, since many children, especially those going to school, are either already communicants or are attending the catechumen classes, and are therefore subject to the Church laws of discipline. But, as our quotation from the report of the 1932 Council meeting has shown, this sanction is not powerful enough. In theory, the Church expects its unmarried members to live chastely; in practice, action is taken only when a girl becomes pregnant. And even the most regular church-goers among the younger people do not regard it as wrong to indulge in sexual relations, provided that they can avoid conception. It is characteristic of their attitude that when I was once discussing with a young man his religious and moral convictions, he included in the list of sins not sexual intercourse in general, but sexual intercourse on Sundays! Moreover, by stressing the European notions of individual responsibility and individual salvation, the Church has weakened the traditional ideal of group solidarity, just as its substitution for ancestor-worship has deprived the father of his ancient role of family priest, formerly a powerful sanction for his authority.

Still more far-reaching have been the effects of labour migration. Where the father of a family goes out to work, his often prolonged absence frees the children from the main instrument of domestic control. They take little notice of their mother, especially if she has a lover or indulges too freely in drink, as sometimes happens while her husband is away, and they tend to do much as they like. This is particularly true of the school children, who for a considerable part of the year, while the other people are out at the fields, remain in the villages with hardly any supervision at all. A father on his return may therefore find that not only his wife but his children too have fallen into bad habits; and while it is easy enough to deal with the younger ones, the older sons do not submit readily to being disciplined. Labour migration has opened to them also a new and easy way of escape from the severities of parental control, and any harsh chastisement, to which formerly they would have had to yield with as much grace as they could muster, is now merely an added inducement for seeking work in the towns. Isang has frequently complained that the Union authorities seldom try to send back youths who had left home without the consent of their parents, a complaint suggesting that such desertions are common enough to be a problem.

In the towns the young men experience the relative freedom of a different culture, in which the domestic sanctions no longer affect them directly, where the laws and taboos of tribal life may be broken with comparative impunity, and where the authority of the father and the chief is replaced by that of the employer and the policeman. They enter into individual contracts, and secure earnings formerly unknown; they acquire new habits and new tastes, and also new vices. On their return home they soon become intolerant of the traditional forms of family control. They realize that their parents depend upon them for the money with which to pay taxes and meet other wants, and that in consequence they have acquired a new importance in family life to which the old conceptions of discipline must yield. They seldom put all their savings at the disposal of their father, or remain to help in the ploughing; they object to being sent to the cattle-posts, and prefer to swagger through the village streets and spend their time with the girls. Comparatively well dressed, and perhaps with money to spend, they readily attract the women, whom they are then able to seduce fairly easily. As we have seen, the day has passed when every young man's wife was selected for him; often enough, he now makes his own choice, and only when he has succeeded in winning the girl does he ask his parents to arrange the marriage. In exceptional instances he may even take up permanent residence with his wife's people. The reason commonly given is that he finds it easier to get on with them than with his own parents – a significant commentary on the decay of family solidarity.

Of course, not all the children are disobedient or undutiful. There are families in which they seem genuinely fond of their parents, whom they treat with all the respect and deference that could be desired; there are many others in which the mutual relationship is at least friendly and pleasant, and the rare quarrels that occur are comparatively trivial in nature. But there are still others in which disputes are fairly common. A child may deliberately and persistently refuse to do as it is told; a daughter may be lazy and worthless; a son may dissipate the family cattle, refuse to work with his parents, or fail to support them in their old age. Cases are known of children openly despising their parents, swearing at them obscenely or even assaulting them. On the other hand, parents also may be responsible for the breach. A father may consistently favour one son by allocating him more cattle than the rest, or he may allow a second wife to use property belonging to the estate of the first; he may punish his children excessively, or fail to provide them with clothes and other necessities; he may try to force his daughter into accepting a husband she does not want, or may refuse to let his son marry as the latter wishes. The opportunities for discord are many, and to overcome the difficulties requires a sympathetic understanding and patience which not all Kgatla parents or children possess.

Usually, if a dispute cannot be settled within the household, it is dealt with at a general gathering of the family-group. The issues involved are fully and openly discussed, and the relatives try hard to effect a reconciliation. An erring child is shown the evil of his ways, and punished if necessary; a stern and unsympathetic father is warned that his attitude is very unwise if he wishes to retain the affection and respect of his children. But if all efforts fail, the matter is referred to the headman of the ward, and if sufficiently serious it may ultimately come to the chief. In every instance the court aims at reconciling the contending parties. It appeals to their reciprocal obligations. If either is blatantly in the wrong he is punished, an offending child invariably more severely than a guilty parent. If it is evident that the breach cannot be healed, a separation is ordered. The son may then build his own home in another part of the village, or go to live with some other relative more sympathetically inclined, or migrate to the towns. His father may also be ordered to give him his due share of the family estate, in which case he will be debarred from inheriting in future. Accusations of sorcery, an almost invariable symptom of family disunity, begin to figure prominently in such cases, and instances are even known where children have tried to poison their parents, or parents have used the same weapons against them.

The case of Ramotsei provides a useful illustration. While at the cattle-post he used to beat his younger brothers excessively and ill-treat them in other ways. They often complained to their father, who, finding that his remonstrances did not help, began to ignore Ramotsei's right, as eldest son, to be consulted in all family affairs. On several occasions they came to blows. Ramotsei then became attracted by a certain girl, whom he wished to marry; his father refused to let him do so, whereupon he went to stay with her at her home. She became pregnant, and he repeatedly asked his parents to 'seek' her for him; they always refused, saying that he was an ungrateful and disobedient son. At last he bought medicines from a doctor with which to kill his father. He put them into the old man's food, but was seen doing so by his little sister. She ran to warn her father, but missed him on the road, and when he came home he ate the porridge awaiting him. He became violently sick, and vomited several times, but managed to recover. He brought Ramotsei before the chief, who made the boy produce the rest of his medicines and swallow them before all the people. Fearing that he was going to die, Ramotsei started to run away. He was caught and locked inside his father's house, but broke out and made his way to his girl's home, where after a serious illness he soon died.

Two other cases that recently came to court afford a further insight into the disputes that may occur. Kabelo, an unruly and disobedient son, became very sick in 1938, and accused his father of bewitching him. The old man finally lost patience, and told him to clear out of their home. For spite Kabelo thereupon burned his father's yokes, sold some of his cattle and repeatedly swore at him. He was tried before their ward-head, who said that if it were not for his illness he would have been sentenced to imprisonment and cuts; as it was, he was fined an ox, and told that his conduct would henceforth be under close observation. Again, at the beginning of 1939, Lekwalo quarrelled with his father over the disposal of some cattle hides. He said that his father had caused the cattle to die by bewitching them. When the old man threatened to beat him for this impertinent accusation, he resisted violently, and injured his father badly. For this he was sentenced by the chief to receive eight cuts in the Government gaol.

The conditions of modern Kgatla life almost inevitably produce strained family relationships. On the one hand we have parents still demanding unhesitating respect, obedience and service, and asserting their traditional right to control the lives even of children who are fully mature. The children, on the other hand, grow up today in an environment where the old domestic sanctions have lost much of their force, and where new influences of many kinds offer opportunities for greater personal freedom. The son who formerly depended upon his father for wealth is now himself often the main support of the family; even daughters are no longer bound to remain among their own people, but can always escape to the towns, as in fact some of them do. Parents have had to adjust themselves to a situation in which their authority is no longer unassailable or inevitable, and in which they depend upon their adult children for maintenance to a much greater extent than before. Many of them have succeeded in doing so, and are sufficiently reasonable not to make exorbitant demands. Moreover, the training a child still receives at home, and especially the traditional cohesion of the kinship group so directly impressed upon him there, establish patterns of behaviour that civilizing influences may blur but cannot altogether eradicate. Nevertheless, there is enough discord these days between parents and children to make the people unhappy. 'We never heard of these things until the white man came,' old Rakabane cried to me, and his words were echoed by many another grey-beard with whom I discussed the problem of modern youth.

And as a final indication of the distress in which parents sometimes find themselves, let me quote once more from the correspondence of the widow, one of whose letters we read at the end of Chapter 5. Writing to her second son in Johannesburg, on 1 January 1937, she says:

My beloved son, I greet you very much. I myself am sick, I am suffering from an ailment of the chest, it seized me last Christmas; I am unable to eat, and I am weakened by emptiness from hunger. The sickness is weighing down upon me, and I fear that I may die before I see you again. My heart is very sad because of the way in which I have been treated by your elder brother, he has treated me just like a dog. I should so like to see you again. My child, how terrible it would be if you came here and found my grave already dug! Cannot you get a pass and come here quickly to see how your elder brother is stirring up strife? Our cattle have gone, he has squandered them all. And even as far as ploughing is concerned, I cannot plough; he ploughed for himself alone; he told me that I would not live to see this year, but yet here I am, abandoned in your father's home. My child, I put all my faith in you alone; and I say that I would rather you called me (to Johannesburg) to end my days there, than that I should die here deserted. I have received the soap that you sent me. I am, your mother.

10. The Stability of Marriage

THE PERSONAL FACTOR

In the last few chapters we observed Kgatla family life as revealed in economic activities, the daily routine of the household, the sexual relations between husband and wife, the production and rearing of children and the responsibilities and burdens of parenthood. We saw that in each case tribal law and custom prescribe how the members of the family should behave towards one another, and we saw also that through the influence of Western civilization the traditional standards of conduct have changed in many respects. Here and there, too, I cited instances to illustrate how far people do or do not conform to these standards in practice. This particular topic may now be examined more fully, for it provides a criterion by which we can judge Kgatla marriage. The relationship that should exist between husband and wife is conventionally defined, and various forms of pressure are used to secure its attainment. But since marriage normally entails long and intimate association between people differing in sex, temperament and other individual characteristics, we have to ask if the variety found among the Kgatla makes for personal contentment, or instead produces unhappiness and conflict. There are, of course, likely to be ill-matched couples under almost any system of marriage, but we are perhaps justified in assuming that where discord is common social conditions are also partly to blame.

There is one important point to which reference must immediately be made. Among the Kgatla a person's marriage was formerly arranged by his parents and other senior relatives; and since procreation, not companionship, was the main object, mutual attraction of the young people themselves counted for little, and their preferences were seldom seriously considered. Now and then a boy or a girl might rebel against being forced into an unwelcome match, but in the main, as far as our information goes, children seem to have submitted willingly enough to their destiny. Today, although arranged marriages are still fairly common, most people choose their own mates. This means that personal attachment has become far more important than before. People do not marry each other merely because their parents wish it; they often marry because they like each other, and feel that they could live together happily. To the desire for children has therefore been added the desire for a more lasting association with some one attractive and congenial.

It must be remembered, however, that in the old days parents choosing a bride for their son were usually anxious to find a girl with qualities likely to ensure a stable marriage. They judged her not merely by the standing and reputation of her family, but by her own conduct and character; she must be of respectable birth, but she must also have the makings of a good wife – industry, modesty, chastity, obedience and amiability. The young man of today, while not as a rule indifferent to such qualities, is influenced also by direct personal attraction. And, as some recent instances have shown, his judgement may turn out to have been somewhat rash, for a bedworthy body and fascinating ways do not in themselves guarantee that the girl will be equally suitable in other respects. Sometimes, too, his choice leads to friction with his parents, which, while it may have the effect of attaching him more closely to his wife, occasionally also furnishes him with a grievance against her which he is not slow to exploit when squabbles occur.

Nevertheless, modern Kgatla marriages usually rest on a more satisfactory personal basis than those of former times. The young people have had the opportunity of getting to know each other fairly intimately beforehand; they start married life not as actual or comparative strangers, but as friends and companions, and probably even as established lovers in the physical sense. Their mutual adjustments have already been largely made, and do not, as in the old days, have to begin with marriage itself. Newly-married people appear fairly often to be very fond of each other and to enjoy being together, which does not seem to have been at all common formerly. Elderly informants with whom I discussed the matter said that mutual affection between the spouses, if it existed at all, developed only after they had learned by lengthy experience to understand and appreciate each other's good qualities. And it is significant that in polygamous households the favourite wife was seldom the woman first married in obedience to the will of the parents, but one whom the husband had afterwards chosen for himself.

But while instances of happy marriage do occur, particularly among the young people, it cannot be said of the Kgatla in general that husband and wife tend to be very devoted or attached. At best they usually like and humour each other, but as often as not they lack mutual sympathy and understanding. Even newly-married people are inclined to drift apart after a few years of comparative bliss, and although they may remain on fairly good terms they sometimes turn to others for stimulus or satisfaction. And often, as far as I could judge, husband and wife merely tolerate each other's presence, and go their own ways whenever possible, while at times they are notoriously estranged.

Temperamental differences of course account for some of this. Most Kgatla strike one as sociable, patient, good-natured and occasionally even cheerful. But the querulous and exacting woman is common enough, and so is the sullen or quarrelsome man, while the scandalmonger, the habitual idler and the aggressive busybody, are types well recognized by the people themselves. And under the influence of liquor, when tempers often rise high, some men and women reveal a streak of viciousness and indifference to the sufferings of others that may go far to explain the unhappiness of their spouses. But while personal characteristics like these may affect individual cases of marriage, the general absence of enthusiastic cooperation between husband and wife is due also to certain social factors.

To start with, there is little intimate contact in everyday life. Married people do of course necessarily have a good deal in common. When the husband is at home, he and his wife share the same hut, they often eat together, and they may entertain or go visiting together. They contribute jointly by their efforts to the maintenance of the household, and work side by side in some agricultural activities; they are jointly responsible for bringing up their children, although the main burden really falls upon the wife; they must consult each other in the management of household affairs and the disposal of property; and they participate together in family and kinship celebrations and councils. Even so, there is little real comradeship between them. They have few opportunities or facilities for joint recreation and amusement, and husbands generally prefer to spend their leisure time, not in the company of their wives, but in gossiping or drinking beer with other men. Formerly the lack of companionship was probably even more marked, for it was considered unbecoming for a man to associate with the women by day; he was expected to remain at the council-place if not otherwise engaged, and returned home only towards sunset. Today there is not the same separation of the sexes in social life, and during visits or informal beer-drinks men and women often sit, talk and joke together with good-humoured familiarity. It is nevertheless seldom that husband and wife see much of each other except at night, and still more seldom that they talk together frankly about their respective private affairs.

More important still, married people hardly ever live together all the year round. Even if the husband is not away in European labour centres, his occupations inside the Reserve frequently take him from home. Both he and his wife are therefore separated from time to time. This sometimes makes them appreciate each other more when they come together again. As one woman put it, referring as usual to sex, 'When your husband comes back, he has more desire for you, and more potency, and this renews your love.' But the general effect is to widen the gap between their respective interests and sympathies. Labour migration, in particular, is creating a good deal of dissension. I have already discussed at some length its bearing upon marital fidelity, and shown that it frequently forces a wife to seek sexual relief in the arms of a lover, a procedure seldom welcomed by her husband even if he is forced to condone it. During his absence, moreover, she enjoys a relative freedom to which she was not formerly accustomed, so that on his return he may also find that she will no longer submit so readily to his authority. Occasionally, too, he fails while away to send her money or other necessities, with the result that she has to struggle hard to maintain herself and her children, and consequently becomes very bitter about him. It is only within relatively recent years that extensive labour migration and prolonged absences abroad have come to bulk largely in Kgatla life. Their influence is therefore a feature not of the old but of the modern marriage system, and as such it may go far to counteract the advantages derived from greater freedom in choosing a partner.

The polygamous tradition provides another fruitful source of discord. Although it has made the people more tolerant of sexual laxity than is usual in Western societies, it has by no means overcome jealousy and possessiveness. In fact, the word *lefufa*, whose primary meaning is 'jealousy', is also used for 'polygamy', an extension that Kgatla explain by pointing out how seldom it is that co-wives can live together amicably. And although polygamy itself is nowadays rarely practised, concubinage is very common indeed. While many wives do not object particularly to their husbands' infidelity, provided that they are not themselves neglected, many others resent it bitterly; and if they are not content to make jealous scenes or to administer love-potions, they may respond by taking lovers of their own. And some are unfaithful without even an excuse of this sort, but merely because they are attracted by someone else, and do not mind the risks that may be involved. Infidelity, or the suspicion of infidelity, is therefore among the most common causes of conflict between husband and wife, and although in itself it is not usually considered sufficient ground for divorce, it certainly contributes greatly towards the estrangement of spouses.

The barrenness of a wife may likewise make her husband resentful and bitter. I have already stressed several times the Kgatla conception of marriage as a union designed for the production and rearing of children; and although personal attraction has today become an important motive, it is still subordinate to the desire for offspring. And what frequently happens when a marriage is childless is well described in the following text, written by Sofonia, which will supplement what I have previously said on the subject:

'Mostly people divorce when they get no children. After they have been married for a couple of years, and there is no child, the husband begins to say, "It is your fault, because before I married you you used to sleep with many boys." Sometimes it is the wife who says, "You are weak, your strength is gone, you should have impregnated me already."

'And this thing continues, bringing violent quarrels between these two people, till the man looks round for a concubine, and he sleeps with her to get children. Then there is a great quarrel, which will bring war between them. The wife goes to doctors, and asks for medicines; she uses them to try and separate these two by breaking their love. If her husband learns what she is doing, he thrashes her very severely, and she complains to her relatives and friends. Then people ask him, "Why are you so cruel, that you marry a poor child, and then treat her so badly?" He replies, "It is my wife who is the cause of all these troubles," but this is just to comfort himself, for he knows that it is not true.

'Sometimes the wife then tells the people that she wants to go back to her mother's home. She says to her husband, "What can I do, when you make such a fool of me?" And he replies, "Well, you can do what you like, because I don't see what use you are here; I thought that you were going to bear children and help me, but I see that you don't help me at all." Then the wife says, "All right, if you give me the road to go my parents will be pleased, because when you married me they said to you, 'Take her, and if you get tired of her bring her back while she is still alive.' Now I am pleased, because you send me back to my home still living, and not yet dead." She takes her blankets and goes back, and tells her parents what has happened to her.

'Then her father and a friend go to her husband's place to inquire into the matter, and the husband calls his people too. He begins to make excuses, saying, "The woman is very lazy, and refuses to go when I send her. Again, she looks for medicines to kill me, and she says that I am using other women in the town. And because I hate to be insulted by a woman, I said to her, 'I don't like this.' Then she became sulky, and went away. She wants to divorce me, and I said, 'All right, you can do what you like.' "

'This reply is brought back to the woman, and they say, "State what you know." And she says, "I am glad that you have given me the chance to speak." She begins to talk a lot, saying all that she was doing, and how she was treated. "First my husband comes home in the morning, just about dawn, and I don't know where he was all night long; but I hear that he sleeps at so-and-so's place. He treats me as if I were just a thing in the house, just something to stamp corn; but I don't want to work for other women's husbands. And again he says that I am too bad, I don't bear children, and the taste of my body is not good, because I used to sleep with many boys while I was still young, that is the reason why I don't bear children. But I don't know how to remedy all these things, because I haven't got the power to do so. He is the one who gave me the road to go, so I told him, 'I am now going,' and I went, and so we parted from each other. But I say that I don't want to go back to this man again, because I don't want to work for other women, because I have got sense."

'Then her parents say, "But divorcing is no good." And the husband says, "Well, if my wife does not agree, I have got nothing to do with her, I don't want any more troubles, I don't want a woman who becomes a snake and bites me." And the wife says, "All right, I don't mind either, but I want the things for which we worked together." Then the parents on both sides say, "All right, it is finished, let us go home, but we are going to take this matter to court." '

Kgatla convention, again, is strongly opposed to social equality between husband and wife. In law the husband is the undoubted head of his family. As such he has considerable authority over his wife. She must obey his commands, account to him for her movements, and defer to him in all household affairs; when he is home she cannot go visiting in other parts of the village without his permission; she may have her own property, but cannot dispose of it without his knowledge and consent, nor can she take legal action against outsiders except through him as her guardian and representative; and if she misbehaves he is entitled to thrash her. Even the newly-married man of today who is very fond of his wife expects her to be meek and obedient, and to pay him the respect due to a superior. At the same time a husband should not be despotic. He is expected rather to protect his wife, treat her kindly and considerately, comfort her when she is in sorrow, and stand by her whenever she gets into trouble with others. The reasonable husband makes his authority felt only when really necessary, and prefers to leave the actual running of the home in the hands of his wife, and to interfere as little as possible with her management of the young children, the foodstuffs, and the huts and their furnishings.

But not all men interpret their matrimonial obligations in this way. Several of those whom I questioned said that the main thing in marriage is to keep the wife firmly in her place. 'The husband must conciliate his wife if he wants to have a good home,' said Masilo, 'but on the other hand he must beat her so that she should fear him.' And Modibe, a man on notoriously bad terms with his wife, expressed himself much more violently:

'There is no special treatment for women,' he said; 'a woman is a dog; what she wants is a rod, because she wishes to make you her servant. What I don't like about women is that they are a low class of people, and the only way to keep them straight is to beat them with a cane. You must never listen to what they say, they tire you out and make you lose hope, they are full of roguery, and don't aim at anything good. So I don't think there's any reason why we should be asked how we behave to our wives, for they themselves don't behave at all; they are dogs that we took from their mothers' homes, and when they come here they want to be the owners of the place. If it were not that the old people say, "The woman builds up the home," I should long ago have sent back my wife, but I keep to the law of my fathers.'

When men think like this, it is no wonder that to some women the dominant feature of married life, as it affects themselves, is the insistence upon humble subservience to the husband in everything, and patient acceptance of his scoldings and punishments. As described by Naome, an elderly woman, the relationship between spouses can hardly be termed one of equal consideration:

'When a woman is married, she must try her best to please her husband; she must cook for him, spread his blankets (i.e. make his bed), and speak peacefully to him. The first thing to learn is that they should report all domestic affairs to each other, but the main thing is to give the husband food: no matter if there is scarcity, the husband must get food, and the wife should rather sleep hungry. Since the husband is the lion in the house, he can send me whenever he likes, and I cannot complain but must obey him. When he gets angry, I must keep my mouth shut. In the old days, a wife could not answer back, but now it is no longer so, and women quarrel with their husbands. According to law, when my husband beats me I have no right to strike back nor have I the right to swear at him, for a wife is called the servant of her husband. But we women also complain that when a husband is angry, and we beseech him to keep quiet, he should do so, because if not he makes us cry, for a woman's heart is light. And even then they always beat us for crying like this, they say we are just being cheeky.'

And there is a well-known song that women neglected or ill-treated by their husbands often sing to themselves as they sit weeping at home, or when, with their friends, they grow melancholy over the beer-pots:

> I have been oppressed by my husband,
> for he treated me like a dog;
> I long for my father and mother,
> for he treated me like a dog;
> if he does not love me,
> why shouldn't I go back?
> for he has treated me like a dog.

When it is realized that a dog's life among the Kgatla is usually one long round of curses, blows, and starvation, no other comment is needed on the hardships under which some women suffer.

In practice, however, a wife does not usually resent her husband's exercise of his marital power, provided that he does not abuse it, and within the household her lot is far from intolerable. She works hard enough at her many domestic duties, but has considerable freedom of movement, often visiting her relatives and friends, and taking part in most local festivities and excitements. As she grows older, and her children begin to relieve her at work, she gradually attains a more comfortable position, and, if she is the mother of several sons, she will be regarded with honour and treated with respect by her husband and his relatives.

In recent times, too, the wife has acquired more opportunity of asserting herself. If her husband marries her for love, and not merely because his parents have chosen her, she has a strong personal hold over him. The decay of polygamy, and the introduction of Christian ideals of married life, have led her to expect and demand greater consideration. The spread of education has likewise contributed towards making her more confident and independent in her attitude. Labour migration, too, by drawing her husband away from home for lengthy periods, has increased her spirit of freedom. Theoretically, she is under the control of his senior relatives during his absence, but in practice she is certainly less restricted in her actions, and she seldom fails to take advantage of this as far as her personal life is concerned. Moreover, as sometimes happens, she may be the more dominant personality, and despite the formal restrictions to which she is subject, she may actually be the real power in the household. I know several men who are notoriously governed by their wives, and who despite the gibes of their fellows have never been able to gather sufficient courage to try exerting their legal authority. But men like these are not often found, and the average Kgatla husband lives up to the maxim: 'A man is the god of his wife.'

It is evident, then, that the Kgatla conception of marriage does not make for loyal companionship and deep personal attachment between husband and wife. The unequal social status of men and women, the lack of daily intimacy in married life, the nature of the authority vested in the husband, the polygamous tradition and its modern manifestations in sexual promiscuity, and the growing spirit of revolt on the part of women, all render difficult the attainment of enduring harmony, and on the other hand readily facilitate discord. The frequency with which disputes occur shows this very clearly. Many squabbles are of course comparatively trivial, and likely to occur in any household. There may be momentary differences of opinion about the treatment of children, especially when, as often happens, each parent accuses the other of oppressing or neglecting a child, or of teaching it bad manners. A wife may complain that her husband does not provide her with clothes as good as those of other women, or that he stays out too late at night, or that he pays no attention to her requests or advice, or that he forces her to sleep with him when she is unwilling. The husband in turn may accuse her of being lazy, careless, or improvident, or of gadding about too much, or of not having food ready for him when he wants it, or of being cheeky when he admonishes her. Quarrels over matters like these are a common feature of family life, even when the couple are normally on fairly good terms, and they seldom last long or lead to an open break.

More serious are the quarrels arising from infidelity. A casual affair may be forgiven, but when the husband continually neglects his wife for a concubine, or she prefers a lover to him, jealous scenes are frequent and often violent. The wife's complete barrenness, again, or at least her failure to bear a son, may rankle with her husband and embitter him. If she is persistently lazy and does not carry out all her household tasks, or if she has a shrewish disposition, he soon becomes impatient with her, and resorts to forceful means of correction. The wife, on the other hand, may find grounds for lasting resentment in his failure to provide properly for her and her children, in his squandering money on drink instead of on household necessities, or in the severity with which he habitually treats her. Such differences are frequent enough to make many a marriage unpleasant for both husband and wife, and it is mainly owing to the stabilizing influence of their relatives, as we shall shortly see, that they continue to live together as well as they can.

From the wife's point of view, the happiness of her marriage sometimes depends not so much upon her husband himself as upon his parents and other relatives among whom she is living. While she generally manages to get on fairly well with them, it happens now and then that they grow jealous of her and begin to dislike her, especially if they feel that her husband is devoting all his attention to her and is not supporting them as liberally as before. They will then start grumbling, possibly with justice, that she is lazy, disobedient, or flighty in her conduct; they will continually run down her family; and if her husband takes her part will accuse her and her parents of having won him over by the use of love-potions. She, on the other hand, may have cause for complaint in the burdens they thrust upon her, and in their attempts to restrict her from visiting or entertaining her friends; and should she still be childless after a few years, she will readily attribute this to their evil dispositions or their use of sorcery. Occasionally, if she finds life with them particularly difficult, she may even persuade her husband to come and live with her permanently at the home of her own parents.

The story of Manyama provides a case in point. After living for the first six months of marriage with her parents-in-law, who made her work very hard and allowed her little freedom, she went home to her mother for her first confinement. While she was there her parents-in-law removed all her belongings from the hut she had occupied, and put them into a store-room at the back, where they intended her to sleep in future. During her confinement, moreover, they neither brought her food nor sent any of their children to stamp corn for her, nor did they even come to see her. As soon as her seclusion was over, they wanted her to come back and start working at once. She refused, saying that if she were to live together again with them they would only quarrel all the time. Since then, nearly five years ago, she has been living at her mother's home, and her husband, who is exceptionally devoted to her (he is the man whose letters I quoted towards the end of Chapter 5), joined her there on his return from Johannesburg. Her second pregnancy, incidentally, ended in a miscarriage, and naturally enough the diviners attributed it to *dikgaba* (malevolent thoughts) emanating from her parents-in-law.

SEPARATION AND DIVORCE

The domestic quarrels to which I have just referred are not as a rule serious enough to cause a final split between husband and wife. An exchange of verbal abuse is often sufficient to clear the air, and to lead to the resumption of peaceful relations. But if a husband is short-tempered, or very annoyed with his wife, he may beat her with a leather strap or a stick. This is an accepted form of chastisement, to which most women are apparently reconciled. It is only if the husband administers it with little or no justification, or with excessive brutality, that the wife will feel really aggrieved, or that she will receive any sympathy from others. And, as Masilo said: 'If you beat your wife now, let it be a long time before you beat her again; don't beat her too often, or she will begin to despise you.' Occasionally a man will also punish his wife by going to eat and sleep with some other woman, but as this is likely to make her still more angry he does not do so unless he wishes to be deliberately vindictive.

A woman when annoyed with her husband generally sulks for a day or two, and refuses to talk to him or to pay him any other attention. It is considered wrong of her to swear at him obscenely or to resist him forcibly if he beats her, and any such action on her part will not only cause him to beat her more violently, but will also make her forfeit public sympathy. Her principal weapon, and one which, according to female informants, is usually an effective means of bringing a husband to heel, is to deny him sexual intercourse, 'even although he implores you; but if you still refuse, he will try to compel you, and when you keep your legs together he will pinch them to force them apart'.

If a husband continually neglects or ill-treats his wife, she may complain to his parents or other senior relatives. They question the two about their differences, and after pointing out where the fault lies implore them to live together peacefully. The husband is reprimanded, and warned that he is not entitled to treat the woman as he likes: she is not only his wife, she is also the 'daughter' of his senior relatives, who sought her for him, and with whose cattle her *bogadi* was given, so that if he behaves badly towards her he will be offending them as well. If this warning does not help, and he persists in his conduct, she ultimately leaves him, and takes refuge with her own family.

A husband, again, if he has any serious complaint against his wife, should likewise report her to his senior relatives, who will reprimand her. But if he becomes alienated from her, he more usually diverts his attentions to some other woman. He may also cease to plough for his wife, and to provide her with clothes and other necessities. If he actually wants to get rid of her, he will remove her belongings into the courtyard and lock her out of the hut, so forcing her to return to her parents for shelter.

A wife's flight to her own people is the customary procedure whenever a serious break occurs between her and her husband, or even when she has been more severely thrashed than usual. She remains with them until he comes to ask her to return. This he will generally do soon enough, for he may have no one in his compound to cook for him and to look after the children, while his neighbours will mock him for having to sleep alone. If he does not come, his wife's parents will after a while send for him, or may go themselves to ask for an explanation. A meeting is then held, at which the parents and close relatives on both sides are present. Husband and wife are each asked to state why they have separated, and the rights and wrongs of the matter are fully discussed. A determined effort is made to bring about a reconciliation, and to induce the couple to live together again. If the wife is found to blame, her parents scold her severely, and perhaps also beat her. If the husband is the offender, he will likewise be scolded and warned to be more considerate in future. If his conduct has been particularly reprehensible – if, for instance, he followed his wife to her parents' home and beat her there – he may even be made to pay them damages for the insult. She is then sent back to his home, accompanied by one or two female relatives who bring with them porridge and beer for a small reunion feast.

The circumstances under which women leave their husbands are illustrated by the following instances. Senna and his wife were together at the fields preparing to bring their harvest home.

He went to visit a neighbour, and during his absence his herd-boy lent someone else a thong used for roping cattle. Senna came back drunk and quarrelsome, and on discovering that the strap was missing scolded his wife for not looking after his property, and thrashed her so severely that she bled. She ran for refuge to the hut of her paternal uncle close by, and after staying there a few days went to her mother's home in Mochudi. A fortnight later, when the people had come home from the fields, Senna was called to his mother-in-law's compound. He came with one of his uncles, and was confronted by his wife, her mother, her paternal uncle, and her brother. They inquired why he had behaved so brutally, and pointed out that he could not reasonably expect a woman to look after such things as cattle-straps. They blamed him for getting too drunk to know what he was doing, and told him that before his wife would be sent back to him he must pay them an ox as damages for shedding her blood.

Another man, Rapula, stayed out very late several nights in succession, visiting a concubine. His wife in revenge kept him out of her hut three nights running, by locking the door and refusing to admit him when he came home. Infuriated by this, he at last broke through the wall and forced his way in. She hid behind the door, and as he came in struck him with her fist and knocked him to the ground. Then she ran at once to the ward-head to complain that her husband was assaulting her. The ward-head came back with her, and on inquiry found that it was she who had attacked her husband. He left them, but came the following morning with a whip, which he handed to Rapula, saying: 'Get out into the open and fight, and we shall see if a woman can treat her husband as an equal.' Rapula began whipping his wife, in front of the people gathered round to watch, and within a few minutes she broke away and fled, weeping bitterly, to her parents' home. She stayed there for two days, and was then sent back, before Rapula had come to seek her. Despite the provocation she had had, public opinion condemned her strongly for having assaulted her husband, a thing no wife should ever do, and even her parents refused to sympathize with her.

A somewhat similar case was that of Mampe. Her husband,

Mongale, was cohabiting with another woman whom he planned to make his second wife. This so angered her that she went one night to the compound where he was sleeping with this woman, and stood in the middle of the courtyard shouting and swearing at him obscenely. For this he took her to court. The chief said that no wife had the right to follow her husband into another woman's home or to swear at him, and she was therefore given six cuts with a cane. A little later Mongale fell ill, and Mampe ran away from him and went to live with another man. We shall see below what happened after this.

Modiane, again, was forced by her parents to marry a man whom she disliked intensely. She ignored him as much as possible, and refused to let him consummate the marriage. He went off to work at the mines, and on his return found her pregnant by a lover. Roused to jealous anger, he beat her so violently that she aborted. Thereupon she collected all her belongings, and went back to her own people. A week later he came with his relatives to ask for her, but her parents refused to send her back. When I again visited Mochudi six months afterwards, she was still living apart from her husband, who in the meantime had taken no further steps in the matter, although his friends were urging him to divorce her.

Modibe, whose opinion on the treatment of women I quoted above, was perpetually quarrelling with his wife and thrashing her, especially when he was drunk. She herself was very cheeky, and frequently gave him good reason for his anger. On one occasion, in 1933, he became so annoyed with her that he cut her skirt from her body and threw it into the fire. She took up a stick and tried to assault him, but he snatched it from her hands and beat her severely instead. She ran home to her parents. Next day Modibe came to fetch her, but her father refused to let her go back, and reported the matter instead to the ward-head. Modibe was summoned and tried, and the court not only made him pay his father-in-law an ox as damages, but also thrashed him. His wife was then taken back to him. The following year he quarrelled again with her after a beer-drink, where, he alleged, she had paid far too much attention to another man. On their way home they kept swearing violently at each other, until he lost patience and started to assault her. She ran off to her parents, and when I left Mochudi two months later was still living with them. Modibe had done nothing in the meantime to get her back.

As some of these episodes show, if a husband treats his wife very badly, or she fails to pay him proper respect, the offender may be tried publicly and punished. It is seldom, however, that matrimonial disputes do come to court. They are dealt with first at a gathering of the two families concerned. Here, as we have seen, every effort is made to bring the couple together again. The attempt is generally successful. The wife goes back to her husband, and they carry on once more as well as they can. Many a marriage owes its continued existence to the part thus played by the relatives in restoring peace between husband and wife, and in using their influence and authority to rebuke and punish the offender. It is not easy to flout their will, for they figure too prominently in one's life, and their advice is generally sound enough to provide a basis, even if only temporarily, for more satisfactory relations in the future.

If, however, the relatives are unable to patch up the quarrel, they refer it to the court of their ward-head. Here the whole matter is, as usual, investigated afresh, and another attempt is made to reconcile the couple. The husband, if found greatly to blame, may also be punished and made to pay damages to the wife's parents, while if on the other hand she is at fault she will be severely reprimanded or thrashed. Public opinion does not allow spouses to injure each other with impunity beyond certain limits, but, justice having been done, it then tries to bring them together again. But if the wife refuses to go back to her husband, or if he does not want her again, the case is sent to the chief's court. Formerly, it is said, all matrimonial disputes were finally settled in the court of the ward-head, who, if unable to reconcile the couple, would divorce them. Nowadays, however, such cases are almost invariably sent to the chief. He too tries to effect a reconciliation, but failing this he will dissolve the marriage, and will also decide what must be done about the children, the *bogadi* and the household property. He may likewise, if circumstances warrant it, punish the one who is obviously to blame for the breach.

In every instance, therefore, first the relatives and then the tribal authorities try to prevent the marriage from breaking up finally. This point needs to be emphasized, for it is one of the strongest forces making for stability. Recognizing that husband or wife may have just cause for complaint, they reprimand or punish the offender, but then urge the couple to try living together again. That their efforts are generally successful is shown by the fact that divorce is not at all frequent, despite the many domestic quarrels that occur. Comprehensive statistics are not obtainable; but of 304 marriages in genealogical records that I collected only nine had been dissolved, while of the eighty-eight cases tried in the chief's court, during the period July 1935 to June 1939, only two were for divorce. To the husband a divorce means at the least that he deprives himself of a very useful servant. Hence it is usually only if his wife is barren and unruly, or repeatedly unfaithful, or neglects her household duties completely, that he will insist on getting rid of her. A wife, on the other hand, loses the prestige and material advantages of being a married woman, and is generally also deprived of her children. She will therefore seek to divorce her husband only if he persistently ill-treats her or fails completely to maintain and support her.

I have already quoted, in Chapter 7, the cases of Ramfatshe and Mmadikhukhu, whose marriage was dissolved because the wife refused to grant her husband sexual access but nevertheless became pregnant by a lover, and of Ramasilo and Dorika, where the husband's infidelity coupled with his breach of an important sexual taboo was the immediate motive for his wife's divorcing him. A few other instances will help to illustrate the variety of factors that may lead to divorce.

Ditlhare took as his second (bigamous) wife a woman named Mmamoseki. He made excessive sexual demands upon her, and thrashed her whenever she refused to sleep with him. Her senior co-wife also treated her very badly, making her do all the more irksome domestic tasks. Unable to bear this any longer, Mmamoseki left her husband and went home to her parents. Ditlhare came to fetch her back, but she refused to go, and her parents supported her. The case ultimately came before the chief. Ditlhare insisted that he wanted Mmamoseki back, but both she and her parents refused to have anything more to do with him. Seeing that there was no possibility of reconciliation, the chief dissolved the marriage; but, finding Mmamoseki to blame, he ordered her to be thrashed, and, since she had no children, her *bogadi* was to be returned. Ditlhare was however told to give her a few head of cattle to support her in future.

Ramanakana became mad: he used to rush wildly about the village, he could never settle down to work, and he beat his wife frequently for no apparent reason. At last his parents told her that she had better go back to her own people, since it was obviously impossible for her to continue living with such a man. The matter was referred to the local court, which agreed that a divorce was desirable. The wife was allowed to take her children with her, so that she could look after them until they were grown. No penalty was imposed upon either her or her husband, since she was not to blame, while he could hardly be considered responsible for his actions.

Pholoma married Tsholofelo in 1931. In 1934 she left him and went back to her own people. He came to ask for her, but although her family wished her to go back she refused. She said that he had never once attempted to have intercourse with her, so that she was still barren; that during the two years he worked in Johannesburg he had sent her nothing; and that since his return he had not ploughed for her. Pholoma retorted that the real trouble was that Tsholofelo had many lovers, whom he had often found in the house, and that unless she gave them up he would continue to neglect her. After several futile discussions between the two families and at the local court, the matter came before the chief. Here it was decided that Tsholofelo's troubles were due to her own misconduct, and, since she refused to go back to her husband, the marriage was dissolved, and her father was ordered to give back her *bogadi*. The judgement was duly entered in the court record-book. The District Commissioner, on reading it, pointed out that, since the marriage had taken place in church, the chief had acted beyond his powers in trying the case. It was therefore brought up again, this time in the court of the District Commissioner, with Tsholofelo as the plaintiff; and she was granted a divorce on the grounds of her husband's malicious desertion and failure to support her.

As this case shows, the chief's jurisdiction in matters of divorce does not extend to people married by the missionary or by any other recognized marriage officer of the Protectorate Administration. Such people have, since 1891, been subject to the local European laws regarding marriage. This means that they can be divorced only in the court of the District Commissioner, and that the grounds for divorce are limited to adultery or malicious desertion by either husband or wife. Formerly it meant also that the injured party could claim a favourable division of all the property in the joint estate, and obtain custody of the minor children. These provisions, as we shall see, conflicted in several respects with tribal law and custom. Very few Kgatla, however, realized the implications of the Church marriage. To them it was primarily a religious ceremony, and they expected that if they were divorced questions of property and the custody of children would be dealt with as usual according to tribal law. On discovering their mistake, they became more and more reluctant to sue for divorce in the European courts, and persisted in bringing their disputes to the chief. At last, in 1925, Isang as regent wrote to the High Commissioner, pointing out the difficulties that were involved.

European marriage [he said] is respected, recognized and encouraged among my people, but that form of marriage is primarily resorted to for religious reasons, and without any intention that it should exclude traditional tribal intervention in possible disputes. As this side of the question becomes more clearly realized, it operates to discourage European marriage. While any people can be induced to try a new form of marriage, I find that in marital disputes my subjects cling most tenaciously to Native notions of propriety, and it is almost inconceivable to them that they should regularly resort to the Magisterial Court for the adjustment of these affairs.

In view of this increasing reluctance to submit marital issues to the European courts, I am constantly asked to exercise jurisdiction in such matters, and my refusal simply results in the matters being left unsettled. Wives and minor children remain without any claim whatever upon the property of an absconding husband, and the deserted spouse is left without support or the possibility of remarriage. Remarriages perforce condoned by me, under Native law, sever the parties from their Church. With the increase of European marriages, it is noticeable that parties who are unhappy enough to have disputes are rendered lawless; it is a most unhappy consequence of the acceptance of the Christian rites that such penalties should ensue.

On the other hand, though my refusals to adjudicate have not availed to send the parties to the European Courts, my attitude has been subversive of tribal prestige and authority, and I feel it a distressing circumstance that the authority of the chief and the *Lekgotla* [tribal council] should be weakened without alternative provision being made on lines acceptable to the majority of individuals concerned.

As a result of his representations, the Bechuanaland Protectorate Native Marriages Proclamation of 1926 was issued. It reaffirmed that, in marriages solemnized by missionaries or other recognized marriage officers, the only authority that can grant a divorce is the District Commissioner's court, the chief having no jurisdiction in the matter. But it went on to provide that if the parties concerned applied formally to the District Commissioner, he could order that questions of property should be dealt with, not according to European law, but by a Native chief and according to Native law. This did not satisfy some of the other chiefs in the Protectorate, and after discussion with them the Proclamation was amended in 1928. As it now stands, it provides that when Natives married under European law are divorced, their property shall be dealt with afterwards by the chief in accordance with Native law. If they prefer to have it dealt with according to European law, they must apply specially to the District Commissioner, and satisfy him that their mode of life is such that it would be 'just and equitable' for the civil law to prevail. So far no Kgatla have exercised this option, and indeed only two cases of divorce have been tried in the District

Commissioner's court since 1926. In this connection, however, it must be remembered that only about one marriage in seven takes place in church and so becomes subject to the civil law.

Under tribal law, when a couple are divorced their household property is divided between them according to the circumstances of the case. The corn in their granaries is measured out by baskets or bags, and portioned out equally between them. Personal belongings, like clothes, go with their respective owners. Domestic utensils, like baskets and pots, are usually taken by the wife, unless they have all been provided by the husband, who may then be allowed to keep some behind. The compound remains his, and so do the fields he had procured for the use of his wife. Any fields that she may have received from her parents, however, revert to her own people. The household cattle all belong to the husband. But if the wife has no children, and also no cattle of her own, she may be awarded a few head, say two to four, to support her in future. If she has children she usually receives no cattle at all, as it is assumed that she will be able to live on the *bogadi* retained by her parents. She can also take back any property she may have acquired in her own right, whether by gift or by purchase, but if she has children she must leave all her cattle behind to be inherited in due course by them.

If there are children of the marriage, the husband cannot as a rule recover his *bogadi,* even if he is the innocent party. It is only if the children are not actually his, but the offspring of an adulterer, that he is given the right to choose between them and the *bogadi*. Such cases are however very exceptional, and if there are children by the husband himself he can never regain his *bogadi*. If on the other hand the marriage is barren, he may, according to circumstances, be allowed to recover his *bogadi*. Formerly he was entitled to it in every instance, even if the wife was the innocent party. Chief Lentswe, however, introduced a modification that is still in force. If the husband has ill-treated or neglected his wife, and so given her just grounds for divorce, he must forfeit his cattle. But if she is held to be at fault, as in the cases of Mmamoseki and Tsholofelo quoted above, the *bogadi* must be returned. 'If the girl tosses her head (at her husband)', says the relevant proverb, 'the cattle will toss their tails (in the face of her father when they leave his kraal).' In such cases the same number of cattle must be returned as were originally given, the people among whom they were distributed being responsible for replacing them. This may be one of the reasons why they are usually so anxious to avert a divorce, although of course it cannot apply to those cases where the marriage is fruitful.

The children of a marriage invariably belong to their father if *bogadi* has already been given. If still young, they may go with their mother to be brought up by her and her people, and when old enough they return to their father. In the meantime he must continue to support them by sending them occasional gifts of food and clothing, and he should visit them from time to time to see how they are faring. If none of them is still an infant, the mother may nevertheless be allowed to take one or more daughters to help her at her home. The father must however contribute to their support, conducts their marriages, and owns the *bogadi* received for them. If he himself has not yet given *bogadi* for his wife, the children in theory all belong to her people, and in case of divorce go back home with her. They have then no claim on his estate, while any *bogadi* subsequently received when the daughters marry is taken by the mother's parents. Usually, however, a man who has not yet given *bogadi* for his wife will hurriedly do so when the trouble starts, so as not to forfeit his rights to the children. It is therefore only in exceptional instances that a woman will receive custody of all her children. But the latter then have the right, when grown up, to return to their father, provided that he is willing to receive them and pays the customary maintenance fees to their mother's people.

Tribal law differs from European law not only in the provisions governing property and the custody of children, but also in the facilities it provides for divorce. It does not usually regard adultery in itself as sufficient ground, but is on the other hand more generous than the European law, and in effect grants a divorce whenever the couple find it impossible to live together satisfactorily as husband and wife. The exact technical details are of minor concern, the degree of estrangement being the more important factor. People married in church are thus at a disadvantage compared with the rest, for unless they can produce evidence satisfying the conditions of the European law, the District Commissioner is unable to divorce them, no matter how unhappy their marriage may be. Furthermore, they must pay various stamp fees and other dues before their case can come to trial, and sometimes find it necessary to employ lawyers to argue for them, since they are unfamiliar with the procedure. For these reasons Isang, at the meeting of the Native Advisory Council in 1939, asked that the chief should be given jurisdiction in all cases of divorce, no matter how the marriage was contracted. It is unlikely that this will be done, but some of the other anomalies arising from the differences between European and Native law are now being investigated by the Administration, and legislation will probably soon be introduced to remove them.

The introduction of Christian marriage not only had the legal consequences already described. In its early years it provided another new ground for divorce, because the Church would not accept polygamists as members, and laid down that they had to get rid of all their wives but the first if they wished to join. Lentswe, for instance, sent away his two junior wives when he became a Christian, and I have several other instances in my genealogies where the same thing was done. The children by these wives usually remained with the husband, but the women were given cattle and other property for themselves, and many afterwards married again. The Church law, although still in force, is nowadays hardly ever applied, as very few men indeed become professing Christians once they are polygamists. It is more usual, in fact, for men to leave the Church in order to take an additional wife.

THE STATUS OF DIVORCÉES

Both men and women may marry again after they have been divorced. Men almost invariably do so, but the women are apparently not regarded with favour as possible wives. 'Seize the breast of a widow,' says the proverb, 'that of a divorcée is unstable,' i.e. she is considered a typical example of feminine frailty, a woman who may as readily leave her new husband as she did his predecessor. Much, however, depends upon the circumstances under which she was divorced. If she has no children, and her husband took back his *bogadi*, she can be married again without any difficulty. But if he did not recover his *bogadi*, and especially if there are also children by the marriage, she will not be so readily married by someone else. 'Relationship-in-law does not rot,' goes the saying. A man once married into a family is still regarded as its son-in-law even in case of divorce, so long as he has not taken back his cattle; and there is nothing to prevent him and his former wife from living together again if they wish. And if someone else wants to marry her instead, her parents should let her ex-husband know, so that he may have the opportunity of taking her back if he wishes and she also is agreeable. Should he make no attempt to do so, he is held to have renounced her permanently, and she is free to get married again. Her new husband must however also give *bogadi* to her people, otherwise the children he begets by her may be claimed by his predecessor.

In practice it is seldom that a divorced woman is married again if she has sons by her ex-husband. 'A bull's mother is not taken in marriage,' it is said. She is held to be under the power of her sons, and even if she marries again she is expected to return to them when no longer able to bear, or they may themselves take her back. Her present husband cannot object if she wishes to return, nor can his predecessor, for she will be going to her own sons, who will feed and support her.

The story of Mongale, to which I have already referred, provides a case in point. After marrying Mampe, he decided, much to her disgust, to take a second wife. While he was still conducting the betrothal negotiations for this woman, he became so ill that he was unable to look after himself. Mampe decided that this was a good opportunity for revenge, so she left him and went to live with another man named Tsome. Mongale recovered from his illness, and married the second woman. He paid no further attention to Mampe; he did not try to get her back, nor did he plough her fields or support her in other ways. This was taken as a sign that he no longer recognized her as his wife. She lived for some years with Tsome, who treated her rather badly. At last she became ill and very weak, and in despair sent to Mongale for assistance. He replied by saying: 'I am going to take you back, because when you deserted me you left me a son, and it is he who will have to look after you. But I claim as my own the daughter you have borne to Tsome; she is "the child of my cattle", because when you ran away I did not ask for the return of my *bogadi*.' Tsome raised no objection, and Mampe with her daughter went to live with Mongale. The daughter grew up, and in due course was married to a man who gave *bogadi* for her. Tsome thereupon claimed this *bogadi*, saying that he was the father of the girl. The chief, however, ruled that as Tsome had not given *bogadi* for Mampe she was never his wife, but only his concubine; Mongale therefore had all along been the girl's legal father, and as such was entitled to the *bogadi* now given for her.

A divorced woman until she marries again lives in the home of her father or brother. While there she is subject to his legal authority, and is supported by him. But she is regarded as an adult woman capable of looking after herself, and usually little objection is made to her becoming a concubine. Her family, in fact, rather welcome it, for it means that her lover will help to support her. The few divorced women I knew who were living at home all had their steady lovers, and several had borne children, but in no case had action been taken against the lover for seduction. In theory the children such a woman bears may be claimed by her former husband if he had not recovered his *bogadi*, but in practice it is seldom that he avails himself of this right unless he takes her back as well. Her lover can obtain the children either by marrying her with *bogadi* or by paying the usual maintenance fees to her guardian. Failing this, they remain with her, and are held to belong to her own people.

11. Death and its Social Consequences

THE LIVING AND THE DEAD

Our discussion of matrimonial disagreements and divorce showed once again that among the Kgatla marriage unites two groups and not merely two persons. The interest taken by kinsmen in the relations between husband and wife is due only partly to solicitude for the welfare of the couple. The passage of *bogadi,* and various other features of marriage, confer certain rights upon the husband's people and impose certain obligations upon the wife's. It is this as much as anything else that makes both families endeavour to prevent a final separation which will disturb the existing relationship. The same tendency is seen in the usages connected with death and widowhood. In Kgatla law death does not immediately dissolve a marriage. Except under special circumstances, a widow remains attached to her husband's people and must continue to bear them children, while on the other hand a widower still has certain claims upon his wife's parents, especially if she has died barren. The surviving spouse, moreover, is ritually purified and observes various mourning usages for a year or so after his bereavement. These serve in the first place to express formally the sorrow felt at the loss of one's mate. But since they are prescribed by law and custom, and must be observed whether there is true sorrow or not, we may regard them as still another duty imposed upon people as part of their marriage, even although the person because of whom they are carried out is no longer alive.

Before proceeding to describe these usages, I wish to deal briefly with the Kgatla beliefs concerning the fate of the dead, for they will help to explain the behaviour of mourners. In the old days, men dying at home were buried in the cattle-kraal of their family-group or ward, and women in the back-yard of their compound. The corpse was laid out by some old people under the direction of the deceased's maternal uncle, whose duty it was 'to handle the putrefaction of his sister's children'. A man was buried with his weapons in his hands, a woman with her hoe and some seeds of every cultivated grain; both were also dressed in the clothes they wore when alive. 'They were then equipped for their journey to the world of the dead, where a man would continue to herd his grandfather's cattle, and a woman to cultivate the soil.' Finally, the corpse was wrapped in old skins, but for a man of some importance the wet skin of an ox specially killed for the purpose was used instead. The grave was a round hole, with a niche to one side, in which the body was placed in a crouching position, with the head facing west, 'so that he was ready to get up and walk to the place where the souls of the other dead had gone'.

As these customs indicate, the Kgatla believed in the survival of the dead. It was held that the souls of dead people became spirits, which ultimately found their way to a world vaguely located somewhere underground. Here they led a life very similar to that on earth. But they continued also to take an active interest in the fortunes of their living descendants, over whose behaviour they exercised a powerful control. They rewarded with good health and prosperity those who treated them with becoming respect and obedience, but punished with sickness, economic loss, or other misfortune those who neglected them or who offended against the prevailing social code, of which they were the guardians. In order, therefore, to retain their favour, no opportunity was lost of propitiating them. The worship of the dead was in fact the outstanding feature of Kgatla religion.

Each family was held to be under the direct guidance of its own ancestors, who in turn were interested only in the affairs of their own descendants. They retained the individual characteristics they had possessed while alive, and their importance as deities was determined largely by the status they had enjoyed on earth. In practice worship was generally directed only to those more recently dead, like a father or grandfather, whose personal peculiarities were known and remembered. The head of the family, as senior living representative of the ancestors, conducted the rites. He sacrificed and prayed to the dead whenever they revealed themselves through dreams or calamity or in some other form that the diviners interpreted as a sign that they were offended. He also invoked them on all important domestic occasions, like birth, marriage, or the undertaking of some new enterprise, when he offered them libations of beer or sacrifices of fowls, goats, and in emergencies even cattle, and prayed to them for continued guidance and help, or thanked them for the blessings they had sent. His role of family priest gave him considerable authority over his dependants; they could not approach their ancestors except through his agency, so that if they quarrelled with him they were cut off from the deities controlling their welfare. A special ceremony of reconciliation was then necessary before he would again sacrifice on their behalf.

The introduction and spread of Christianity and other European influences have profoundly affected the old religious system. Burial customs have altered considerably. Influential men are occasionally still buried in their cattle-kraals, but all other people, except the young children, are now buried in special graveyards on the outskirts of the villages. As soon as anyone dies, the women around him start wailing loudly. This conventional signal attracts all the neighbours. The women enter the compound and join in the wailing, while the men go to sit silently at the council-place, unless asked to help in the preparations for burial. Messages are meanwhile sent to the near relatives, who must immediately abandon whatever they are doing and go to the stricken household. The maternal uncle is still responsible for laying out the corpse. A dead person is buried in the clothes he liked best when alive, but not, as a rule, with any of his other possessions. Whenever possible, he is put into a coffin made of wooden planks covered with black print; the materials are bought in the store and knocked together by a carpenter or blacksmith. Failing this, he is buried in some old skins or blankets, but also in a horizontal position.

The funeral is held as soon as possible, preferably on the very day of the death. If it takes place on the following morning, the sympathizers spend the night with the bereaved family, the women sleeping or wailing in the compound, while the men sit or sleep at the council-place. The coffin is carried to the graveyard by hand, or transported by wagon or sledge. As it leaves the compound, the women burst out again into very loud wailing, and then fall silently into procession behind the men. At Christian funerals, however, all sing hymns as they slowly walk along. The grave, dug by some volunteers under the direction of a near paternal relative, is a fairly deep rectangular hole without a niche. The surviving spouse throws in the first spadeful of earth, and is followed by the close relatives in order of seniority. After the grave has been filled in, a mound of stones is erected over it, with a big slab planted upright at the head. The graves of the royal family, who have their own burial-ground behind the Mission station, are sometimes covered instead with inscribed tombstones of European type. If the dead person was a Christian, he is buried with the appropriate church service, conducted by the missionary or an evangelist. There are no corresponding rites at heathen funerals.

All the people present at the funeral return to the stricken household. Here they are given water to clean their hands (formerly also their feet) from 'the contamination of the grave'. The women then make unleavened porridge for them to eat. It may not be seasoned with anything, 'for it is sadness', but some medicine is added to the portion eaten by the newly-bereaved widow or widower. The following day, or as soon after as possible, an ox or a goat is slaughtered for the feast known as 'sadness'. The meat is cooked and eaten on the spot by all the relatives and close friends of the family, who must be specially invited for the occasion. It may not be salted or seasoned with any relish. The bones are afterwards carefully gathered together and burned, to prevent anyone from stealing them to bewitch the surviving members of the family. These funeral feasts, which were held also in the old days, are still observed by Christians as well as by heathens.

Modern beliefs concerning the fate of the dead vary considerably. Hardly any of the younger people know just what is meant by the term *badimo* (ancestral spirits), and many of their elders also are unable to explain it clearly. Professing Christians have accepted the Church doctrine of immortality. They say that when a person dies his soul, according to his behaviour on earth, goes either to Heaven, where it lives in eternal peace and happiness, or to Hell, where it will burn for ever. The idea of resurrection has apparently made little impression upon them, and many are openly sceptical, pointing out that no one has yet seen a man risen from the dead. Some of the heathens retain the old belief that the soul goes underground to the world of the dead, but they seldom profess to know what happens to it there. Others maintain that it is simply blown away by the wind, so that when a person dies he is annihilated, just like an animal. Most of them are familiar with the Christian teaching, but scoff at it, particularly at the doctrine of resurrection. 'Then also,' said Natale, 'they tell us that the soul of a dead man goes to Heaven. But who has ever seen it going there? And why is it that only people go to Heaven, and not cattle? What then happens to cattle, for they also die?'

Both Christians and heathens also speak freely of *dipoko* ('ghosts', from the Afrikaans '*spook*'), a conception which, as the name suggests, is almost certainly borrowed from Europeans. They say that if a person, after death, regrets the cattle and other wealth he left behind, he will haunt the places he frequented while alive. His soul rests in the grave by day, but emerges at night and wanders about in human or animal guise seeking its lost treasures. People are afraid of these ghosts, and will therefore usually avoid a graveyard at night. There seem to be no other customary usages relating to them, except that occasionally, when a wealthy man is buried, some coins are put into his coffin to prevent him from becoming a spook.

Ancestor-worship itself has virtually disappeared. Some magicians do on occasion still invoke the spirits of their ancestors, especially when preparing their medicines or performing an important ceremony. But even they seem to have abandoned the more elaborate routine offerings and sacrifices. Among the rest there is now no form of organized religion at all outside

Christianity. It is usually only in sickness that the influence of the ancestors is still recognized, for *dikgaba* is held to be the punishment they inflict on someone who has violated the social code by offending against a senior living relative. This type of sickness, as we have seen, cannot be cured until the injured relative washes the patient with medicines and prays for his recovery. Even Christians continue to practise the rite, although generally aware that the prayers are really directed to the ancestors.

Both the traditional beliefs and modern Christian teaching encourage people to hope that they will meet again the relatives and friends of whom death has deprived them. To a few this may afford some consolation, but the majority certainly do not have much faith in it. 'If God really listens to our prayers', they say, referring to the doctrine of resurrection, 'Why can't He send back the dead person for whom we are longing, so that we can talk to him, if only once, and then he can go back again, and we will believe it all.' This statement, and the many others like it that were made to me, show that sometimes at least there is genuine sorrow at the loss of someone beloved. The mourning ceremonies are then more than a mere formality, but provide a recognized channel for the expression of true grief. My impression, however, is that people fairly soon recover from the loss of a husband or wife. It is seldom that a dead spouse seems to be permanently regretted, and considering the relations that usually exist between married people while both are alive this is not unexpected. Kgatla usage, too, does not encourage enduring grief. The mourning ceremonies allow a decent interval for the expression of such sorrow as there may be, but both widows and widowers, if young enough, are then expected to resume married life with someone else. To remain faithful to the memory of a dead spouse is considered unnecessary in all but the old, and in practice, however acute the sense of bereavement at first, most people seem after a year or two to resign themselves to the inevitable, and to be more concerned with their own fate in this world than with the prospect of rejoining in the next those whom they have lost.

MOURNING OBSERVANCES

While the beliefs and practices relating to the dead have so greatly changed, the old mourning ceremonies have survived relatively intact. In the first place, a surviving spouse must be specially purified immediately after his bereavement. The reason usually given for this links up with the theories of 'hot blood' that I have already discussed. It is held that, owing to the intimate sexual association between husband and wife, their 'bloods' have intermingled in their bodies. When one of them dies, the 'blood' of the other misses its counterpart, and so becomes 'hot'. The survivor himself is said to be 'sick', 'because his blood needs the dead person's'. Should he go about he will also injure people, cattle, and crops, and keep away the rain, for wherever he treads the ground will become scorched. It is therefore essential that steps should be taken as soon as possible to 'cure' him. This was formerly considered so important, particularly because of the dangers threatening the rain, that the chief or village headman, as soon as any death was reported to him, would himself send one of the recognized 'tribal doctors' to purify the survivor. Lentswe after he became a Christian no longer followed the custom, but Isang during his regency revived it. Nowadays, the mourners may themselves summon a doctor known to be skilled in the work, but if necessary the chief will still recommend one. Even members of the Church adhere faithfully to this purification, and in fact most of the ceremonies I saw or which were described to me were performed in the families of professing Christians.

From the moment a death has taken place, the newly-bereaved spouse remains inside his compound. Until he has been purified, he may not go outside, except perhaps to attend the funeral or to relieve himself, nor may he eat anything at all or wash himself. He spends most of his time lying down in his hut, for 'he is a sick person, made weak by sorrow and the loss of his mate's blood'. The purification ceremony is held either on the day of the funeral itself, or as soon afterwards as possible. If for any reason it is delayed, the old woman looking after the survivor gives him a drink of water cooked with the bark of a certain tree. This medicine is termed 'foolish water', because it is held to dull the senses and relieve the anguish of the heart. He is then free to eat and drink other food before the doctor comes.

The details of the ceremony vary considerably from one doctor to another. The general procedure, however, is fundamentally the same. The dead person's family slaughter a goat. The doctor cuts up the roots and bulbs of certain plants, especially those used in making rain, and puts them into a potsherd standing on the fire. As they burn, the mourner crouches over them so that his face is completely bathed in the smoke. The doctor then grinds the ashes to powder, which he divides into two portions. He sprinkles one portion over the inflated large intestine of the goat, with which he beats the mourner on the loins 'to reverse his entrails', 'because they have been disturbed by the loss of the blood to which they were accustomed'. Some doctors, however, mix the powder with the roasted and ground entrails of the goat, and smear the mixture into small cuts made on the joints of the mourner's body. Others mix the powder with the bran of newly-stamped corn, and rub the mixture all over the mourner's body to 'cleanse' him. The second portion of the powder is given to him to take with his food. Some meat from the foreleg of the goat is roasted; he dips a small piece into the powder, bites it and spits it out, dips another piece in and swallows it, and then eats what is left. Some of the powder is also cooked with porridge, which he eats in the same way.

This rite concluded, the mourner remains in his compound for six days, mostly lying down in his hut. During this time he is waited upon by a female relative past the menopause, 'because the hands of an old woman are not hot'. She prepares all his food, and attends to his other wants. He eats with the left hand, which is normally taboo, 'but he is still unclean, so that he cannot eat with the right hand like anybody who is happy and joyful'. He also takes some of the medicinal powder with each meal, in the manner already described. On the seventh day he is free to go about again, and to eat meat and porridge in the normal way. But the first time he drinks beer or milk after his bereavement, he uses the powdered medicine again in the same way as with the other foods. This method of eating is identical with that formerly observed at the tasting of the first-fruits, and, like it, is known as 'to bite'. It evidently symbolizes his entry into a new mode of life.

The doctoring and seclusion just described do not apply to widows or widowers whose marriage was childless. 'They have nothing to be sorry for,' said Rapedi; 'they are both boys, there is no blood in their body from any man or woman; it is just as if they had not been married at all. It is only when they have had a child that their blood has been changed, and that they suffer from "mourning sickness".' The same explanation was given by other informants. It illustrates once again the dominant role played by child-bearing in the Kgatla conception of marriage. But the mourner is as usual given 'foolish water' to take before he eats or drinks anything, 'so that his heart must not be heavy'. He also 'bites' any food that he eats for the first time, and he carries out the various other usages described below. The brothers and sisters of a dead person observe no special mourning usages, while his parents and children are as a rule only shaved.

Once the essential preliminary rites have been performed, the mourner is allowed to mix again with the people of the village. But on some suitable occasion afterwards, generally within a week or so, but sometimes much later, he and his children all have their heads shaved as a sign of mourning. The hair is cut round the sides and back, but not on the top. The surviving spouse and the last-born child are shaved at the home of the wife's people, whether it is she or her husband who is dead; the older children are shaved either there or in their own compound. The shaving is done in each case by a senior female relative. Thus, when Phiri died in 1932, his older children were shaved in his own home by his paternal aunt; the next day his widow and his youngest child went to her brother's home, where they were shaved by her paternal uncle's wife.

The occasion is usually celebrated by a feast. While the mourners are being shaved, the wife's father or brother slaughters a goat, whose meat is immediately cooked. Each of the women attending the ceremony brings with her some corn in a dish, from which the bereaved spouse takes a few grains, which he bites and spits out. This is done to prevent the corn in their fields from getting spoiled if at any time he goes past with 'the smell of death' still clinging to him. 'He tastes the corn of all his neighbours, so that this corn must not fear him.' The rest of the corn is made into unleavened porridge for the feast. The food is eaten by all the people present, the principal mourner first tasting it. Some of the meat is wrapped in the skin of the goat, and taken home by him, together with a bowl of porridge. There it is eaten by his local relatives and friends. A widow's parents also provide her on this occasion with the black clothes she must wear as a sign of mourning. She changes into them before going back to her husband's home.

When a woman has died, her husband gives her parents an ox or a goat to notify them formally of their loss. He may bring it on the day he goes to them to be shaved, but generally leaves it for a later occasion. He is in any case accompanied then by his children and some of his other relatives. The animal is driven into the cattle-kraal and tied to a post; its right ear is cut off and sliced to pieces, which are tied with sinews round the necks of the widower's younger children and their maternal cousins. This is done to prevent the latter from falling sick when playing with the orphans. The animal is then killed and eaten. The meat must be finished on the same day, and the bones are all thrown into the fire. No such rite is performed when a husband dies. But if he was a ward-head, or a man of some standing, his heirs, if they can afford it, should send an ox from his herd to the chief's council-place. It is killed immediately on arrival, and is eaten by all the men who are there.

In addition to these special rites, all newly-bereaved spouses observe the various usages incumbent upon people with 'hot blood'. They should, for instance, scatter *mogaga* peelings before them whenever they go anywhere for the first time since their bereavement, smear wet cow-dung on the wall of a hut when they first enter it, refrain from visiting sick people or confined women and abstain altogether from sexual intercourse. The period for which they must behave like this is generally said to be a year; some informants, however, maintain that it ends, according to the season, either when the harvest has been reaped or when the first rains have fallen. The survivor is then free to marry again, subject to the regulations dealt with below. But, if his previous marriage was fruitful, his 'blood' must be 'joined' with that of his new mate before they have sexual intercourse. As we have already seen, both are cut on the pubis, and blood from the wounds of the one is transferred to the wounds of the other. This will prevent them from suffering the misfortunes held to result from coitus with a 'hot-blooded' person.

It is not only a person's own family who are affected by his death. His relatives and friends also must observe certain rules of conduct. In the old days, as soon as a death had taken place, everybody in the village had to abstain for several days from all but the most essential activities. The people either sat idly at home, or, if acquainted with the stricken family, went to condole with them. Nowadays, the general taboo on work is no longer observed, but a dead person's neighbours usually wait a day or two before resuming their normal occupations. Some, especially the close relatives, sleep at the compound for a few days after the funeral to comfort the bereaved. During this time other relatives, friends, and acquaintances, keep coming there to condole. A man and a woman, both very close relatives who attended the dying person, are appointed to receive them, according to their sex, and to tell them how he became ill, and how he passed away. These formal visits are considered obligatory, especially for relatives, whose failure to come would arouse great resentment. If away from home, a man must call on the survivors as soon as he returns, even if several months have elapsed since the death.

THE FATE OF WIDOWS

Her period of mourning over, a widow's attachment to her husband's family nevertheless continues. It is her duty to remain with them, and normally she does so. Her eldest son takes his father's place as head of the family, and becomes responsible for supporting and maintaining her and her other children. In a polygamous family, the father is succeeded by the eldest son of the great wife, while the eldest son of each minor wife takes charge of her and of the property belonging to her house. But in matters affecting the household generally, she remains under the authority of the main heir, who looks after the common interests and matrimonial affairs of the whole family. The same principle is observed in the family of a man who married again after the death of his first wife. The latter's eldest son succeeds to the status and responsibilities of his father, while the eldest son of the second wife becomes her special guardian if old enough.

If the widow is still fairly young, and especially if her sons are all minors or she has none at all, her fate may be settled in various ways. In the old days custom demanded that her husband's younger brother, even if already married, should 'enter her hut', so that she might continue to bear. He was not regarded as her husband, but merely as her guardian, and apart from cohabiting with her he protected and supported her and her children, and looked after her husband's estate. The children he begot by her were legally her husband's. 'They are the children of the dead man's bones,' it was said, or 'of the rafters (of his hut)', or 'of his cattle', i.e. of the *bogadi* paid on his behalf for their mother. They were entitled to inherit from his estate, and if he had died without a son the first boy afterwards born to the widow succeeded him as head of the family. When Mare, one of the early Kgatla chiefs, died without male issue, his widow was taken over by his half-brother Teke, to whom she bore a son named Kgwefane. The boy was accepted as Mare's legal son and heir, and on attaining manhood duly became chief of the tribe.

The widow was not bound to accept her husband's younger brother as lover. She could choose any close relative-in-law whom she liked, and who was also willing to enter her hut. The matter was usually arranged by discussion soon after the period of mourning was over. A small feast was then held, at which she publicly indicated her choice. She sat in the centre of the court-yard next to a large covered pot of beer. Her husband's next brother went to the pot and uncovered it. If she did not want him, she replaced the lid. The man next in order of seniority then came forward in the same way. This continued until she left the lid lying where it was and began to serve out the beer, showing thereby her acceptance of the man who had uncovered it. In such cases he was generally either a junior paternal uncle or a paternal cousin of the husband. But in a polygamous family the eldest son of the great wife was sometimes allowed to take over his father's junior widows. Hence the saying: 'The man who lies with his "mother" is not killed, for he is begetting his younger brother.' Occasionally, too, a man might be allowed to 'inherit' his maternal uncle's widow. But an elder brother could not enter the hut of his junior.

Should the widow refuse to accept any of her relatives-in-law, 'they would regard her as a dog; why does she want to leave the group into which she was married, and to which she is bound by *bogadi*?' If their efforts to persuade her were futile, they could take the matter to court. Here, if she still refused, she was if childless sent back to her own people, who had to return the *bogadi* given for her. She was then free to marry someone else. But if she had children, she could remain where she was, although her relatives-in-law would then probably neglect or ill-treat her. If, on the other hand, none of them wanted her, as seems to have sometimes occurred, she could either continue to live among them and accept as lover another man of their ward, or she could go back to her own people and then marry some one else. She could not admit a man from another ward into her hut while still at her husband's home. This was considered adultery, for which both she and her lover might be punished. She belonged to her husband's people, and it was only by returning to her parents and reverting to the status of a daughter that she obtained the right to accept an outsider.

The 'inheritance' of widows is nowadays forbidden by the Church to its members. Some of them nevertheless practise it secretly, and the majority openly defend it. In *Lesedi la Sechaba* for March 1934, for instance, two of the young 'intellectuals' of the tribe criticized certain of the Church laws relating to marriage. They said about this particular custom that, owing to the

Mission attitude, a Christian widow was now afraid of always consulting her husband's brother, lest she be suspected of immorality with him; the result was a weakening of the friendly relations that should exist between her and the man mainly responsible for her welfare. Among heathens the custom still meets with general approval, and indeed public opinion tends to condemn a man failing to observe it. One of the complaints often made against the ex-regent Isang, even by Christians, was that he had not entered the hut of Seingwaeng, widow of his elder brother Kgafêla. I was told that the council of headmen several times asked him to do so, but that, for reasons of his own, he always refused. She was therefore 'looked after' instead by Bakgatla, her husband's half-brother, to whom she bore two children, who both died while infants.

Nevertheless, although it is still considered correct for a widow to be taken over by a close relative-in-law, the custom is not as extensively practised as might be expected. In 1935, of the twenty unmarried widows in Makgophana ward who were known to have lovers, only three had been properly 'inherited': one by the husband's junior paternal uncle, another by his younger brother, and a third by his son with a former wife. These figures, as far as I could observe, are apparently not exceptional. It must be remembered that even in the old days people were not absolutely forced to follow the custom, although social pressure was always very strong. Today, with the spread of 'civilized' ideas, they can avoid it more easily. Informants, at least, always refer to it as optional though desirable, and not as compulsory.

Where the widow is 'inherited', the traditional laws of legitimacy still prevail: the children she bears to her lover are held to be those of her late husband. They never call their begetter *ntate*, 'father', but refer to him in terms of the legal relationship in which he stands to them, e.g. as *rrangwane,* '(junior paternal) uncle'. If he is already married, he lives in his own home, but visits the widow periodically to sleep with her. If unmarried, he may come to live permanently at her compound until he takes a wife of his own. He can even marry the widow herself by giving a second *bogadi* to her parents. The children he begets by her will then be regarded as his, and not as his predecessor's. This form of marriage prevailed in the old days also, for I have several instances in my genealogies of its occurrence. It was, however, not as common as the practice of merely cohabiting with the woman, the necessity of giving fresh *bogadi* apparently being an obstacle.

If the widow is not taken over as concubine or wife by a relative-in-law, she can, if still fairly young, be married by some one else. Usually the matter is first discussed at a family gathering. If no one is willing to enter her hut, or she refuses the volunteers, she will be allowed to go back to her parents' home if she wishes. Her children if still young also go with her, so that she may look after them, but their father's relatives must contribute to their support. She can then be 'sought' in the usual way by a prospective husband, who must give *bogadi* to her parents in order to obtain the children he himself has by her. He has no claim to the children of his predecessor, unless the latter had not given *bogadi*. He may, however, help their mother to look after them until they are old enough to return to their own people. But it is said that he generally shows a marked preference for his own children by the woman, and tends to neglect or ill-treat those by her former husband. This is one of the reasons why it is sometimes held that a widow with children should not marry again.

The great majority of widows do actually remain among their husbands' people without remarrying: in Sikwane village (1929) and Rampedi ward (1932), of forty unmarried widows thirty-six were living with their husbands' people, while only four had gone back to their own paternal homes. If the woman has no adult sons, her husband's younger brother or next senior relative becomes her guardian. He looks after the cattle and other property of her husband's estate, from which he feeds and clothes her and her children and helps to plough her fields; he also assists her if she is involved in a court case, watches over the welfare and interests of her family generally, and in consultation with her arranges the marriages of her children. His responsibilities cease when her eldest son becomes a member of an age-regiment and so attains legal majority. But if there is no son, she remains dependent upon her guardian as long as she lives.

The guardian sometimes carries out his duties faithfully, especially if he has entered the woman's hut. Sometimes, however, he tends after a while to neglect his trust. He may fail to continue supporting her and her children, he may appropriate for his own use the cattle of her husband's estate, or he may pay little heed to her difficulties and troubles. Isang himself told me that he regarded the traditional system of guardianship as bad, for it can easily be abused. The opportunity of despoiling the estate is so convenient that not everybody is able to resist it, nor are all guardians equally willing to carry the burden of looking after another family as well as their own. The woman in such cases will appeal to her husband's other relatives, who are expected to intervene on her behalf. Often enough, however, they too tend to be unsympathetic, especially if she has no sons, and has not accepted one of them as lover. They leave her out of their family discussions, give her little help in work, and do not check the behaviour of her guardian as they should. This is of course exceptional rather than the rule, but many a widow nevertheless has to struggle hard to support herself and her children, and her life is sometimes pretty miserable. As one informant said, 'She lacks all comfort except when drinking beer, and then she manages to forget her troubles for a while.' In the last resort, however, she can always appeal to her own people, who will help her to bring the matter to court. Cases of this description are frequent enough to show that widows often have good cause for complaint. If it is proved that the guardian has not carried out his duties properly, he will be punished, or, if the chief thinks it advisable, he may be relieved altogether of his trust, which is then handed over to some other man, possibly of the woman's own family.

Three recent cases will serve to illustrate this. Mmamolebatsi, after the death of her husband, came under the guardianship of his younger brother Rateeng. He soon began to neglect her, failing to plough for her or to sell cattle for her and her children;

and when she complained he replied that he did not like the man she had taken as lover. She therefore went back to her own people, who appealed to the courts. Rateeng was fined an ox or three pounds, and warned to look after her properly in future. Gaenaope, again, had as guardian her husband's younger brother Andria. Because she was barren, both he and his father objected to her; they neither ploughed for her, nor allowed her to use her late husband's cattle. Her own people then took up the matter. It went through several minor courts, and ultimately came before the chief. The evidence showed that Andria was planning to appropriate the cattle. The chief therefore ruled that Gaenaope's people were to look after them for her until she was dead, when they were to be brought to him for distribution among her husband's relatives according to the customary rules of inheritance. Andria was also fined an ox for his behaviour. In the third case, the guardian of a widow and her daughter began selling her husband's cattle for his own benefit. The chief heard of this, although no formal complaint had been made, and after inquiring into the matter he gave the guardian a few animals as 'mourning gift' from his brother's estate, and placed the rest under the care of the wife's brother, who was to look after them for the daughter until she was married.

As the case of Mmamolebatsi shows, difficulties may arise from the widow's choice of a lover. Sometimes she lives chastely after the death of her husband, but generally, if not too old, she 'shares her blankets' with another man. Even if he is not actually related to her husband, there is seldom any trouble so long as he is of the same ward. Her relatives-in-law may in fact be relieved, for he helps to support her by ploughing for her and by providing her and her children with clothes. The children she bears him are then readily accepted as those of her late husband. But if her lover is an outsider, and especially if he gives her no help, the men of her husband's ward may object to him and make her life a misery. They regard her conduct as reprehensible, saying that if she must have a lover she ought surely to take one of them, considering that they are the people expected and entitled to look after her. They may therefore try to prevent him from visiting

her, and if she persists in seeing him may even drive her back to
her own people.

A dispute that came to court in 1935 provides a case in point,
and illustrates also some of the difficulties that may arise even
now from the custom of 'inheriting' a widow. Phalane had been
adopted by his maternal uncle, and on the latter's death took over
his widow, by whom be begot a son named Nyekge, and a daughter. Some time afterwards he married, in church and with *bogadi*,
a woman named Leepi. He had intended also to marry the widow
with whom he was consorting, but died before giving *bogadi* for
her. Leepi then wanted Nyekge to enter her hut, but he refused,
proposing instead Lesira, the son of Phalane's elder brother. The
rest of the family agreed with his choice. Leepi, however, did not
like Lesira, and twice repulsed him when he came to her at night.
She then became attracted by Radinamune, the son of Phalane's
sister, and wanted to take him as lover. But because he did not
belong to their ward, although he was related to them, Nyekge
and the rest of the family objected. She nevertheless allowed him
into her hut. Nyekge discovered this, and turned him out. She
continued to receive him, however, and ultimately became pregnant by him. Nyekge thereupon thrashed her and ordered her to
return to her own people. When she refused, he brought her
before their ward-head, who upheld his decision. Leepi appealed
to the chief. The latter ruled that Nyekge, in acting as head of the
family, had exercised an authority that was not his, for legally he
was the son not of Phalane but of Phalane's maternal uncle, the
promised *bogadi* never having been given for his mother. The
men of his ward were therefore fined eight head of cattle for
wrongfully supporting his pretensions. At the same time, it was
held that Radinamune had been at fault in visiting and impregna-
ting Leepi against the express wishes of her husband's people, so
he was fined six head of cattle and warned to stay away from her
in future. The judgement does not record what happened to her.

THE REMARRIAGE OF WIDOWERS

We have just seen that in traditional Kgatla usage a woman after
the death of her husband was taken over by his younger brother

or some other close relative, whose duty it was to look after her and to raise up seed to the man on whose behalf *bogadi* had originally been given for her. A similar custom prevailed when a married woman died. Her husband, if he wished, could then claim another woman from her parents to replace her. He was not required to give fresh *bogadi* for the substitute wife, nor were any of the customary wedding ceremonies held when she came to live with him. She was placed in her predecessor's compound, looked after her children, cultivated her fields, and had the use of her cattle. Any children she herself bore the husband were held to belong to the dead woman's house. In a polygamous household this meant that they ranked according to the latter's position, and if she had died without an heir any son borne by the substitute would take precedence over the sons of junior wives.

The woman selected as substitute was generally the dead wife's younger sister, who was considered the most suitable person to look after her children. So much importance was attached to this that at one time a woman, even if already married, could be taken from her own husband and sent to replace her deceased elder sister, especially if the latter's husband was closely related to them. Normally, however, if there were no unmarried younger sister the wife's people would select another relative instead, like a maternal cousin or niece. In law they were originally obliged to provide such a substitute if requested, especially if the wife had died childless. But if they were not satisfied with the way in which her husband had treated her, they might refuse, but then had to return her *bogadi*. Chief Lentswe, however, abolished this liability, maintaining that the wife's parents were not to blame if she had died without issue. Moreover, nothing could be done if they had no suitable daughter or other relative to give.

The husband also was not bound to ask for a substitute, although it was considered desirable that he should do so if his wife had left him children, since if he married a stranger she would not look so well after them. Genealogical records show that in fact he seldom took one, unless his wife had died barren or with children who were still fairly young. Old Rakabane, after carefully describing the law relating to this practice, said, in reply to a question, that he had not himself sought a substitute after the death of his first wife, 'because he was tired of following all the old customs'! Most often, indeed, a second wife was actually not related at all to her predecessor.

Today the custom of claiming a substitute from the wife's parents is still practised at times. Ramotsei, for instance, first married Bahumi. She became too sick to attend to her household duties, so he took an additional wife, who was not related to her. Bahumi died in 1928, leaving behind several adolescent children. Ramotsei, fearing that they would not live harmoniously with his other wife, a fairly young woman, asked for and was given Bahumi's younger sister Mapula to take her place and look after the children. Similarly, Radithlhomeso, after the death of his first wife, married her young sister, and Motlalefe, on the death of his, married her maternal aunt's daughter. Moeketse, again, when his wife died without issue, asked her parents for a substitute. They replied that they had no other daughter or suitable relative to give, but promised to help him find a second wife and to contribute towards the *bogadi*. On the whole, however, the custom is tending to disappear, and the wife's parents are certainly no longer bound to provide a substitute, nor can the girl selected be forced to go to the man, as was formerly the rule. It is only if there is general agreement between all the parties concerned that the husband will marry another woman of his wife's family. He then need not give *bogadi* for her.

A widower generally marries again, especially if his children are still fairly young, or he has none at all; but if he is an old man with married children he will rely upon them instead to look after him. Unless the new wife is closely related to her predecessor, he must give *bogadi* for her as well. She is expected to look after her step-children as if she were their mother. She often tends, however, to favour her own children instead, and even if she has none may still neglect or ill-treat those of her predecessor. Quarrels arising from this are fairly common, and at times even come to court. In 1929, for instance, I was present at a case where a woman complained that her step-daughter, who was little younger than she, had gone away and left her to do all the hard work, and on coming back had assaulted her. The evidence showed, however, that it was she who had driven away the girl by ill-treatment, and that the fight had actually been started by her. The case was therefore dismissed, and she was warned to behave herself in future. Instead, she almost immediately afterwards left her husband and refused to go back to him. He therefore divorced her and, since she was childless, recovered his *bogadi*.

Should the husband not marry again, the children if young are taken to live with some close maternal relative, like their grandmother or uncle. Their father remains at his own home, where his female relatives cook for him and do what other work is necessary. The children stay with their mother's people until old enough to look after themselves. The boys then return to their father, but girls often remain where they are until they get married. While the children are with their mother's people, their father must plough for them, clothe them and send them occasional presents of food. Should he fail to do so, and afterwards when they are old enough wish them to come and work for him, he will have to pay maintenance fees to his wife's people.

If both parents are dead, the young children are looked after by the wife of the eldest son, if he is already married, or else by one of their married sisters. If none of the children are married, they are taken over by one of their grandmothers, while their paternal uncle looks after their property. Failing a grandmother, they may be entrusted to a paternal aunt, but more often than not they go to live with their mother's people until they are old enough to return to their father's home. The preference usually given to maternal relatives is explained by the statement that they are more tenderly inclined towards the children, who also have the right to be supported by them from the *bogadi* received for the mother.

INHERITANCE

The death of a person, finally, raises the question of what must be done with his property. This is dealt with according to various traditional rules, which reflect once more the patrilineal bias of Kgatla society. It is not unknown for a man to inform his close relatives that after his death he wishes certain cattle or other property to be given to some one in particular. His wishes are generally respected, for, as the proverb says: 'The word of a dead person is not violated.' But if in them he departs to any considerable extent from the ordinary rules of inheritance, and deprives anybody of his due rights, the aggrieved person will appeal to the chief to adjust the matter. Usually, therefore, a man wishing to make special provision for his younger children or other people will do so during his lifetime. Property thus donated does not form part of his estate to be dealt with afterwards by the customary rules of inheritance.

When a married man dies, leaving a wife and children of both sexes, his eldest son becomes the main heir, even if there is an older daughter. He inherits all the cattle that, at the death of his father, had not been allotted or donated to any special house or person. He must, however, out of them give his younger brothers one or more each as 'mourning gift'. He also inherits the cattle specially assigned to his mother's house. He was formerly entitled to them all, but is nowadays expected to provide for the other children of that house. He generally keeps the majority for himself, and distributes the rest in decreasing numbers according to the relative ages of his brothers and sisters, the latter receiving proportionately less. If any of these children had already received cattle from their father during his lifetime, their share of his estate is almost always fairly small. But if no such provision had been made for them, they are entitled to a 'reasonable', but unspecified, proportion. The eldest son also inherits the common household fields, and such uncleared land as had not been specially allotted. Fields assigned to a particular house remain in the hands of the widow and are not divided until after her death. The huts, with all their furniture and utensils, likewise remain her possession. Wagons, ploughs, guns, and similar male effects, with any money left by the dead man, all go to the main heir, if not previously allotted to any house or person. But he should again make adequate provision for his brothers and sisters if this had not already been done. Clothes and similar personal effects go as a rule to the dead man's maternal uncle, or the latter's successor, who divides them at will among his own paternal relatives.

The estate of a polygamist is divided according to the same principles. All cattle, fields, wagons, money, and other property, not assigned to any particular house or person, are inherited by the eldest son of the great wife. He also takes the cattle and other male effects specially allotted to his own mother's house. The eldest son in every other house inherits its corresponding property. Similarly, on the death of a widower who had remarried, the eldest son by the first wife is the main heir, and succeeds to the general household property and the property of his own mother's house, while the eldest son of the second wife inherits the property specially assigned to her. But both here and in a polygamous family, the heir in each house must provide for his full brothers and sisters as already indicated. If the husband had during his lifetime failed to assign property to his second or junior wife, her children can now claim such an allotment from the main heir.

When a married man dies, leaving a wife and daughters, but no sons, his estate is looked after by his younger brother or next senior paternal relative. This man, as we have seen, must maintain and support the widow and her children from the property entrusted to him. Formerly he was the ultimate heir after she was dead and her daughters married, unless she had borne a son to the man entering her hut. Such a son, being regarded as the legitimate child of the dead husband, would then be the heir to his estate. Nowadays, if the widow does not bear a son by an authorized lover, the cattle and other property pass to her daughters when they get married, although the guardian is entitled to a share. The right of daughters to inherit in preference to a paternal uncle or other male relative is an innovation probably derived from European law, but I have been unable to discover the exact circumstances under which it came to be locally adopted. It shows, however, that the family is no longer so greatly merged in the kinship group, but is tending to acquire more individuality, and it is of course also an important change in the status of women.

A childless widow, again, must be supported from her husband's estate as long as she remains at his home. On her death it passes to his younger brother. If, however, she marries again, or goes back to her own people for any other cause, she must be given some cattle according to the wealth of the estate, while the bulk of the property belongs to her husband's nearest male relative. But the case of Gaenaope, which I quoted above, shows that there is now a tendency for the estate to be regarded as the widow's property even if she quarrels with her relatives-in-law, and not until she is dead does it revert to them. In the very unlikely event of there being no male heir at all, the estate falls to the chief.

When a married woman dies, leaving a husband and children, her personal belongings and domestic utensils go to her daughters, the eldest taking most and providing for the others. Her clothes go to the family of her maternal uncle, together with some pots, baskets and similar utensils. Any cattle she may have had remain under the care of her husband, but must ultimately descend to her own children, among whom they are divided according to relative age and sex. The huts and fields allotted to her likewise remain under her husband's control, and are usually not divided until after his death. They are then as a rule inherited by those children who have not yet obtained fields of their own, the youngest child, irrespective of sex, having priority. If all the children already have fields, the eldest son inherits his mother's, but usually distributes some among his younger brothers and sisters. The compound ultimately becomes the property of the youngest son. Failing any sons, a married daughter with her husband and children may remain in possession if they have been living there, or it may be taken over by one of the dead man's brothers who has not yet a compound of his own. Often enough there may be no one caring to claim it, in which case it remains standing empty, and can then be dealt with by the ward-head as he pleases.

When a married woman dies without issue, her property is

inherited by her sister, if afterwards married by the husband. If this is not done, the property given to her by her husband, including the huts and furniture, fields, cattle and domestic utensils, remains with him and can be given to a second wife. But any fields, cattle or other property, that the dead woman may have brought with her into the marriage revert to her own family.

The estate of an unmarried man falls to his father, if still alive. Failing this, it is divided among his younger brothers, the one linked to him having the preferential claim. Failing a younger brother, an elder inherits, and if there are no brothers at all the estate goes to the nearest paternal uncle or his senior male descendant. The estate of an unmarried woman similarly falls to her mother or her sisters, those not yet married taking priority. If there are no sisters, a maternal aunt inherits. This applies more particularly to such property as fields and domestic utensils. Any cattle the woman may have had will be inherited by her linked brother, or failing him by her father. But if, although unmarried, she has children of her own, they will inherit all her property.

The estate of a dead man is usually not divided until some time after his death, and often not until his widow is also dead. If the surviving members of the family get on well together, there is no haste over the division, but if there is any dispute or ill-feeling, it may take place as soon as possible. Enough time is generally allowed for the cattle to increase so that each child may receive a 'reasonable' number. In any case, the estate is seldom divided while the main heir is still a minor. It is looked after in the meantime by his guardian, who hands it over to him when he comes of age. He may elect to divide it then, or prefer to wait until his younger brothers have also grown up. He must, however, consult his senior paternal relatives regarding the division. It is also the rule, especially when a big estate is involved, that the chief should be informed and his consent obtained before it is dealt with. Any property disposed of by the guardian or main heir before the estate is finally divided must be satisfactorily accounted for, and if any debts had been incurred by deceased they should be paid before the heirs take their share.

The division of cattle and other livestock generally takes place at the family cattle-post, where all the animals are brought together. The main heir goes there with his younger brothers and sisters, and a few senior relatives as advisers and witnesses. He then proceeds to allocate the cattle, sheep, goats and other property, among those entitled to share in the estate. If, as frequently happens, the minor heirs are not satisfied with what he gives them, they can appeal to the ward-head. If unable to make a satisfactory adjustment, he refers the matter to the chief, who orders all the cattle to be brought to the council-place. Here he inquires publicly into the reasons for the dispute. He either upholds the original division, or divides the property afresh, paying due regard to the claims of the main heir. One of the cattle is usually slaughtered for the men present to help him, and he may also take for himself a fee of from one to three head, or even more, according to the wealth of the estate. The house property and personal effects inherited by women are generally divided among themselves in the compound, the eldest daughter presiding with the aid of her senior relatives. If there is any trouble, which is seldom the case, the matter would be referred as usual to the ward-head and possibly even to the chief.

12. The Family in Tribal Life

We are now in a position to review generally the structure and functions of the Kgatla family, and the transformations it has undergone as the result of contact with Western civilization. It will have been gathered already that there has been no uniformity of change, and that the family is today not nearly as homogeneous as before. Some of its traditional features have disappeared completely, or else have become much less common. Others persist strongly, or have perhaps been modified only slightly. A few people have gone as far as possible in adopting the new practices brought in by the Mission and other civilizing agencies. Others, again, are conservative enough to adhere fairly closely still to many ancient usages. Despite such variations, certain main trends of development are readily discernible, and in order that we may visualize them clearly I propose, at the risk of some repetition, to summarize briefly the outstanding characteristics first of the traditional Kgatla family and then of its modern successor. This will assist us to consider afterwards how the changes have affected the position of the family in tribal life as a whole.

The old Kgatla family, in its typical form, was a polygamous unit in which each wife had a separate rank and establishment. The majority of families were actually monogamous, but certain matrimonial customs and laws of property, succession and inheritance were all based upon the conception of polygamy. A man's first wife was sought for him by his parents, preferably from among his close relatives. His other wives, if any, he usually chose himself. After the betrothal had been confirmed, he cohabited with the woman for some time at her parents' home before bringing her to live among his own people. His marriage to her was not regarded as legally valid, nor could he claim as his own the children she bore him, until the cattle known as *bogadi* had been given for her. These cattle were contributed jointly by his father and other relatives, and were divided among the wife's people, especially her father and maternal uncle. Like the discussions preceding the choice of a wife or the approval of a suitor, *bogadi* showed that a marriage involved not only the two spouses themselves but also their kinsmen.

Marriage served, among other purposes, to regulate sexual relations. Premarital chastity was an ideal, the attainment of which was attempted by segregating the older boys and girls, and by condemning child-bearing by an unmarried woman. Extramarital relations, again, were punished as unlawful, except when practised to raise up seed to an impotent or dead husband. Sexual intercourse was normally considered proper only if the couple were married to each other. Even then its pattern was culturally determined, in that it was prohibited on certain occasions and prescribed on others. But the main object of marriage was the production of legitimate offspring. Only married women were entitled to bear children, and if an unmarried girl did so both she and her lover were punished severely, while their child had no legal claim upon its father. Large families were the ideal, and it was partly for this reason that polygamy was practised. Children of both sexes were desired, to ensure adequate help in all the household tasks. Daughters were a source of wealth through the *bogadi* received for them, but sons were preferred, for they would perpetuate the father's line and inherit his property and rank. Various special customs were therefore practised if a woman was barren or produced daughters only. These included magical rites to make her fruitful, the adoption of a child from some near relative, the provision of a 'substitute wife' by her family, and the employment of an authorized lover 'to enter her hut' and raise up seed to her husband. The last two customs were practised also when either wife or husband had died. They indicated once more that marriage was in part a contract between two families, each of which had to ensure the fulfilment of the associated obligations if its original representative was unable to do so himself.

Parents were responsible not only for rearing their children, but also for training them in subsistence activities, moral conduct, and other tribal customs and beliefs. This was almost all the direct education that a child received until it attained physical maturity, when on being initiated into its age-regiment it was given a short course of instruction in adult behaviour by selected old people. The members of a household contributed jointly to its maintenance, by producing their own food, building their own homes, making the greater part of their clothing and domestic utensils, and doing all their own housework. The relevant tasks were portioned out among the men, women and children, according to a culturally standardized division of labour, so that the activities of each supplemented those of the rest. Polygamy was a great advantage in this respect, for it meant that more people were available for work. Land, livestock, dwellings, agricultural produce and other household property were controlled by the husband and father, who allocated them for use among his dependants. He was the legal head of the family, entitled to the obedience, service and respect of his wives and children, and he was responsible in law for their dealings with outsiders. He also prayed and sacrificed for them to the spirits of his dead ancestors, employed magicians to perform the various ceremonies believed to ensure good health and prosperity, and arranged the customary celebrations whenever a member of the family was born, initiated, married or buried. On his own death his eldest son (by the great wife, if he was a polygamist) succeeded him as head of the family, and inherited all the property that had not been distributed among the 'houses' of the wives. The other sons received some of the cattle assigned to their mother's 'house', while daughters inherited her domestic utensils and fields.

Some reference should here be made to the general status of women. They were regarded as socially inferior to men, and in Kgatla law were always treated as minors. Before marriage a woman was under the authority of her father or guardian, while after it she came under the control of her husband, and, on his death, of some other male member of his family. She could never sue independently at court, she could own property but might not dispose of it without her guardian's consent, and she could not inherit cattle or other livestock from her father or husband. Women took no part in the government of the tribe; they did not attend the tribal assemblies, and all the political offices were kept exclusively in the hands of men. Even in family life preference was given to males, and a woman bearing daughters only was held to have failed in one of her most important duties to her husband. Certain activities, too, were assigned to men only, others to women, and neither sex would readily undertake work normally performed by the other. The ritual impurity associated with menstruation imposed upon women various taboos and other observances peculiar to their sex. They were also excluded from taking a leading part in sacrifice and other active phases of ancestor-worship. At feasts and on other public occasions when both sexes met, men and women always sat in separate groups, while in ordinary social life they had little in common.

The modern Kgatla family does not perform all the functions noted above. Some have been taken over, either wholly or in part, by specialized agencies that formerly did not exist in the tribe. The change has been most marked in religion. With the acceptance of Christianity, the Churches have become the dominant religious units, and people who are not professing Christians have no organized system of worship. The family has therefore lost its ancient role of serving as the social basis for the tribal religion. It is still the centre of birth, marriage, death and similar rituals, but owing to the introduction of Christianity the details of the ceremonies now observed may vary considerably from one family to another. Magic, too, is no longer as uniformly employed as before. Some people use it on almost every conceivable occasion. Others, still a small minority, claim to dispense with it altogether, except in case of disease. Between these two classes are the great bulk of the people, including many Christians, who rely upon it in some situations only, and do not feel the need for it in others. There is accordingly far less homogeneity nowadays in the ritual life of the family.

Similarly, the schools introduced by the Mission and afterwards developed by the Administration have taken over to some extent the task of educating children. But, unlike the Christian religion, school education has not deprived the family of an ancient function; it merely supplements, and does not replace, the teaching given at home. The household remains the chief educational unit in the tribe, and most children receive no other training for their future calling than is provided at home. Half of them do not go to school at all, and are therefore influenced by it only indirectly. Of the rest, the great majority stay at school for only two or three years. Here they receive an entirely new kind of training, especially in the rudiments of literacy, which the family is unable to provide. But knowledge of the tribal culture, and especially of the farming pursuits they will have to follow as adults, still reaches them mainly at home. The few able to carry on further with their schooling can, however, learn to become teachers, artisans, etc., and in any case they acquire a good deal of knowledge alien to the rest of the tribe. School education has therefore created new lines of social differentiation. In this respect it corresponds to Christianity, which also is not universally accepted by the Kgatla, and so distinguishes people from one another.

In economic life, the family has lost much of its traditional self-sufficiency. Although in the main it still produces its own food and builds its own home, it has become increasingly dependent upon outside markets like the trading-stores for most of its clothes, utensils and other manufactured goods. The consequent decay of local industries has deprived both men and women of tasks in which they formerly engaged. On the other hand, the desire for imported goods, and the necessity of paying taxes, levies and other cash dues, have forced people to seek new sources of income, the most important of which is wage-labour for money. The result has been a change in the traditional division of labour between the members of the household. Most of the younger men, whether married or not, spend a good deal of their time working in European industrial or farming areas, and through the money they earn contribute more than before to the support of their families. A few other men have taken up specialized occupations at home. But they all still rely upon farming for the great bulk of their food supply. Their absence abroad, however, or their preoccupation with other tasks at home, means that they cannot as a rule participate very greatly in agriculture and other domestic work. The attendance of children at school has also to some extent deprived the family of labour resources it could formerly command. As a result, many women have been burdened with more work than before, and where, as occasionally happens, a husband while away fails to provide for his wife, she may be almost entirely responsible for maintaining herself and her children. A few women have engaged locally in such new occupations as teaching, nursing or domestic service for European residents, and others go to work abroad, but the majority are still concerned primarily with running their homes and cultivating their fields.

The production and rearing of children are still among the main tasks of the family. But it has become less exclusively the reproductive unit. In contrast with the trend of development in European societies, the proportion of unmarried mothers has increased very considerably. Their children are still considered illegitimate, but the woman herself and her lover are no longer punished as severely as before. Some of the customs traditionally associated with child-bearing in marriage have also decayed. The taking of a substitute wife or the entering of a woman's hut are both less commonly practised. Polygamy, again, has declined so considerably that very few men can nowadays have as many lawful children as in the old days. The later age of marriage, and the lengthy absences of men working abroad, may also have contributed to reduce the size of the family. Statistical evidence is not available, but the Kgatla themselves maintain that women nowadays bear fewer children than formerly. The spread of venereal diseases, another innovation, makes it probable that their contention is not unfounded.

Marriage continues to regulate sexual relations, which are still considered improper except between husband and wife. But premarital affairs are now treated much more tolerantly, and have become the rule instead of the exception. Married men, again, unable or unwilling for religious or economic reasons to have more than one wife, take concubines instead, while married women, during the absence at work of their husbands, seldom remain faithful for long. It is therefore no longer so exclusively within marriage itself that people find sexual satisfaction. On the other hand, the greater role played nowadays by personal attraction in the choice of a mate probably serves to enhance the pleasure husband and wife get from sleeping together. There is, nevertheless, a good deal of maladjustment. This may have existed in the old days also, but the frequent separations of the spouses, and the infidelity of one or both, are contributory factors that have been greatly intensified more recently.

In tribal law, the head of a family is still the guardian of his wife, and of his children as long as they live with him; he controls their movements and property, and is responsible for their debts and civil offences. In marriages contracted under European civil law, a wife was at first theoretically entitled to new property rights and other privileges. These, however, were never accepted inside the tribe, and since 1926 have in effect also been excluded from the provisions of the law. But women married under civil law are entitled to divorce their husbands for adultery, a right that does not extend to others; they can also resort independently to the European courts, and are trying to enforce the same right for the tribal courts, although hitherto with little success. In other respects, too, the status of women has changed. Daughters are now entitled to share in their father's estate, and failing sons they are the main heirs in preference to a paternal uncle. The great majority of Church members are women, while four times as many girls as boys go to school. Women are therefore on the whole the more 'educated' section of the tribe. Some, as teachers, dressmakers, nurses or domestic servants, have also attained a measure of economic freedom. The result of all this is that they have become more independent in their attitude, and less submissive to the men. Nevertheless, they are still obliged to live either among their own people or among their husbands', and are perpetually subject to the authority of a male guardian. It is therefore as yet impossible for them, while still inside the Reserve, ever to feel completely emancipated. This applies as much to widows and divorcées as to wives or unmarried daughters.

Adult sons, again, are in European law individually liable for the payment of tax. This implicit recognition of their independent status, however, is not acknowledged in tribal law. But they are notoriously tending to act with more freedom than before, and no longer look always to their father for advice and approval. Many, for instance, now choose their own wives instead of relying upon their parents to do so for them; occasionally a man may even go to reside permanently among his wife's people, an innovation often regarded with disgust, but illustrating the decay of parental control. Daughters, too, have much greater say nowadays in the choice of their husbands. In practice, therefore, the head of a family is less powerful than he used to be, although in tribal law the traditional ideal persists of a husband's dominance and his wife's subservience, and of unquestioning obedience to parents by children.

There have been other changes in marriage itself. The traditional wedding ceremonies have been supplemented by the corresponding Christian rites, which, although practised by a minority of the people, are now considered more respectable. Polygamy, the inheritance of widows and the taking of a substitute wife are forbidden by the Church to its members, but even among the heathens they are no longer so extensively practised. Child betrothals have virtually disappeared. Marriages with relatives or neighbours are still common, but wives are now more frequently taken from strange families. Finally, people seem to marry somewhat later in life than they formerly did, a fact partly responsible for the changed attitude towards premarital unchastity. But betrothal negotiations are still conducted along the same lines as before, and *bogadi*, at one time prohibited, is now again an essential part of marriage. The two features traditionally considered necessary to validate a marriage are therefore still retained, even where the couple are married in church and so under European civil law.

The family remains the only unit providing people with a home. But, more than ever, it is mainly the women and the younger children who participate habitually in the domestic community of life. The traditional separation of the sexes in everyday social intercourse has largely broken down, but most men, especially if they go to work abroad, spend a good deal of their time away from their wives. The older boys still live mainly at the cattle-posts, or also go out to work abroad, and the children attending school stay alone in the villages for part of the year while other people are at the fields. The members of the family tend therefore to be more scattered than formerly, and as a result it is seldom that relations between them are very intimate. The older men, who no longer go to work abroad, see more of their families than do the rest, but even they are so often away at their cattle-posts and elsewhere that there can be little companionship between them and their wives.

THE FAMILY AND OTHER SOCIAL GROUPS

The survey just given has shown that in the old days many of the activities making up the culture of the tribe were centred in the family. It was the outstanding reproductive, economic, educational and religious unit; it regulated sexual relations; it was the basis of the legal and administrative system; and it was the unit of domestic life, inadequate although that life was judged by ordinary European standards. Nevertheless, the family was not a completely self-contained body. In carrying out its functions, it relied to a varying extent upon the cooperation of other people, including above all its near relatives. People were not free to live where they chose. Children until they married belonged to their father's household. A son, after some time, then built his own home, but as close as possible to his parents, and in any case within the same ward settlement. He was accordingly always surrounded by his paternal kin, and remained in some degree under the authority of his father or eldest brother. So, too, a married daughter usually lived in the same village as her parents, and sometimes even in the same ward if her husband also belonged to it. She kept in constant touch with her relatives; and her brothers, as the maternal uncles of her children, figured prominently in her domestic life.

The circle of kin helped to sustain the individual family. A married man's relatives and relatives-in-law helped him whenever necessary with labour and with gifts of food and other commodities, lent a hand in bringing up and instructing his children, protected him in his dealings with outsiders, participated in all his domestic discussions and celebrations, and intervened whenever a serious dispute arose in his household. His paternal relatives were the more closely bound to him, in law as well as by contiguity of residence. They provided the guardian of his wife and children after his death; they ultimately inherited his property if none of his wives bore him a son; they could be held responsible for paying his debts if he was unable to do so himself; they worshipped the same ancestors as he; and the man senior to the rest in line of descent was the head of his family-group and so exercised some authority over him. His maternal uncles, however, were also intimately attached to him by various economic and ritual ties, and had an important say in the regulation of his domestic affairs. The individual family, therefore, although a distinct unit with clearly specified functions, operated more as part of an interdependent kinship group than as an autonomous body.

Almost all the major social units in the tribe were composed of allied families grouped together on a local basis. Several closely related families, living in adjacent compounds, made up the family-group; several family-groups, occupying the same well-defined portion of a village, made up the ward; and several wards, concentrated together in an isolated settlement, made up the village. These three forms of grouping constituted the basis for the system of local administration. Within each, the head of the leading family was accepted as paramount over the rest. In a family-group, the man senior to the others in line of descent from their common ancestor was the 'elder'; in a ward, the elder of the senior family-group was hereditary headman of them all; and in a village the headman of the senior ward was the chief's local representative and governor.

In each case the senior authority was politically superior to the lesser authorities in his own group. They obeyed his commands, carried out his instructions and referred to him all cases that they were unable to settle or with which they were not competent to deal. An appeal also lay to him from their judicial and executive decisions. But within the limits of his own group the elder of a family-group, the head of a ward or the headman of a village, had undivided power; he regulated the economic, judicial, administrative and on occasion also the military and religious, activities of his immediate dependants. In carrying out his duties he was helped firstly by his brothers and other close paternal relatives, and, in such groups as the ward and the village, by the heads of the remaining family-groups or wards respectively. The system of administration was thus one of ever-increasing jurisdiction extending upwards from the head of the household, and converging in the person of the chief, who governed the whole tribe with the aid firstly of his own paternal relatives, and then of a formal council comprising all the headmen of villages and wards.

The only well-defined social unit cutting across this symmetrical system of family aggregations was the age-regiment, consisting of all people of the same sex and approximately the same age. But even here members of the same ward always constituted a separate group in their regiment. Inside this group they ranked according to the relative status of their family, and the man or woman senior to the rest acted as their sectional leader. There were no organized professional or occupational bodies. Some people, in addition to carrying on the same subsistence activities as the rest, made objects for sale to others, or supplemented their income by the practice of magic. But specialists of this kind were never formally grouped together into a separate social unit. There were also social distinctions of various kinds based mainly on hereditary rank and wealth, but these distinctions too were not reflected in the existence of special forms of grouping. Except for the age-regiments, the family and the larger groups directly derived from it constituted the principal units of social organization; and in the main each family was a replica of the rest, leading the same sort of life and performing the same functions.

Today the family is no longer so conspicuously the basic unit of the whole tribal system. The traditional grouping into family-groups, wards and villages still persists, and the administrative system founded upon it continues to operate. The judicial powers of the ward-heads, however, have been curtailed by the Administration, and their religious and military functions have disappeared. Their economic and administrative functions, especially in regard to land tenure, have on the other hand been but little disturbed. The kindred generally, too, is still a very influential factor in domestic life, although it is no longer so important in economic affairs, now that new opportunities of making a living have developed.

Contact with Western civilization has led to the formation of new social groups, and to the introduction of new special agencies. These have between them taken over some of the functions previously performed by the family, so that there is now greater division of labour and consequent interdependence within the tribe as a whole. The churches and schools carry out activities that used to belong very largely to the family; the European traders and blacksmiths, and such Kgatla craftsmen as dressmakers and carpenters, have added to the range of specialists whom people employ; the Mission hospital and the various Government departments, including the railway and post-office, have provided new services which also cannot be duplicated by the average family. In social life generally there now exist organized religious and educational groupings, and new distinctions based on the degree of 'civilization' to which people have attained. The structure of the tribe has therefore become much more complex.

All these changes have reduced the importance of the family in tribal life. It was formerly the group within which people had their home, obtained sexual satisfaction, begot their children, made their living, conducted their worship and other ritual observances, received education in tribal practices and beliefs, and were made responsible for adherence to the recognized standards of social control. Today a man generally obtains sexual satisfaction from other women as well as his wife, and women often bear children before they are married; people rely upon the trading-stores and skilled craftsmen for many of the goods and services they desire, and upon employment by Europeans for the money with which to purchase these commodities; they go to church if they are religious, and send their children to be taught in school. Except for religion, these different activities are still partly carried on by the family itself, which continues to have sexual, reproductive, educational and economic functions; but the last two it now shares with the schools and other new agencies, while the first two are no longer so exclusively associated with marriage. It is only in regard to the provision of a home and the enforcement of certain legal rules that the family has not been supplemented or displaced by alternative agencies, but in both spheres its efficiency has nevertheless been diminished.

THE MAIN CAUSES OF CHANGE

In trying to explain the changes summarized above, we must note once again that all appear to be due, directly or indirectly, to the introduction of Western civilization. But the Kgatla were not exposed suddenly to the whole of this civilization; it spread to them gradually, and many of its characteristic features never reached them at all in their home. This point needs elaboration, for in it lie some of the reasons why only certain changes have occurred and not others. We may roughly distinguish four main phases of contact: an early period in the Transvaal, from *c.* 1835–69, leading to the withdrawal of the Kgatla into Bechuanaland; a middle period, from *c.* 1870–1900, confined mainly to the introduction of what the Europeans regarded as indispensable religious, political and economic institutions in the form of the Mission, the Pax Britannica, the trader, taxation and labour migration; a later period of relative quiescence, from *c.* 1901–20, during which these institutions gradually established themselves in tribal life; and a modern period, only recently begun and by no means ended, of more intensive political, economic and social change.

Moreover, contacts between the Kgatla and Western civilization have in the main taken place on two fronts, differing considerably in character. Since the Kgatla came to Bechuanaland, and especially since that Territory was made a British Protectorate, they have occupied a Reserve within which no European may own land. A few people live and work there as Government officials, missionaries, traders, doctors and blacksmiths, but these Europeans, with their families and assistants, do not number more than about fifty in all, in contrast with the 16,000 Native inhabitants. European visitors, both official and private, are now so often seen in the Reserve as no longer to arouse special comment, but the average tribesman does not as a rule have any dealings with them. The Reserve is also bounded on three sides by blocks of European farms, with whose occupants, too, the Kgatla seldom have much to do. On the other hand, most of the able-bodied men go periodically to work in the Transvaal and other European centres. But here they are themselves a negligibly insignificant minority, and so scattered about that as a rule they can lead no corporate life at all.

The Europeans resident among or visiting the Kgatla revealed to them new forms of dress and decoration, speech, and material culture in general. The missionaries introduced a new form of religion, with its associated places of worship, ritual, organization and morality, a new system of education, and new forms of medical treatment. The Administration introduced its own officials, taxation in money, new laws and penalties for their breach, new courts and methods of procedure and various services designed to promote economic development. The traders, again, brought in the manufactured products of Western civilization and a new system of trade.

Many aspects of Western civilization, however, did not reach the Kgatla at home. The local white residents are too few and too isolated to convey more than a superficial idea, even to their own servants, of European domestic and social life. Still less can they reflect adequately the social and political organization of their own people. It is equally impossible for the Kgatla in the Reserve to learn much about the industrial aspects of Western civilization, apart from the slight glimpses they obtain of modern forms of transport and a few other mechanical contrivances. These missing traits are fully presented only to the men going to work in the towns. On the mines and in other industrial undertakings they encounter the white man's technical achievements in the most developed South African form; as domestic servants they observe fairly intimately the patterns of European domestic and social life; while in the streets they find additional features of material culture, social intercourse and the regulation of public life. But all this they must leave behind when they return. It does not as yet exist in their home, and can only indirectly through them affect those remaining there.

The aspects of tribal life first influenced by the impact of Western civilization were therefore the economic, religious and political. Economic life was disturbed by the introduction of manufactured goods, by taxation and by labour migration. In religion the difference between Christianity and ancestor-worship was sufficiently marked to make them incompatible, while the attack upon other forms of ritual was designed to produce a definite break from 'heathenism'. Political life generally was altered by the imposition of British rule and by the forcible diminution of the powers and functions of the tribal authorities. Social organization, and domestic and communal life generally, were not at first directly affected, apart from the changes in marriage and other customs attempted by the Mission. It was only after the carriers of Western civilization had been active for some time that their influence extended to these other spheres as well, owing mainly to the more intensive development of Christianity, education, trade and labour migration.

As far as the family is concerned, Christianity was the most directly subversive factor. The Mission introduced a new form of religion, whose acceptance meant the abandonment of the

domestic cult of ancestor-worship; it also brought new forms of
wedding and death ritual, baptism and confirmation ceremonies,
schools and ideals of sexual morality, which either supplemented
or modified traditional aspects of family life; and it forbade polygamy, several of the customs practised to ensure the birth of an
heir, and various kindred usages directly connected with marriage. For its acceptance, however, it had to rely almost entirely
upon persuasion and propaganda, and the sanctions it introduced could affect only its own followers. For nearly thirty years
after it came to the Kgatla, it laboured with but little success,
making only a few converts and exercising no great effect upon
tribal life generally. Then, in 1892, it achieved the notable
triumph of securing the adoption of Christianity as the official
religion of the tribe when Lentswe was baptized. Since he, as
chief, was also the great tribal rainmaker and magician, he accel-
erated the decay of the old religious system by the marked encouragement he gave to Christianity, and by abolishing many
ancient ceremonies for whose performance he was directly responsible. Professing Christians are still in a minority, but the
heathens also have discarded ancestor-worship, and many of
them have been influenced indirectly in regard to marriage
customs by the example of the converts. They have imitated the
chiefs and other prominent tribesmen, even although they have
not gone so far as to become members of the Church.

The ultimate acceptance of Christianity was therefore due
mainly to the personal influence of the chief, by far the most
important man in the tribe. The same factor played a great part
in the adoption of other aspects of Western civilization. Both
Lentswe and Isang were men of exceptional ability and enterprise, and through sheer force of personality and the tremendous
prestige and authority attaching to them as chiefs were able to do
much for the advancement of their people. They realized that
Western civilization was coming to stay, and, in the words of
Isang, that 'in adapting ourselves to this same civilization lay our
future as a nation'. Lentswe's acceptance of Christianity was due
partly to his hope that the missionaries would protect him from
undue exploitation by other Europeans and help him in pro-

moting the welfare of the tribe. He supported their educational activities, and also encouraged his men to seek work abroad in order to acquire 'useful objects'. Isang during his regency followed the same policy, and actively fostered economic progress and education. All these developments reacted in time upon the structure and functions of the family: they disturbed the traditional organization of labour, led to more lengthy separations between husband and wife, introduced new ideals of women's place in the home and provided new agencies to carry on activities previously performed by the household.

The Mission, in pursuing its general policy of spreading Christianity and 'civilizing' the tribe, tried to discourage and even abolish various practices connected with family life. It met with some success, especially in regard to polygamy and certain other matrimonial customs. But the people resisted several of the changes attempted, and here the Mission policy had to be abandoned. The most conspicuous example is *bogadi*, which, after being prohibited for the tribe as a whole, was afterwards allowed for the heathens, and in the end, due mainly to Isang, came to be accepted as an essential part of the church marriage itself. The Mission tried also to prevent marriage between church members and heathens, threatened to expel from church any person resorting to a Native magician, and forbade converts to attend heathen ceremonies, even when relatives or friends were being married or buried. In all these instances, too, it met with active opposition or passive resistance, and the laws concerned are no longer in vogue.

Isang's attitude in regard to *bogadi* was part of a general attempt he made to retain, and where necessary revive, what he regarded as 'good old' customs that were falling into decay. Thus, he insisted upon the proper celebration of marriages and the prompt payment of *bogadi*, and revived the ritual purification of widows and widowers. His object in all this, he told me, was to develop among the people a feeling of patriotism, of pride in their own culture, in so far as it was not blatantly in conflict with general social and material advancement. The encouragement he gave to the retention of old practices and beliefs

served obviously as a powerful check against their disintegration.

The Administration, unlike the Mission, had the power to
enforce the changes it introduced, which the people had little
alternative but to accept. But its policy in the main was to preserve and utilize Native laws and institutions as far as possible, so
that apart from a few changes considered necessary in the
interests of 'peace, order and good government', it interfered
hardly at all with social and political organization. In regard to
family life, it did provide that all people married in church
should come under the European civil law, which meant their
practising monogamy and accepting new conceptions of property rights and grounds for divorce. But Isang secured an am-
endment of the law, so that, in case of divorce, questions of
property and the custody of children are now dealt with according to traditional usage. By imposing taxation the Administration also affected indirectly the relationship between parents
and adult sons. But it did not concern itself at all with the traditional marriage customs, rules of inheritance and other family
usages of those people, still the great majority, who do not get
married in church. Any departure these people may have made
from ancient usage are due to other factors than legal compulsion by the Government.

So far, then, the factors I have been discussing affected directly only that portion of the tribe which accepted Christianity
to the extent of joining the Church. The people concerned came
under the laws framed by the Mission for the guidance of converts, and so had to depart in various respects from traditional
usages relating to marriage and the family. Unwittingly, too,
their marriages subjected them to the provisions of the civil law.
The rest of the tribe were not bound by the same moral and legal
obligations. Imitation probably led some to adopt the type of
wedding ceremony developed by the Church, and to discard
customs regarded as 'abominable' or 'repugnant', but they were
not compelled to do so, and have on the whole remained more
conservative.

The economic factors had a more far-reaching influence since they extended to the tribe as a whole. They affected not only the traditional division of labour, but also the social cohesion of the family. Labour migration, especially, has led to prolonged separations between husband and wife; the result is that women have not only obtained greater personal freedom as well as increased domestic responsibility, but also indulge to a much greater extent in illicit love-affairs. Adult sons, similarly, have in many families become important contributors to the support of their parents through the wages they earn; consequently they feel entitled to claim more independence than they formerly enjoyed. Labour migration, moreover, has opened a way of escape from the burdens of tribal and domestic authority. Formerly there was no hope of breaking loose from one's family except by the dangerous method of fleeing to some other tribe. Today, however, people can move about much more freely and safely than before. This is due mainly to the development of new transport facilities, especially the railway, and to the abolition of inter-tribal warfare owing to the extension of European rule all over South Africa. Many of the people going abroad, ostensibly to work, never return at all, or stay away so long that they may be considered as lost to the tribe. The proportion does not seem to be as great as the people often maintain in conversation (the few figures I have suggest that it is about one in twenty), but the fact that such losses do occur indicates a growing distaste for conditions at home.

All these factors, then, have tended to break down the traditional family organization and to create greater social diversity and interdependence. On the other hand, there have also been certain influences making for continued stability, or at least slowing down the rate of change. We have already noted the recognition given by the Administration to Native laws and institutions, and the efforts made by Isang to retain or revive certain traditional usages. Christianity and education, again, are not legally enforced upon the tribe as a whole, and still affect directly only a minority of the people. Moreover, many of the influences already discussed are of comparatively recent origin. Although the Kgatla have been in contact with Europeans for just over a century, Christianity did not really become established until 1892, European civil law was introduced in 1891, taxation was first imposed in 1899, and education made comparatively little headway until the first decade of the twentieth century. Labour migration, most important of all, did not attain really grave proportions until after Isang had become regent in 1920, when there was a general spurt in economic development as well as in education. It is therefore only for the last fifty years or so, and in several instances only for the last twenty years or so, that disorganization has been actively stimulated. Against it, however, two other factors have been steadily operating: the continued importance of subsistence farming in economic life, and the continued influence of social pressure by the kinship group.

We saw in a previous chapter that despite the many changes in economic life, the Kgatla still depend upon farming for their food supply. No matter in what other ways it obtains additional income, every family, from that of the chief downwards, still cultivates the land and keeps livestock of some kind. It also builds its own home, and does all its own housework. Wealthy people may have servants to help them, but the average family depends for the necessary labour upon the exertions of its own members. A husband looks to his wife and daughters to do most of the agriculture, housework and building; a wife looks to her husband and sons for help in ploughing and reaping, transport and building, and for the care of the cattle and small stock. The family is therefore still a cooperative group whose members rely upon one another for maintenance; and this normally serves to ensure its continued existence. Under the present conditions of tribal life, neither men nor women can permanently fend for themselves; the stage has not yet been reached when one can purchase board, lodging and all other domestic attentions. It is partly for this reason that people are generally reluctant to seek a divorce unless their marriage has become almost completely intolerable. They appreciate the discomforts that would arise from separation, and, as is shown by the procedure followed when a woman runs home to her parents, they are generally prepared to make allowances for each other in order to retain the services upon which they respectively depend.

The nature of the pressure exerted by the relatives has been repeatedly described in preceding chapters. Marriage is still considered a union between two groups and not merely two persons, and the respective kin of husband and wife continue to take an active interest in the welfare of the couple. The rule persists that a married man must build his home close to his paternal relatives, and it is only exceptionally that he is allowed to live somewhere else. The great majority of couples are therefore immediately surrounded by people entitled and expected to intervene in case of trouble between them, and the loss of social esteem and of indispensable services that may result from ignoring these people contributes greatly to the stability of marriage. For women, especially, there are as yet no alternatives inside the Reserve other than married life or continued dependence upon their own relatives, and the former, with the higher status it commands, is the more widely preferred.

Despite the many factors making for disruption, the Kgatla family has therefore not broken down to any considerable extent. Some of these factors have only begun to operate fairly recently, others affect only a portion of the tribe. But the general structure of the family has obviously altered, and it is certainly less self-contained and united than before. The disappearance or decay of certain functions it used to fulfil have diminished the range of direct cooperation among its members; the increased scattering due mainly to labour migration and education has meant that there is less intimacy now in everyday life; and the conflict between the traditional ideal of the husband's dominance and the freedom claimed today by his wife and children has led to many painful disagreements. The Kgatla family is not on the whole a group in which affection, loyalty, and companionship, are dominant features; it is often enough little more than a prosaic partnership for economic and social purposes, and for the production of legitimate offspring. And Western civilization, through the changes it has produced, must be held mainly responsible for the lack of happiness and contentment now so frequently observed in married life, although there is little to suggest that even in the old days these emotional satisfactions were a common feature of the Kgatla family system.

The European influences, however, have not operated in a uniform direction. Some have tended to loosen the ties uniting the family, and therefore produce instability; others have created a new basis for harmonious relations among its members. The same set of influences has at times even operated in both directions, by breaking down the former cohesion and simultaneously producing conditions for a new type of relationship that may or may not be more enduring. The 'emancipation' of women and children, for instance, although disruptive of the traditional family ties, may yet possibly succeed in developing those conceptions of human personality that many thinkers believe to be the only suitable psychological foundations for stable personal relations under modern conditions. We cannot therefore regard 'disintegration' as synonymous with 'demoralization'; the process at work may perhaps be more accurately described as one of 'reconstruction'.

The influences tending to weaken the family are primarily economic and religious. Their specific effects are to divest the family of certain functions. It ceases to be the channel for the satisfaction of religious needs; it is no longer economically self-sufficient; and it is less important for judicial and administrative purposes. Because of the greater social specialization, children are less dependent on parents and less mindful of filial obligations; the social importance of producing children has diminished; husbands are not so dependent on their wives; and the family is less intimately connected with other social groupings. Sexual desires, economic and cultural wants and educational needs are satisfied to a greater extent outside the family units. In addition to the loss of functions, there is, finally, a greater scattering of the members of the family, due to the absence of husbands, sons and even daughters in European centres.

On the other hand, there are certain factors that may be regarded as creating new ties among the members of the family. There is a greater measure of individual freedom, e.g. in the selection of a mate and the status of wives; the removal of sexual restraints might be held by some sexologists to provide greater possibilities for the satisfactory adjustment of relations between husbands and wives; the Christian ethic provides a moral sanction for fidelity and the endurance of the marriage bond; and Western teaching stresses the importance of basing social relations upon a high regard for human personality.

But these constructive forces have as yet been imperfectly realized, and are less potent than the disintegrating tendencies. There is often a conflict between traditional social forms and new ideas, between modes of behaviour and legal and conventional rules. Christianity and education encourage concepts of equality between the sexes, while the law and the economy preserve the subordination of women, with limited exceptions, e.g. the right of women to inherit property, and the openings for wage-earning by females. The change in the position of widows owing to the decline of polygamy and the adoption of Christian ethics has not been accompanied by a corresponding change in the legal status. The *femme sole* has emerged, but there is as yet no place for her in the legal system, or in the political life of the community. The possibility of giving institutionalized expression to new concepts and modes of life is further handicapped by the disorganization consequent upon the migration of men to European labour centres. The prospects of creating stable, well-adjusted marriages upon a new basis are considerably discounted by the complications resulting from the absence of husband and father from home. It is perhaps this factor, more than any other change in the family, that has produced the features which indicate the undermining of respect for moral principle and of regard for stability in family life.

Index

More about Penguins
and Pelicans

Penguinews, which appears every month,
contains details of all the new books issued by
Penguins as they are published. From time to
time it is supplemented by *Penguins in Print*,
which is a complete list of all books published
by Penguins which are in print. (There are well
over three thousand of these.)

A specimen copy of *Penguinews* will be sent to
you free on request, and you can become a
subscriber for the price of the postage. For a
year's issues (including the complete lists) please
send 25p if you live in the United Kingdom, or
50p if you live elsewhere. Just write to Dept EP,
Penguin Books Ltd, Harmondsworth, Middlesex,
enclosing a cheque or postal order, and your name
will be added to the mailing list.

Some other Pelicans on Anthropology are
described on the following pages.

Note: *Penguinews* and *Penguins in Print* are
not available in the U.S.A. or Canada

The Greek Myths

(Volumes One and Two)

Robert Graves

Not for over a century, since Smith's *Dictionary of Classical Mythology* first appeared, has the attempt been made to provide for the English reader a complete 'mythology', in the sense of a retelling in modern terms of the Greek tales of gods and heroes. In the two volumes of this book Robert Graves, whose combination of classical scholarship and anthropological competence has already been so brilliantly demonstrated in *The White Goddess* and *The Golden Fleece,* supplies the need. In nearly two hundred sections, it covers the Creation myths, the legends of the birth and lives of the great Olympians, the Theseus, Oedipus, and Heracles cycles, the Argonaut voyage, the tale of Troy, and much else.

All the scattered elements of each myth have been assembled into a harmonious narrative, and many variants are recorded which may help to determine its ritual or historical meaning. Full references to the classical sources, and copious indexes, make the book as valuable to the scholar as to the general reader; and a full commentary on each myth explains and interprets the classical version in the light of today's archaeological and anthropological knowledge.

Not for sale in the U.S.A.

Pelican Anthropology Library

Kinship and Marriage

Robin Fox

We are so accustomed to our own marriage and family
customs that we tend to think of them as norms of human
behaviour. But systems of kinship are not immutable;
other cultures – both primitive and modern – have operated
modes of determining kinship and controlling marriage
and inheritance significantly different from ours. This
volume in the Pelican Anthropology Library is the first
introduction to these alternative systems of social
engineering, many of them of a fascinating elegance and
complexity. By analysing the pressures which mould each
of them, Robin Fox gives us a fresh insight into the
workings of our own customs. He also suggests a tentative
solution to the problem of the incest taboo. This is the
first time that all the theories of kinship and marriage
have been analysed within a single framework of argument
in terms intelligible to the layman.

Ever since Captain Cook first used the word in his
account of the Polynesians, the strange phenomenon of
taboo has fascinated laymen and scholars alike. It has
been absorbed into the language of psychology and has
been applied, often carelessly, to a wide and varied range
of human customs and beliefs. Franz Steiner's now classic
study examines critically the taboo theories of Frazer,
Freud, Levy-Bruhl and others, and clears up much of the
confusion surrounding a mysterious facet of human
behaviour.

'His book will be found to be of great value to anyone
interested in the idea of taboo and to those who in the
future tackle once more the problems it raises . . . it states
in small compass, but with equal learning and wit,
everything of any significance which has been written
about taboo' – Professor E. E. Evans-Pritchard

Pelican Anthropology Library

Totemism

Claude Lévi-Strauss

The so-called 'problem' of totemism, which was once
seen as the embryonic form of all religious belief, has
for long exercised the minds of anthropologists. From
McLennan's famous pronouncement in 1869 that
totemism was simply 'fetishism plus exogamy and
matrilineal descent' to Sir James Frazer's portentous
publication in 1910 of the four volumes of *Totemism and
Exogamy*, the institution was accorded a special and
honoured place among anthropological studies.

In his short essay Professor Lévi-Strauss analyses the
totemism theories of Boas, Evans-Pritchard, Radcliffe
Brown and others and then, in what is in effect a
demonstration of structuralist anthropology at work,
demolishes the 'problem' by suggesting that the whole
concept has been a figment of western minds, intent on
classifying everything and determined to relegate certain
human mental attitudes to the realm of the 'primitive'.
The work makes surprising (and convincing) reference to
some neglected observations of Rousseau and Bergson
and leads on naturally to Lévi-Strauss's famous book,
The Savage Mind. It stands, in fact, as an excellent
introduction to the structuralist approach and to the thought
of one of the most distinguished and interesting minds
of our time.

'Totemism has been anthropologically démodé for many
years, but Lévi-Strauss's sharply provocative analysis has
thoroughly shaken out the dust' – *New Statesman*

Not for sale in the U.S.A. or Canada